TRADITION AND INNOVATION IN CHAUCER

Also by Derek Brewer

CHAUCER
CHAUCER AND CHAUCERIANS (*editor*)
CHAUCER AND HIS WORLD
CHAUCER IN HIS TIME
CHAUCER: THE CRITICAL HERITAGE (*editor*)
CHAUCER: THE POET AS STORYTELLER
MALORY'S *MORTE D'ARTHUR* (*editor*)
PROTEUS
SYMBOLIC STORIES
THE PARLEMENT OF FOULYS (*editor*)
WRITERS AND THEIR BACKGROUNDS: GEOFFREY CHAUCER
(*editor*)
ENGLISH GOTHIC LITERATURE (*Macmillan History of Literature*)

TRADITION AND INNOVATION IN CHAUCER

Derek Brewer

Macmillan Press London

First edition 1982
Reprinted 1983

Published by
THE MACMILLAN PRESS LTD
London and Basingstoke
Companies and representatives
throughout the world

ISBN 0 333 28427 5

Typeset in Great Britain by
Computacomp (UK) Ltd, Fort William, Scotland
and printed in Hong Kong

To Geoffrey Shepherd

Contents

Preface

The essays in the present volume have all, except the first, been printed before in widely-scattered periodicals, and they are now reprinted with minimal alteration so far as possible in the order of publication. Although the essays were published separately and may be read independently they are interrelated. They represent an overall view of Chaucer and his relationships both to the literary culture of his own times and to our present attitudes. Chaucer is both traditional and innovatory in a highly characteristic way. The underlying interest is in the kind of new use that Chaucer makes of traditional material. He himself was well aware of what he was doing.

> For out of olde feldys, as men seye
> Comyth al this newe corn fro yer to yere,
> And out of olde bokis, in good fey,
> Comyth al this newe science that men lere.
>
> (*The Parlement of Foulys*,
> ed. Derek Brewer (1960) pp. 22–5.)

The general method is to attempt to re-create the 'culture-patterns', at once generally historical and highly personal, of the imaginative world which Chaucer, to adapt Wordsworth's phrase, 'half creates and half perceives' in his writings.

DEREK BREWER

Acknowledgements

In the case of those essays which are reprinted full details are given of the original publications. I should like to acknowledge with gratitude the permission to reprint which has been accorded to me by the original publishers.

1 The Archaic and the Modern

It is axiomatic that humanity needs images (or symbols, or models) of many kinds by which to grasp reality. Those recognisably fictional images comprising literature and the fine arts are not the least important for us as a mode of coming to terms with life and death. Since we exist in time, the sequence of images of a similar or related kind constitutes the core of the history of any art. The sequence is most clearly to be recognised in the history of the fine arts, for example in the sequence of paintings.

Each successive image can be located at the intersection of two main 'vectors' or lines of force. One is the 'tradition', that is, both the similarities between a sequence of images and our sense that these similarities are normative, our recognition that they show how such images *should* appear. The other vector may be summed up as the demands which contemporary experience makes upon the images. Each vector is the resolution of many forces, not always compatible with one another. The vector of tradition is complex in the images themselves and the skills required in creating them. The sequence of images that compose the essential thread of the tradition is historically interrelated, not a mere succession, but not (usually) causally related as we often think historical accounts should be. The vector of contemporary demand is even more complex and variable, comprising as it may social, economic, political, psychological, personal factors, whose strength and relative proportions will vary with each work of art.

Works of art of the same kind in the same tradition differ from each other because the two vectors are never the same. The existence of the latest work of art, as T. S. Eliot long ago noted, in itself changes the nature of the tradition. It has added something to the tradition which cannot but be different, however slightly, from what has gone before. The addition is not merely cumulative; it interacts and changes the composition of the whole. The very existence of a living tradition implies constant innovation. Children are different from their parents.

The vector of contemporary demand may no doubt be thought of as the main agent of change. The functions we require of the image inevitably change, sometimes to such an extent that the sequence of images itself suddenly decays. A dramatic representation of such a change may be seen in isolated splendour in the sequence of decorated ancient Greek pottery. It moves from geometrical pattern to progressively more richly realistic though idealised representations which in the fifth century achieve one of the peaks in the world's art. Then within little more than 50 years that achievement apparently became no more attainable, or desired, and the art collapsed.

When we consider the two vectors in literature we have a further complication in that the medium of language is, unlike stone or paint, itself already a very complex system of images, subject to exactly the same sort of conditioning from tradition and contemporary requirements. The verbal work of art is carved out of an art of verbal work. Even to write *about* literature is in some minor way to be writing symbolic fictions, creating a series of images. Even if a satisfactory history of literature is possible we are certainly very far from achieving it.

A work of art, being a complex image, or system of images, of what some human beings wish to think about, will itself by definition generate its own meanings, through its interaction with those who contemplate it, whom it works upon, and who lend it their own energies for it to release. In the end we recognise a major work of art by the richness of meanings that it generates in its own and successive generations. The systematic quality of the work of art, the complexity of relationships within itself that also relate to the rest of experience, is the measure of its greatness. Beauty, goodness, even truth, and certainly relevance, are *ir*relevant to its success, except as paraphrases or colourings of its capacity continually to generate meanings in receptive minds. The multiplicity of facets of any work of art, especially of verbal art, ensures that the meanings are multiple, not easy to define, not simple or even difficult logical statements, but subjects of continuous exploration. Hence the myriad books on Shakespeare's works. Hence also the uselessness of a good deal of evaluative criticism. At the end of an exploration of the meanings of a work of art (and if the end is not too far off the work is by definition minor) it may be of use to say that such a poem is better than such another, and so is more worth reprinting, or editing, or even rereading. But the exploration needs to be done first. In the case of major works the exploration is continuous; that is how we know they are major works. When a given author produces a series of works relationships are inevitably set up between them which allow the whole *oeuvre* (we need the distinctive French word) to be taken, if not as one work of art, at any rate as a systematically related series whose relationships from individual work to work (prose or verse, fiction, philosophy, science or edification) constitute further meanings which illustrate the elements.

Such is one justification for collecting the present set of essays. Another is the attempt to explore some special aspects in the case of one peculiarly rich and rewarding author of the intersection between the two vectors of tradition and contemporary demand. Contemporary demand in this case is mainly seen in the mirror of the perceived world which the work itself offers in its subject-matter. This 'mirror' is an image, subject to the laws of images, including tradition, and not a realistic document of the kind used by the historian (though historians increasingly realise how 'fictional' or symbolic are their plainest documents). The image must be explored as an image.

II

There is at all times a tension between tradition and experience, and all living, as well as all language and art, is a continuous attempt to reconcile the two. At some periods the speed of perceived change is unusually rapid, or affects particularly sensitive areas of life. The latter part of the twentieth century is clearly, or seems clearly to us, such a period, and perhaps makes us particularly sensitive to the general phenomenon. The seventeenth century in England is another period, in our eyes, of such enhanced speed of change, though consciousness of it was much less widely diffused through society as a whole. In that century we see gathering speed those changes which are associated with the empirical scientific revolution, and with which ought also to be associated the effective development of Neoclassicism, as I have argued in parts of this book and elsewhere.[1] The begetter and the product of the seventeenth-century revolution can be usefully called the 'scientific' mind. It seems to be an especially vigorous manifestation of a new compulsion exerted by new insight, new experience, upon ancient tradition, a compulsion so urgent as to constitute a heavy attack.

For literary critics the phenomenon I am referring to may seem little more than a restatement of T. S. Eliot's famous 'dissociation of sensibility' which he located in the seventeenth century—a view which has been strongly attacked.[2] There are certainly parts of Eliot's formulation, for example the apparent claim for overall and once-for-all change, which need to be modified. Nevertheless it represents an important insight. The problem can now be better investigated in the context of what was perhaps at the back of Eliot's mind when he wrote: the much older and still continuing debate amongst the anthropologists which has often centred on the dichotomy between two modes of thought—that using magic and myth set against that of science and history, concrete against abstract, oral against literate, and so forth. This debate 'has been the commonplace of anthropological discourse since its beginning'.[3] It is associated, as in J. R. Goody's *Domestication of the Savage Mind*, with the concept of the 'savage' mind. The 'savage' mind is a splendidly confident expression by the nineteenth century of its own intellectual civilised superiority over 'inferior' societies, pre-literate, pre-scientific, etc. It now begs too many questions and I prefer to substitute for it a more neutral term, the 'archaic' mind, though like any single term that too is awkward and requires qualification. It has the advantage of an historical base of sorts in what we know of certain ancient societies, including our own, which are comparable with modern 'primitive' societies, that is, those with little or no advanced technology, no modern Western scientific knowledge. It corresponds with much of what we experience when we read medieval English and European literature. The disadvantage of the term is that it risks implying a total unity of the mind it describes, and excludes 'non-archaic' characteristics. This I specifically deny. All minds have at least potentially 'archaic' and 'non-archaic' characteristics. All ancient or primitive societies have had and still have the problems of reconciling tradition with experience. All modern societies not only preserve and maintain but even invent and develop 'archaic' responses and attitudes. It is indeed likely that art itself is mainly an 'archaic' activity. The notion of a dichotomy, or binary division, is only a modern simplifying trick of thought which helps to impose some order on the flux of experience, but if we remember that it is only a device, it is useful to summarise the extensive mixtures of mind in ourselves and our cultures as a division between the 'archaic' and the 'scientific'.

The 'scientific' itself is equally awkward a term. It must always imply some degree of intellectual testing of received truth. Sometimes it will be easily equated with scepticism, religious or otherwise; at other times with 'commonsense'; at others with empiricism; or again with utilitarianism. Nowadays science has gone far beyond commonsense. In the sixteenth century it was a matter of commonsense to believe in witches and devils.[4] Nowadays anthropologists are fond of retailing stories from their fieldwork amongst primitive tribes which indicate a strong if controlled scepticism on the part of tribesmen about, for example, the efficacy of rituals, such as that for making rain. It is valuable to recognise this logically incompatible duality of the mind, provided that we realise that the dualism is a simplification of many forces, and that modern, advanced, 'scientific' cultures maintain similar dualities. The proportions and contents of the duality differ according to time and place and people but the crude formal structure is always useful as a way of beginning to understand a culture.

III

It is necessary to qualify the meaning of 'archaic' for the purpose of this discussion. While remembering that the fullness of experience of any individual or culture will always contain more than the dominant tendency, we may characterise the 'archaic' mind as a dominating tendency opposed to the 'modern' or 'scientific' mind. The 'archaic' mind differentiates much less clearly than the 'scientific' mind, is less specialised, in this sense less fragmented. Moral, psychological and material objects of perception, or aspects of objects, are not so clearly distinguished and disconnected from each other. Phenomena are conceived of as indivisible amalgams of personalised and material qualities.[5] The law of gravity is conceived of as 'attraction' (our language retains something of the amalgam) between *objects* which is similar to love or sexual desire between human beings. For Dante, in the last line of the *Paradiso*, 'L'amor che move il sole e l'altre stelle' is the love of God which is also the force which both contains the tides and sustains matrimony, as Boethius thought in the sixth century (*De Consolatione Philosophiae*, ii, metre 8) and as Chaucer thought when he translated (though with a subtle modification) the passage from Boethius in *Troilus and Criseyde*, iii, 1744–71. For the 'archaic' mind cosmology, science, society, morality, personal relationships are all constructed on the same general model and are part of the same general system. An interesting example of this is richly demonstrated in *The Franklin's Tale*. There Dorigen complains to God about the dangerous rocks on the sea-coast which imperil her beloved husband's safe return. When the squire Aurelius attempts to seduce her she softens her absolute denial by saying that she will give herself to him if he gets rid of the dangerous rocks. He produces the illusion that the rocks are gone, to Dorigen's horror. The structure of the story depends on our recognition that there is a connection between the rocks and Dorigen's faithfulness and her husband's honour; between material realities, unpleasant as they are, and desirable moral qualities. An event in the physical world is one in the social and moral world. To sum up, nothing is context-free or self-enclosed.

A further aspect of this is that the 'archaic' mind projects (as it seems to us) the unconscious activities of the mind on to the outside world.[6] The gods, angels, devils, spirits of the middle air, not to speak of fairies large and small, succubi and incubi, may walk amongst men, and trees and rivers may have their inner spirits, as the planets were thought certainly to have their guardian angels or 'intelligences'. A large area of human experience is covered here which needs further differentiation prevented by lack of space, but one caution must be entered. Our own modern experience and language, our modern 'scientific' minds, make such a sharp differentiation between subjective and objective, material and non-material, what is predictable and what arbitrary, that we are always in danger of reading *into* the 'archaic' mind a literalism of belief that it does not aspire to. Literalism, the attempt to achieve an exact correspondence between words and things, though present to some extent in all language, has become dominant only in the modern mind.

Another aspect of the projection by the 'archaic' mind of the unconscious part of the mind upon the external though not *more* real world is that what is 'outside' for us, neutral, without intrinsic value except as we value it, is in a sense 'inside' for the 'archaic' mind, part of its own psychic world, personalised and charged with values, in a way that we now stigmatise as 'the pathetic fallacy'. We 'know' that the sky, clouds, the mountains, the sea, all nature, are mindless purposeless matter; for us of the modern mind values have retreated from the outside world to the sharply differentiated world within our skulls, where they are purely subjective, transient, relative and uncertain. Wordsworth, part of whose greatness as a poet was his sense of his own 'archaic' mind, and part was his sense of it slipping away from him, catches the feeling even as it escapes.

> Great God! I'd rather be
> A Pagan suckled in a creed outworn,
> So might I, standing on this pleasant lea,
> Have glimpses that would make me less forlorn;
> Have sight of Proteus rising from the sea;
> Or hear old Triton blow his wreathed horn.[7]

For the 'archaic' mind the sacred is uncontained, though it may concentrate in holy places as well. The modern mind, in the person of Professor Gellner, formulates this as 'the pervasiveness of entrenched clauses'. The 'entrenched clauses' in this sense are the deeply-held convictions so crucial to one's general world-view that they may be termed 'sacred'; they demand worship, or at least unquestioning adherence. If one of them crumbles, it carries many other beliefs and actions with it. 'In a traditional thought-system, the sacred or the crucial is more extensive, more untidily dispersed, and much more pervasive.'[8] Professor Gellner extends his notion of the 'sacred' to that of the 'crucial'—that is, elements which are felt in a community to demand unquestioned acceptance, and which, if removed, carry away so many other important elments as seriously to imperil the existence of the whole cultural fabric. Such elements are much reduced, at any rate in intention, in the 'scientific' mind.

Their importance in the 'archaic' mind is obviously in part an aspect of the unified, interrelated structure of the 'archaic' mind, but another way of putting the same difference is to say that for the 'archaic' mind knowledge of 'reality' and values seem direct and absolute, so that when such knowledge and value are shaken, 'chaos is come again'; while for the modern 'scientific' mind, knowledge and values seem indirect, relative, subject to continuous change. It is paradoxically much more difficult for the modern 'scientific' mind to be *absolutely* certain. (Modern scientists may be a different matter, because modern science may be believed in, in a quite archaic way, as Gellner points out.)

One may sum up the difference by suggesting that what is absolutely and immediately 'real' to the 'archaic' mind is 'symbolic', provisional, capable of substitution, to the modern 'scientific' mind. The clearest examples are religious. For most medieval men hell was a material place of recognisable physical torment. For most modern Christians the concept of hell is a statement about a person's lack of relationship to God which is capable of many different kinds of interpretation but which, it is safe to say, is practically never thought of as a place with its geographical location in the centre of the earth, where a lot of our dead friends well deserve to be for ever.

Once again I simplify with a binary distinction for the sake of argument a complex differentiation. 'Reality' and appearance were related but not the same in the medieval concept of 'reality' and we should not attribute too rigorous and consistent a literalism to medieval words. Words were instruments of the mind, for persuasion, command, expression, exaggeration, punning, as well as for describing what 'is'. Equally, however relativistic the modern mind, relativism must have a stop if thought is to progress. Something must be axiomatic, taken for granted. No life can be lived devoid of some unprovable convictions, some 'entrenched clauses'. Nevertheless, with these qualifications, it is often easier for the modern mind to see as a symbol what the 'archaic' mind takes as a truth. The difficulty is that the symbol, once perceived as such, loses much of its power, loses its sacredness. As soon as we start taking a story as myth we are saying that it is not 'true'. The modern vulgar use of the word *myth* as a euphemism for *lie* truly represents the natural modern feeling, as the group of modern radical theologians knew who contributed essays to *The Myth of*

God Incarnate (1977). Symbolism is the inevitable concomitant of a world-view which sees materiality as the only 'real' reality, if the phrase may be permitted, but which wishes to take account of other intuitions about the nature of experience. The 'archaic' mind is severely limited in control of the material world, in consistency, and in self-knowledge, but it has an at least psychological bonus in the confidence with which its inclusive world-view can absorb non-material experience and express values: in a word, in its confidence that it can approach reality direct—or that what it approaches direct *is* reality.

The modern mind can never fully recapture in practice the 'archaic' confidence. It is 'never bright morning again', as Wordsworth constantly testifies. Yet literary empathy may do much. Literature, emancipated from 'reality', can on the viewless wings of poesy give us glimpses which may make us both less forlorn at our loss and more conscious of our gains. We can approach the 'archaic' with a genuinely modern absence of our own values in order to sympathise with and in part absorb those of the 'archaic'. We must therefore, when reading traditional literature, not only accept the pervasiveness of the 'sacred', but accept as unchallenged values which the modern 'scientific' mind has long challenged or even demolished. Thus the sacredness of chastity (though mainly for women) has to be accepted as a justifying factor for what the modern liberal imagination too easily qualifies as barbarous, such as many aspects of the structures of honour, and such noble deeds as the father's killing of his own daughter when her honour is threatened. The sacredness of war cannot be understood by the modern 'scientific' mind acting alone (as of course it never does), nor patriotism, nor the sacred obligations of honour, nor the hierarchical structure of society. (The sacred nature of these sentiments is not entirely destroyed even today, for many people.)

These sentiments we need to explore with sympathy if we are to understand the 'archaic' mind, especially in our own culture. This is not to say that every primitive society has the same sacred objects or sentiments. Traditional societies are characteristically moulded by their environment and acquire sufficiently distinctive a configuration of elements for Gellner to emphasise their 'tendency to rely on a socially idiosyncratic notion of the normal, which determines what does and does not require explanation'.[9] Primitive societies in their specific local manifestations differ a good deal from each other within the broad limitations of environmental conditioning—the obvious example is the prevalence of local dialects even today in Europe. Local idiosyncrasy within the general pattern is another demonstration of the power that tradition has to vary while maintaining continuity. The idiosyncrasy of social reality within any society that is capable of establishing its own identity soon becomes marked and is still with us. The idiosyncrasy is reflected in the literature and we should bring the same care of interpretation and caution in value-judgments to the study of medieval literature as an anthropologist would to the study of a primitive tribe in remote parts. We should not assume that our own modern notions of normality or morality are necessarily the same, *or necessarily superior.*

We should not always associate the 'sacred' with the serious. The traditions of comedy, with their derisive abuse, scornful laughter, vulgar bawdiness, physical humiliation, blasphemous jokes, are not less archaic, or even less ritualistic, than high and solemn festivals. They are often the counterpart to such festivals because of the inter-connectedness of the archaic mind, and may be destroyed with them, as happened at the English Reformation. Derision and satire may or may not be innovatory; they are often highly conservative, and associated with the 'sacred'. Sacred and secular are mingled together.

The interlocked, potentially or actually sacred nature of what is perceived by the 'archaic' mind ensures that no act is performed, no thought even thought, independent of its moral, social, religious, consequences. In artistic terms one may say, as Huizinga wrote of medieval art, that all art is applied art. Chaucer revoked his purely recreational poems as immoral. By contrast, the greatest success of the modern mind, which is the achievement of science, has been arrived at by establishing a notionally absolute autonomy for scientific investigation free from any significant constraint. It is objective and context-free. The pursuit of (scientific) truth is regarded both as an absolute in itself, which no other considerations, social, intellectual, political, moral, religious, should hinder, and as a pursuit which is obligatory upon us as a society. Perhaps the classic confrontation of the 'archaic' mind with the 'scientific' is that between the Roman Church and Galileo. An earlier one, less well known but equally emblematic, was the controversy between the impassioned St Bernard and the great analytic theologian Abelard. In a smaller way Chaucer comes to the edges of the 'archaic' mind and refuses to go further when in *The Astrolabe* he denies astrological speculation about the future. Astrology, with all its confusions, was one of the attempts of the fourteenth century to become 'scientific'. But Chaucer advances out of the 'archaic' mind to the extent that at least in his maturity he wrote what he evidently came in the end to regard as purely 'literary', recreational, that is, fictional, works, which did not aim to edify, and which consequently are revoked in the 'Retracciouns' at the end of *The Canterbury Tales.* The autonomy of literature, its freedom from social, moral, religious, economic, context would seem to correspond to the autonomy of science, and would be maintained by all those who today deny censorship. In this respect the 'scientific' mind corresponds to the literary liberal imagination, for which nothing is sacred. Modern literature, like modern science, is context-free, and is also an international, relatively uniform phenomenon.

By contrast, the interrelatedness, the contextuality of all perception, the lack of clear distinction between 'inner' and 'outer', in the 'archaic' mind, create some of the characteristic forms of non-modern literature. The capacity of one object to represent another gives allegory. The interrelatedness of objects, the attempt to assimilate everything to one general system, fosters the acceptability of argument by analogy rather than analysis. Tradition asserts the value of what has long been generally known.

> To works, however, of which the excellence is not absolute and definite, but gradual and comparative; to works not raised upon principles demonstrative and scientifick, but appealing wholly to observation and experience, no other test can be applied than length of duration and continuance of esteem. What mankind have long possessed they have often examined and compared; and if they persist to value the possession, it is because frequent comparisons have confirmed opinion in its favour.[10]

Such works are often at first sight bafflingly illogical to the 'scientific' mind. The heart has its reasons which the mind cannot understand. We murder to dissect. The 'scientific' mind is analytical and seeks logical development. Historically speaking it has been especially concerned with the processes of material cause and effect. 'Archaic' culture of course knows physical cause and effect, but it is willing to accept that other modes of action also exist, in forms of sympathetic magic, for example (which is analogy). It will accept sequences of action not logically and explicitly motivated. Almost all myth has this latter characteristic. Yet he would be a bold (and ignorant) man today who would argue that myth is meaningless or absurd, however grotesquely unrealistic may appear to be the story that it tells. The corresponding example in medieval literature of this connective capacity of the 'archaic' mind, which is so different from the causal structure of the 'scientific' mind, is romance. The structures of romance, though not articulated by material cause and effect, and though not plausible images of everyday life, have an intelligible structure that appeals to the deeper levels of the mind, but they are frequently derided by modern literary exponents of the 'scientific' mind, and also, interestingly, by Chaucer.[11] Such works are acceptable within the society that generates them because their structures correspond to the needs and aspirations of that society, not as analysed in utilitarian terms but as necessary symbols and accepted patterns. An analytical realism is not required; significance and pleasure lie in repetition with variation of images at once familiar and mysterious, which give, and are known to give, reliable satisfactions. The 'archaic' mind is not childish, but a child's mind is largely 'archaic', and the child's acceptance of repetition is a guide to the pleasure the 'archaic' mind takes in such matters. The most obvious example at an adult level of this pleasure that the non-discursive, non-analytic part of the mind takes in repetition is music. Stories, especially non-realistic mythic stories, approach the same category.

The pleasure in repetition, the recognition of symbols, are characteristic of a tradition. It is reasonable to associate the 'archaic' mind with traditional societies, since it is certain that the nature of the 'archaic' mind is to preserve traditional knowledge and ways. Because everything is interlocked with everything else, and the sacred is pervasive, innovation is difficult, small-scale, piecemeal. When everything is interlocked sudden major innovation is liable to destroy the culture as a whole, as we have seen in the twentieth century with many primitive tribes. The 'scientific' mind, on the other hand is characterised by progressive change, generated by its own continuous self-criticism.

IV

There has been much debate whether literacy is the fundamental factor in the change of balance between the 'archaic' and the 'scientific' mind.[12] Literacy is itself a gradual acquisition for an individual, and especially for a society. The change from a purely oral culture to one based on written documents must be slow, and written documents retain something of that fluidity within the norm that, as A. B. Lord showed in the variations of his Yugoslav folk-singers, marks oral culture.[13] But a manuscript nevertheless has more fixity than remembered words, can be checked, even though one manuscript is never an exact copy of another, and literacy thus begins a fundamental change. The change from script to print alters the situation much more radically. The uniformity of the printed book, the possibility of wide dispersion, the absence of the collective 'literary' event for the silent solitary reader who will never know the author, all promote decontextual-isation and the uniformity and predictability required by the 'scientific' mind. Science depends on the huge accumulation of complex knowledge, accurately, uniformly and objectively conveyed, context-free, continuously self-critical. Such a situation is obviously impossible in purely oral conditions. Memory is too variable, diagrams by definition non-existent. Diagrams are a good index of the development of the scientific mind. They are barely possible in manuscript, though with great labour their accurate reproduction can be attempted. However, diagrams in manuscript are notoriously unreliable, as are proper names. Only print can accurately reproduce and preserve complex accurate knowledge, including the diagrams which are so distinctive of the nature of the printed book. So if we wish to draw the sharpest distinction we can between the 'archaic' and the 'scientific' mind we must do it by confronting a purely oral culture with one that has for centuries been based on print. Printing may not be a sufficient cause for the full development of the 'scientific' mind, but it is evidently a necessary one.

Surviving Old English literature is the furthest we can reach back into the 'archaic' mind within our own culture, and work on *Beowulf* conducted without reference to my present theory well illustrates how a critic, expounding the nature of the poetry, may independently come to similar conclusions. Professor Clemoes, in his essay on action in *Beowulf*, definitively establishes certain major characteristics of the poem which clearly reflect, we may say, the 'archaic' mind.[14] It maintains a generalised point of view, not an analytic or separately identifiable one. It uses language concerned with synthesis, with 'unparticularised expressions of analogy ("seahorse" for "ship") or connection ("ring-hall")' (p. 148)—connection which we may call metonymy. The poet is the anonymous 'voice of traditional corporate wisdom' (p. 150). Action, description, actor, all interlace, and both inanimate objects (a boat) and natural phenomena (the sea) are felt to have distinctive beings. There is a sense of the 'inner principles of things', which are not analysed. There are no detachable external qualities, and action is 'an innate, inherent attribute' of the doer, 'it is what philosophers call "immanent" ' (p. 155). 'The sense that action belongs to someone has implications for story-telling. For one thing action itself can become submerged in a way that may offend us moderns. Explanation, comment and digression of all kinds crowd in' (p.159). In other words the interconnectedness of experience is deeply felt, and a (to us) idiosyncratic selection of significance is made. In particular, the sequence of material cause and effect as the basis of progression of a story is not regarded as important—partly because either the story itself, or the *kind* of story it is, its 'rules', being traditional, are already known to the audience. Action is always seen with mental concomitants (p. 164). Events or states of mind are surrounded by interconnected attitudes; actions (in which speech is included) follow 'psychological' requirements, not those of material necessity as would be required of descriptions aiming at a plausible realistic account of the external world. Thus what is 'inside' and what 'outside' the mind is less differentiated; physical objects are themselves, yet are also symbolic. 'The symbols, expressed in traditional language, belong to shared consciousness. They give concentrated form to general experience' (p. 166).

All this clearly differentiates the 'archaic' from the modern 'scientific' mind even in its literary suppositions. Yet even *Beowulf* can be known only because it was written down. The existence of manuscripts is a salutary reminder that these binary distinctions between oral culture and print culture, 'archaic' and 'scientific' minds, are only opposite poles on a connecting axis; such polar distinctions are only conveniences of thought and argument. The actual historical change in our culture was a slow progression from an oral culture, through very elementary forms of writing on sticks and stones, to a developing use of writing and the slow spread of literacy. Even printing was at first seen as little more than a welcome speeding up of the production of manuscripts. (The University of Oxford did not begin to collect printed books until 1530, almost a century after the printing of the Gutenberg Bible, and half a century after Caxton set up in England.) Other factors were needed—the development of humanism, the scientific revolution, in essence a new feeling about 'reality'—for the 'scientific' modern mind fully to evolve. The seeds of these were indeed sown much earlier, and in part at least, as already argued, the 'scientific' mind is the cultural form of mental attitudes that are potential in every mind.

Literature understood in its broadest sense as all writing that is not purely utilitarian is at any time one of the fullest manifestations of the 'mind' of any culture. Man does not live by bread alone but by symbols which are the nearest he can come to formulating for himself the multiple character of 'reality'. Thus all art, much religion, ceremonial, sport and indeed much of the only partially practical needs of food, drink and sex. But *verbal* symbols, which live essentially in the mind, relatively independent of a physical base, with their protean malleability, are peculiarly effective in representing to ourselves our mixed feelings about complex 'reality', and thus of representing the range of a culture. Moreover the passage of time is such that it necessarily deprives even the most utilitarian uses of writing of their utility, leaving them as symbols. An Ancient Egyptian laundry list, Old English laws, an order of battle when the battle is lost and won, all survive as in the broad sense symbolic. The passage of time confers on all documents the status of fictions. As such we can wring out of them far more meaning than their pragmatic authors were ever aware of. Even a laundry list is literature once the washing is done. There are of course grades of meaningfulness in literature, which are probably the only satisfactory basis for literary evaluation. Shakespeare's plays are fuller of meaning than Shakespeare's laundry lists would have been, had they survived—interesting as those would be. The plays are better literature, but art and symbolic status inhere, at a lower level, in the laundry list.

The literature of a traditional culture is a particularly good representative of the culture because it is the product of a whole series of tellers and hearers, writers and readers, throughout several generations, 'a laminated product of accretions, erosions and changes, like a great house continuously occupied by many generations. It partakes of the idiosyncrasy of the culture, and is not less valuable because it incorporates many apparent inconsistencies, 'fossils' of usage, changes of use, elements of which may even be incomprehensible to later generations, but which confer a character, and sometimes an unconscious significance, which enrich even while they are taken for granted, and only valued when destroyed in the name of progress for a would-be utilitarian block of offices.

The literature of a culture is not only a representative of a culture, and an element that must be understood for a culture to be understood; it is in itself an *analogue* of the culture which produces it, capable of being studied as an end in itself. We need then an appropriate anthropology of literature, in which the literary historian will describe and interpret the imaginative but not imaginary world which is created in the literature he studies. He will ideally, like the anthropologist engaged in a comparable study, be 'inclined to respect the intellectual capacities of the tribe he studies'.[15] He will have some extremely intelligent, if often highly eccentric, informants.

The study of medieval English literature is peculiarly relevant to this ideal because although for the English it is bone of our bone and flesh of our flesh, and intimate enough for North Americans and Europeans, and recognisable in its common humanity by other racial traditions, it is markedly *different* in its cosmology downwards from modern, that is, post-seventeenth-century, European literature. The difference is not *total* because complex changes operate over a wide front at varying speeds, and there is an abiding human sameness which always enters the cultural mixture, however strange the culture's configuration. But the change is there.

The notion of a cultural configuration is harder to define than to operate. It is important to the literary historian because willy-nilly he must proceed by detecting characteristic 'periods'. It is easy to mock these. Everyone knows from his own experience that an epoch does not change overnight. Life felt much the same in 1923 as in 1921 although *The Waste Land* and James Joyce's *Ulysses* were both published in 1922. The changes that produced these apparently anomalous and difficult literary works can be traced far back, and novels and poems are still being produced apparently unaffected by their presence. Yet it is not unreasonable to see a new style of literature emerging around the 1920s which is important and can be characterised. The 'style' of an epoch, both of words and 'habit of mind' can be identified by those who are familiar with it. A good student of the eighteenth century can be expected to 'place' an unidentified piece of eighteenth-century verse never previously read by him. Once again the history of art gives clear examples. The art historian can be expected to date, and often to attribute to an artist, a previously unknown painting, on grounds of style. It is true that he can make mistakes, but usually only when he is the victim of skilful forgery, and forgeries seem almost always to reveal themselves as such as soon as they cease to be contemporary with the expert examining them. An eighteenth-century forgery of a work of antiquity is nowadays recognisably of the eighteenth century. This is itself evidence of the existence of a 'period style'. The history of the visual arts gives a useful analogy. Art historians are justified in speaking of a 'Gothic style', of painting, manuscript illumination, wood and stone sculpture, architecture, stained glass, script. The period style can be defined by certain characteristics and by configurations of characteristics. The products themselves are related to each other rather as the members of a family are related to each other, with enough similarities to reveal the connection without all possible characteristics being shared by each individual, which would indeed produce merely a collection of clones. The possibility of establishing in art history a 'family relationship' of works of art, naturally ill-defined at the edges, where second and third cousins, as it were, of the later generations may be more effectively related to someone else's parents or siblings, justifies in principle a similar possibility of establishing such a network of relationships and similarities amongst works of literature as may constitute a recognisable 'period style'. It is equally justifiable to attempt to characterise English medieval literature, and a later essay attempts to establish the configuration of a 'Gothic' period of English literature, in which the work of Chaucer is a significant element.

Once we have established the sense of a Gothic literary period, which with whatever uncertainties and qualifications, may be said to have lasted from about 1200 to about 1600—and in its later years, from 1500, ever more deeply interpenetrated by the modes of the Neoclassical—we may return to the general consideration of its differences especially from the period immediately following. As I have argued the verbal detail of these elsewhere I do not propose to rehearse them here.[16] The reader of medieval English and European literature is not only struck by the major differences between it and modern literature in subject-matter and verbal style: he must also be struck by the *similarities* between medieval literature and European folk-tale, and eventually with profound similarities to other literatures from 'primitive' societies. What I am seeking to establish, taking as a pivot the seventeenth century in English culture, is that medieval English literature, and indeed culture, contain a large component which must be characterised as 'archaic'.

V

The long process of change between an oral culture, mainly 'archaic', and our modern culture, produces a mixture of elements in every period, including even our own (to which the 'archaic' in certain forms of collectivisation has proved enormously attractive). In the culture of the fourteenth century in England we see the predominance of orality, lack of specialised function, interconnectedness of phenomena, absence of clear distinctions between subject and object, dominance of personal relationships, weakness of abstractions, power of the collective over the individual, pervasiveness of the sacred and preference for the customary over rationalised uniformity, which are the marks of the 'archaic' mind. (The 'sacred' here includes both more and less than the specifically Christian or ecclesiastical tradition—it includes, for example, deep-set feelings about honour and social hierarchy to which sometimes churchmen were strongly opposed.) We may sum up this culture as 'traditional'. Like all traditional cultures it changes and develops within quite stable norms.

The literature of the Gothic period is necessarily a traditional literature. Its basis, even in Chaucer, is the telling of stories that are already known, the repeating of commonplaces of description (as that of the beautiful lady, of the arming of the warrior) which are already centuries old. The structures of the stories or even of discursive narrative, like those of folk-tale or fairy tale, are not dependent on the operation of material cause and effect, nor do they aim at a naturalistic representation of ordinary life. Events are interconnected in a multiplicity of ways, and the association of sentiments and objects is often idiosyncratic to the culture (for example, poverty, chastity, stability). There is little sense of individualised character, though traditional types are well recognised and constantly repeated. The language and style of literature are often those of the collective wisdom of tradition and what we now call 'the folk' and then included all classes. It is 'sententious', full of accepted commonplaces, stuffed with proverbs, full of word-play, often general and unspecific, imprecise to our way of thinking, hyperbolical in a way that offends our sense of literal accuracy (knights fighting up to the ankles in blood—how *could* it be so?). In short, we have a developed version of Old English traditional literature, not the same but recognisably of similar kind.

This is extremely different in style and sentiment from post-seventeenth-century literature, as I have already noted. To emphasise the difference is not to make a value-judgment about the respective merits of any period of literary culture, but to assert a preliminary need for understanding the characteristics of any period and particularly for realising the progressively unusual nature of European and American culture since the seventeenth century, and by consequence all cultures in the modern world which largely reflect the 'scientific' mind. In this respect the words of a social anthropologist who has much experience of traditional African folk-tale are a salutary warning:

> to take as our yardstick the present circumstances of literature in Western Europe—or rather perhaps those of a generation or so ago—and assume that this is the standard by which we estimate all other literatures is to show a profound lack of historical and comparative perspective. There is no reason to suppose that our peculiar circumstances are the 'natural' ones towards which all literature is somehow striving to develop or by which it must everywhere be measured.[17]

When we approach fourteenth-century literature in this enquiring mood we find many at first alien structures and we limit ourselves if we do not do justice to the strangeness. There is no point in travelling if you resent change, or cannot detect it. You might as well stay at home or stop complaining when abroad that you can't get what you are used to.

Yet fourteenth-century culture and literature, and the work of Chaucer in particular, do contain tensions and qualities of a kind apparently more radical than normal traditional variation and which from our historical position do seem to lead to the emergence of the modern 'scientific' mind. The production of manuscripts was considerable, and the ability to read, if not to write, may have extended to more than half the total population. Even such a traditional institution as the court had so extensive a documentary base that we have far more records of the life of that minor courtier, Geoffrey Chaucer, than we have of Shakespeare, who lived two centuries later. In the culture as a whole there were increasing possibilities therefore of the preservation, accumulation and testing of knowledge, and of freeing communication from context. There was an increasing sense of the internalised individual as against the external collective, and increasing specialisation of function, especially amongst the citizens of London. London itself resembled the great European towns in the advances in regularising conduct of business, developing a sense of objective, measurable time through clockwork, and depersonalising transactions by the use of money. These tendencies had existed earlier and were moreover only certain threads in the whole tapestry which contained much that was traditional and customary; but innovation and the mixture of tradition and innovation become more noticeable in the fourteenth century.

The mixture is particularly evident in the work of Chaucer, though in his very different, more troubled, way Langland also testifies to it. Chaucer was very advanced for his times and makes an immediate appeal to modern readers. We respond to his realism, occasional bawdiness, satire, irony, cynicism. In *Troilus and Criseyde* and the more or less bawdy comic poems of *The Canterbury Tales* he seems to present to us with as naturalistic an account of life as it might be lived as any nineteenth-century realistic novelist or dramatist. In particular he has a truly remarkable and (for his time) advanced gift for individualistic characterisation, with the corresponding tendency to isolate an individual from his context. Dr Jill Mann concludes her study of Chaucer's description of certain characters in the *General Prologue* with the following:

> The Prologue proves to be a poem about work. The society it evokes is not a collection of individuals or types with an eternal or universal significance, but particularly a society in which work as a social experience conditions personality and the standpoint from which an individual views the world. In the *Prologue*, as in history, it is specialised work which ushers in a *world where relativised values and the individual consciousness are dominant*.[18]

This is an admirable summary of some principal aspects of the 'non-archaic' mind, the modern 'scientific' mind. Even satire, so often conservative, and partly so in Chaucer, is also ambiguous with him. The traditional pattern of the feminine ideal, applied in parodic fashion to the village-wench Alison in *The Miller's Tale*, mocks Alison from a position of social superiority, but that Chaucer could use the tradition so implies detachment from it (see pp. 30 ff). His use of the traditional topos of the arming of the warrior is even more undermining, in complete contrast with the *Gawain*-poet's use of the same topos (see pp. 142 ff). Chaucer's view of the class-structure (see pp. 54ff) is undoubtedly that of the 'new man', the literate layman. In the more general movements of the mind he also shows many advanced characteristics. Linguistically he has a high proportion of new words. This is not to say that he invented them or even that he was the first to use them when he is only *recorded* as the first to use them; but their frequency is significant.[19] It is likely, could we but know it, that some aspects of his syntax, especially in colloquial circumstances, are equally advanced. His use of metre may be speculatively linked with the new sense of regular, clockwork time (though this is the kind of speculation that philologists dislike).[20] In scientific matters Chaucer was at least in the forefront of astronomical popularising by writing his *Astrolabe* in English. His friendship with the Lollard knights[21] and some elements of his work suggest a deep sympathy with this proto-Protestant movement, lay, literate, literalistic, transcending class boundaries. Lollardy was part of the movement that fragmented the archaic holistic structures of medieval religion, though it brought the change by developing tendencies already within the Church and indeed within the New Testament itself.

Our criticism does right to bring out the modernism of Chaucer, and to emphasise these and other characteristics. Yet caution is needed. Chaucer's modernism is closely related to what I have called the Neoclassical period. The creative force of the 'scientific' mind as it evolved was, as it seems, an important element in that period. But the force continues, and yet we begin to see that many of the stylistic aspects of that period are now less dominant. The autonomous individual character clearly distinguished from the event is an example. In the most modern literature it might be argued that the autonomous character is dissolving. A great deal of modern Chaucer criticism actually envisages Chaucer's characters more as if they were autonomous figures in a nineteenth-century realistic novel or play than as if they were truly modern creations. Critics may inadvertently impose upon ancient authors the patterns of yesterday, as Ruth Finnegan observes (above, p. 17). Some of yesterday's patterns may be valid, but distortions arise if objective consideration of the full complexities of the whole text is overlooked. Such consideration shows that modernistic as Chaucer is, he also, like his period, represents many 'archaic' (and timeless) characteristics, along with many that are to be seen as the special configurations of his time. We may take once again the example of characterisation. In Chaucer's works characters are individualistic and autonomous in flashes or short stretches. Only when characters in a story can be seen objectively, set off clearly against the rest (as we first see Criseyde, for example) can we distinguish between objective and subjective, and so plunge into the character's inner mind. Then we can have a sense of the objective external impersonal compulsions of law, as against personal loyalties; only when we can conceive of such external regularities imposed upon the individual can we also conceive of the internal subjective fluctuations of desire and thought, of the relativism of judgments. Chaucer achieves such distinction of subjective from objective with astonishing richness in his portrayal of Criseyde—hence the frequency with which the poem is regarded as a novel. Yet along with this novelty is a variety of 'archaic' elements. Troilus's love is one. Another is his eventual apotheosis, which gives so much trouble to modern readers who must constantly explain it away; and indeed it is, in a sense, inconsistent with some of what has gone before. The story has gaps in naturalistic plausibility, and the attempts to explain them in terms of novelistic (and 'scientific') causality always risk violating the still underlying 'archaic' concepts of honour, love and war. Much of the story is told in the 'archaic' style of the traditional story-teller, sententious, wise, commonplace, reflecting 'what mankind have long possessed', 'have often compared' and 'persist to value the possession' of, 'because frequent comparisons have confirmed opinion in its favour'.

> Swich is this world, whoso it kan byholde.
> In ech estat is litel hertes reste.
> God leve us for to take it for the beste.
>
> (*TC*, v, 1748–50)

This is a sympathetic comment on a commonplace of misery. It is true, resigned, sensible, passive. Why should we assume that it is ironical on the part of the poet? Why assume that it is spoken by a foolish so-called Narrator? Because Neoclassical literary criteria exclude traditional, sententious, proverbial wisdom. 'Make it new!' as Ezra Pound cries. The concept of the Narrator is itself a device of the analytical modern 'scientific' mind, prising apart a narrative style comprised of many different elements. That is legitimate unless it denatures the actual quality of the poem: divorce destroys the marriage; but marriage has to be between two separably conceived people.

The nature of Chaucer's works as a whole is that they constitute an idiosyncratic amalgam of the old and the new, and we must not deny the old. Chaucer was not in rebellion against the dominant forces of the time, and they too were a mixture of the old and the new, like the court and the city which were such strong moulding forces on Chaucer. It would do no harm rather to emphasise Chaucer's 'archaic' qualities. He was a courtier (and it is anachronistic to see him as a bourgeois overawed by the social superiority of his normal company). The court was a network of personal relationships. Class-distinctions easily overlapped in some ways, and Chaucer easily registered a great social range. He presents his work in a social, moral and sometimes religious context. It is not hard for us, while registering the modernity of his poems as autonomous fictions, to see how they also arise out of more 'archaic' attitudes. By their very nature, as retold stories, they are traditional, and it is of the nature of tradition to maintain continuity with change. By a final paradox Chaucer himself recognised the real modernity of his greatest works in such a way as to assert his own final allegiance to the 'archaic': he denounced in the 'Retracciouns' to *The Canterbury Tales* his autonomous fictions, *Troilus and Criseyde* and the rest, because they were not linked to the great 'archaic' web of religious instruction, and were therefore 'sounyng unto synne'. We may say he condemned them *because* they were fictions, relatively context-free, autonomous entertainment, art not applied art. But if we ourselves reject that, to us, incomprehensible rejection; if we express a strong disapproval of Chaucer's 'archaic' values, we are by that very act abandoning any claim we may have to a modernity, to a modern relativism. To like or dislike, to express value-judgments, are themselves 'archaic', not modern. The rejection of the 'archaic' is itself 'archaic'.

2 Love and Marriage in Chaucer's Poetry*

The incompatibility of love with marriage in the poetry of Chaucer is a platitude so widely accepted that it is worth pointing out that it is quite untrue. Chaucer nowhere celebrates illicit love, though it is sometimes material for a joke, or satire. The only exception seems to be *Troilus and Criseyde*, and it may be argued that this exception is more apparent than real.

The Book of the Duchess, though an elegy, records a love-affair which as a matter of historical fact had culminated in marriage—Chaucer's audience knew, without being told, that the Duchess Blanche had been John of Gaunt's wife. It is significant that Chaucer told their story in the terms of fashionable love-poetry. In *The Knight's Tale*, written just before or just after *Troilus*, the aim of each lover is marriage, and each lover expects to win Emily only through marriage. In every one of the legends in *The Legend of Good Women* there is an explicit connection between love and marriage—a connection emphasised by the God of Love in the prologue to the legends when he praises Alceste (*Pro.*, F, 544–6). In the legends themselves every deserted lover is either a wife or has been betrayed by the promise of marriage.[1] The general attitude which may be said to underlie all Chaucer's serious writing about love is set forth most succinctly in the lines concerning Jason and Medea:

> They been acorded ful bytwixe hem two
> That Jason shal hire *wedde, as trewe knyght.*
> *(LGW, 1635–6)*

In *The Squire's Tale* the honourable nature of the falcon's love is emphasised (*CT*, v, 533–4). And, of course, love is perfectly compatible with marriage in *The Wife of Bath's Tale*, *The Clerk's Tale* (though with a difference), *The Franklin's Tale* especially, and others. It would hardly be

* First published in *Modern Language Review*, 49 (1954) 461–4.

worth stating these obvious facts did not even well-known scholars assert
love to be incompatible with marriage in Chaucer's thought, and *Troilus*
appear to be so outstanding an exception.

If, however, we look at *Troilus* without prejudice we find that not only
Troilus himself but also Chaucer treats the love between Troilus and
Criseyde as in accordance with the divine ordering of the world, and as
entirely honourable. The crucial comments come at the end of Book III.
Troilus sings a triumphant song beginning,

> Love, that of erthe and se hath governaunce,
> Love, that his hestes hath in hevenes hye,
> Love, that with an holsom alliaunce
> Halt peples joyned, as hym lest hem gye,
> Love, that knetteth lawe of compaignie,
> And couples doth in vertu for to dwelle,
> Bynd this acord, that I have told and telle.
>
> (*TC*, III, 1744–50)

The song ends,
> So wolde God, that auctour is of kynde,
> That with his bond Love of his vertu liste
> To cerclen hertes alle, and faste bynde,
> That from his bond no wight the wey out wiste;
> And hertes colde, hem wolde I that he twiste
> To make hem love, and that hem liste ay rewe
> On hertes sore, and kepe hem that ben trewe.
>
> (*TC*, III, 1765–71)

Love is the golden chain that maintains and controls the whole universe; it
is the expression of God's creative activity. It would be hard to prove that
such love were in any way immoral. Indeed, the passage from Chaucer's
translation of Boethius's *Consolation of Philosophy* on which this song is
based says of the bond of Love that 'this love halt togidres peples joyned
with an holy boond, and knytteth sacrement of mariages of chaste loves'
(*Boece*, II, metre 8). Troilus obviously must omit the reference to marriage,
since he and Criseyde are not married, but it may be noticed that when their
love is consummated Troilus gives thanks first to Love, then to Love's
mother, Venus 'the wel-willy planete', and then to Imeneus—Hymen (*TC*,
III, 1254–60). There is no doubt that *Troilus* thinks his love honourable.
How are we to reconcile such a view with the facts of the plot which

Chaucer took from Boccaccio, and which tells the story of what is after all no more than a furtive liaison?

It might be argued that Troilus is deceiving himself. If he was, then so was Chaucer, for Chaucer praises Troilus's virtuous behaviour as inspired by love, and says

> For soth to seyne, he lost held every wyght,
> But if he were in Loves heigh servise,
> I mene folk that oughte it ben of right.
>
>   (*TC*, iii, 1793–5)

The only possible assumption is that Troilus 'oughte it ben of right' as well. From this can be drawn only one of two possible conclusions. Either Chaucer is saying openly that illicit love is virtuous and lawful (which is contrary to the whole tenor of his writings, and which any consideration of historical and literary circumstance will show is unlikely); or Chaucer is deliberately *obscuring* the fact of illicit love. There seems to be evidence in the literary practice of the times to show that the second alternative may be the true one.

There is an important distinction to be made in medieval literature between the basic plot or substance of a story (often called the 'matter' by Chaucer), and its presentation or interpretation. The clearest recent exposition of the importance of this distinction is to be found in Professor E. Vinaver's brilliant introduction to *The Works of Sir Thomas Malory* (1947)[2] where, following Chrétien de Troyes, he calls the plot the *matiere* and the presentation the *sen*. Medieval writers did not consciously alter the main outline of the plot; on the other hand they considered themselves perfectly free to alter its significance, to *interpret* it, in any way they desired. A minor example of Chaucer's reluctance to alter the *matiere* even when it seemed to conflict with the *sen* (in this case character) may be found in *The Man of Law's Tale*. In two instances certain actions are reported by his source which Chaucer appears to feel do not accord with the characters of the actors (*CT*, ii, 1009 and 1086). Although his source is quite unequivocal Chaucer in each case adds the doubting phrase 'Som men wolde seyn.' But he does not alter the facts themselves.

Troilus and Criseyde, it may be suggested, offers a major example of conflict between *matiere* and *sen*. The facts of the story of Troilus were a matter of history to Chaucer. Where he diverges from or supplements the facts in his main source, Boccaccio's *Il Filostrato*, it is usually because he is conflating Boccaccio's account with older authorities, such as Benoît de Sainte-Maure, Guido delle Colonne, or Joseph of Exeter (e.g. *TC*, iv, 50–4,

137–8; v, 799, etc.). He respected facts as much as a historian does, and probably felt he had as little warrant to alter them, although it is a commonplace that he entirely altered the spirit of the poem. Thus it would appear that Chaucer retained the plot about illicit love, and built on it a poem about honourable love.

If this be a correct analysis of the situation we shall expect to find some trace of an attempt to account for the discrepancy. The point at which the strain appears is to be found in the *secrecy* of the love-affair. If their love is honourable, why do they not marry? The fact was that they did not, and Chaucer could not alter that. All he could do was in some way to account for it. He reveals his artistry and his honesty by making no effort to invent elaborate reasons which by their very presence would draw attention to what he wished to be ignored. He takes what we can now see to be the simplest and most obvious course—he merely says that these matters are ordered differently elsewhere. He chooses the beginning of Book II for his principal effort to account for the secrecy—a position neither too obscure nor too prominent. He remarks on the different customs of lovers in different lands and ages, for his audience knew well enough that he was writing of events in a far country that had happened long ago. And he very obviously has the curious secrecy of Troilus's love-affair chiefly in mind when he writes

> Ek in som lond were al the game shent
> If that they ferde in love *as men don here*,
> As thus, in *opyn* doyng or in chere,
> In visityng, in forme . . .
>
> (*TC*, II, 38–41)

This plea of different manners goes some way to account for Troilus not marrying Criseyde, but Chaucer deals with his problem mainly by silence. He does everything he can to make us understand that their love is ordained by God (for the planet Venus, as astrologers taught,[3] is the agent of God's Providence), and everything he can to avoid the question at the turning-point of the story of why they did not solve their dilemma by marriage. Of course he was helped in his silence about marriage by the fact that he was writing in a tradition which had often dissociated love and marriage.

It must be admitted that the fundamental inconsistency between a *matiere* of illicit love and a *sen* of legitimate love is an artistic blemish, though of a kind met elsewhere in medieval literature.[4] If, however, we accept this basic inconsistency the poem becomes more comprehensible and even more profound. By recognising the difference between the plot and the presentation we may protect ourselves from the confusion that inevitably follows if we criticise the one in terms of the other as if they were of equal importance and had each the same implication (though we repeat that in a perfect poem there *ought* to be a complete correspondence between the two). Thus we cannot say that Troilus's love is really immoral, because according to the plot he and Criseyde were not married. Questions of morality (if they are important in the poem) belong, like those of character, description, etc., to the sphere of the *sen*, not to that of the *matiere*. Troilus's love is moral and in accordance with the divine ordinance because Chaucer plainly tells us so. For understanding the poet's purpose the *sen* is what is most important, because that is the poet's own contribution, his own poetic feeling about the story. If the *matiere* is the skeleton, the *sen* is the flesh and blood, the very character and soul of the work.

If the argument presented above be correct our opinions about many parts of the poem may be affected. In particular our views about the Epilogue may well be seriously modified. But this rich, subtle, and in some ways illogical ending raises too many problems to be dealt with at the tail-end of an article. It will be enough to say that we shall only begin fully to understand Chaucer's purpose and consequently the degree of his artistic success or failure in *Troilus* and other poems when we take into account such bases of his art and thought as the vitally important distinction between *sen* and *matiere*, and his uniformly exalted conception of love.

3 Chaucer's *Complaint of Mars**

The 'story' in *The Complaint of Mars* of Mars's love for Venus is usually said to be taken from Ovid's account of how Vulcan surprised the lovers at the instigation of the Sun (*Metamorphoses*, IV, 171–89). Ovid's amusing anecdote was undoubtedly the main source of this information in the Middle Ages. But the story was also treated by astrologising mythographers. The earliest of these known to the Middle Ages was Hyginus, who drew on Greek sources now lost. He probably lived in the second century AD but was for long confused with the librarian and freedman of Augustus of the same name. In his *Poetica Astronomica* he refers to the planet Mars, and to Mars's love for Venus, thus:

> Tertia [i.e. planeta] est stella Martis, quam alii Herculis dixerunt, Veneris sequens stellam; hac (ut Eratosthenes ait) de causa: Quod Vulcanus cum uxorem Venerem duxisset, et propter eius observantium Marti eius copia non fieret, ut nihil aliud assequi videretur, nisi sua stella Veneris sidus persequi a Venere impetravit. Itaque cum vehementer eum amor incenderet, rem significans, e facto stellam Pyroenta appellavit.[1]

It is to be noted that Hyginus calls Mars the 'third planet', which may have suggested Chaucer's reference to Mars as 'the thridde hevenes lord' (*Complaint*, 29), for the usual though not the only method of numbering the heavens was from the earth outward, which makes the third heaven that of Venus.

It would be rash to assert dogmatically that Hyginus was certainly the basis for Chaucer's astrological fantasy, for of course Mars and Venus were known as planets throughout the Middle Ages. But no other mythographer takes quite the line that both Chaucer and Hyginus take. It is at least a curious coincidence.

* First published in *N & Q*, 199 (1954) 462–3.

The characteristics attributed to Venus:

> My lady is the verrey sours and welle
> Of beaute, lust, fredom, and gentilnesse,
> Of riche aray—how dere men hit selle!—
> Of al disport in which men frendly duelle,
> Of love and pley, and of benigne humblesse,
> Of soun of instrumentes of al swetnesse;
> And therto so wel fortuned and thewed
> That thorogh the world her goodnesse is yshewed.
>
> (*Complaint*, 174–81)

are not those of the usual heroine of romance; they are the essential characteristics of the planet, as developed by the fourteenth century. The most useful compendium of astrological and mythological knowledge open to literary men of the late fourteenth century was Boccaccio's *De Genealogia Deorum*. Chaucer may have known it, though it is not certain that he did (see Robinson's notes to *The Legend of Good Women* in his edition of Chaucer's *Works*.[2] Boccaccio has a very long entry on Venus the planet, following his favourite astrologers Albumasar and the 'venerable Andalo'. Among much else he says (*De Genealogia*, III, 22):

> Volunt igitur Venerem esse *feminam* complexione flegmaticam atque nocturnam, apud amicos *humilem* et *benignam, acute meditationis in compositionibus carminum*, periuria ridentem, mendacem, credulam, *liberalem*, patientem et levitatis plurime, honesti tamen moris et aspectus, *hylarem*, voluptuosam, dulciloquam maxime, atque aspernatricem corpore fortitudinis et animi debilitatis.

All this signifies great *beauty*, pleasure in the use of precious scents and unguents, enjoyment of sweets, *gambling*, wine, food, all kinds of fornication. She has mastery in splendid works of art of all kinds, *delights in fine clothes*, has pleasure in singing, laughter, dancing, feasts, marriages, and so forth. She is in general a *beneficent* planet, as all the astrologers teach. She presides over friendship. She is the brightest of all planets. Chaucer's stanza is in fact a fair summary and selection of the characteristic traits attributed to the planet.

In the same section Boccaccio has a paragraph elaborating the commonplace that 'God makes nothing in vain' (which occurs elsewhere in Chaucer, e.g. *The Franklin's Tale, CT*, v, 867) and explaining that God made the planets not merely for beauty, but in order to control the earth.

This helps to illuminate Mars's words, ll. 164 ff, rather more directly than the passage from Dante (*Convivio*, ii, 5, 8, 9) referred to by the editors.

All the same, it would again be rash to claim the *De Genealogia* as a certain source. This work, regarded by Boccaccio as his masterpiece, is a compilation of many authors, literary and astrological, a number of whom Chaucer had certainly read. All that can be claimed is that the *De Genealogia* offers illuminating parallels which have not been brought forward before. When these, and the parallel with Hyginus, are duly weighed, it becomes more than ever difficult to accept the theory that Chaucer was writing an allegorical account of a courtier's *amour*, and not a traditionally allegorical account of certain astronomical movements.

4 The Ideal of Feminine Beauty in Medieval Literature, especially the Harley Lyrics, Chaucer, and some Elizabethans*

I. THE TYPE

The formal description of a person is a well-recognised device of many medieval authors. But the extraordinary fixity of the type of heroine so described, throughout the countries and centuries, has never been emphasised as it should be, with all that it implies for the understanding of individual authors and of the modes of literature itself.

As with so much medieval vernacular literature the seed of the idea was first nourished in later Greek and Latin Classical literature and began to undergo its characteristic medieval development at the hands of Latin writers of about the fifth century.[1]

A writer who makes a convenient point of departure for the Middle Ages is Dares Phrygius. Writing probably in the fifth century but deriving from Greek originals of at least as early as the first century, he had himself an enormous vogue in the Middle Ages, and was of course at the fountain-head of the great stream of medieval writing about Troy. In the *De Excidio Troiae Historia* Dares gives a series of brief portraits of the chief persons concerned at Troy, among them Helen, Polyxena and Briseida.[2] Here is the later-Classical ideal of feminine beauty ready to receive its medieval development. Helen, curiously enough, is not described in visual terms, but the other two are each *candida* with yellow hair (*flavis*), and each is clearly of the same general appearance; though Polyxena is tall, while Briseida is 'not tall' and has the joined eyebrows which were a mark of beauty to the Greeks.[3]

However, the first formal description of a beautiful woman that seems to have survived is one written by Maximian in the sixth century.[4] It is so

---

* First published in *Modern Language Review*, 50 (1955) 257–69.

important that it must be quoted again, for it gives the type of all the beautiful women in European literature up till the end of the sixteenth century.

> Aurea caesaries demissaque lactea cervix,
> Vultibus ingenuis visu sedere magis,
> Nigra supercilia, frons libera, lumina clara,
> Urebant animum saepe notata meum.
> Flammea dilexi modicumque tumentia labra
> Quae gustata mihi basia plena darent.[5]

'Milky' whiteness; the golden hair contrasting strikingly with the black eyebrows; the slightly swelling lips; these establish the type to which *every* lady conforms in all the medieval Latin and vernacular literature of Europe. This conformity is a remarkable illustration of the cultural unity of medieval Europe, and of the general aim of medieval writers to achieve a uniform, non-realistic ideal. Nor does the Renaissance make much difference.

Before the twelfth century the description of the beautiful woman does not seem to have been of great importance in literature. The full organisation of the ideal of feminine beauty in formal description is first seen in the work of Matthew of Vendôme, though even here it is only one of several types who are described. He gives an important place to descriptions of persons in the *Ars Versificatoria*, and two examples of the description of a beautiful woman; in each case, be it noted, Helen of Troy.[6] In the first example her hair is golden, forehead white as paper, eyebrows black and thin. The space between the eyes (in contrast to the Greek ideal) is white and clear, a 'milky way'; the face is a shining star; the eyes are like stars. She has a little smile, a nose neither too big nor too small. Her face is rosy, her colouring white and red, like rose and snow. Teeth are like ivory, lips are small, slightly swelling, honeyed. Her mouth smells like a rose, her neck is smooth, shoulders radiant and well spaced (*dispatidi*), breasts small, and figure incomparable.

Matthew's second portrait is more highly wrought still. This time the forehead is like milk, and, like that of Maximian's lady, is *libera*. But there is no difference whatever in the type of many of the comparisons. Eyes are still like stars, teeth like ivory, the neck like snow, and the lady is still narrow down to the waist, with a swelling belly.[7] The skin of her hands is smooth, not slack, her legs fleshy (or white), her foot short and toes straight.

Matthew's lead is followed by the Englishman Geoffrey of Vinsauf. His description of a beautiful woman[8] is much fuller than Matthew's, though

without his trifling indecencies and without a name. Both writers begin
with a reference to Nature who has lavished her gifts on this superb
creature. Geoffrey has the same type—golden hair, black eyebrows, white
skin, long neck (a column), long arms, long thin milk-white fingers, very
small waist, very short foot. Snow, lilies, stars, crystal, are the terms of
comparison. Small variations are introduced; the mouth smells not like a
rose, but like incense: this seems understandably not to have become
popular. Geoffrey says this kind of portrait is perhaps *res quasi trita / Et
vetus*, and goes on to give something much more strange and rare; but the
old-fashioned *formae descriptio* persisted.

The works of these rhetoricians were used as school-books, and their
influence was immense. Chaucer of course knew Geoffrey.[9] They did not
invent the type, but they set their seal upon it. They crystallised in this
respect the concepts held in solution in the mind of ages.[10]

That this type did not depend for its extension simply upon the influence
of the rhetoricians may be shown by its occurrence in writers
contemporary with them, who must have been to some extent dependent
on works similar to the elegy of Maximian referred to above, and on earlier
rhetorical works. An example of the mechanical application of the formula
as it was presumably taught in the schools is provided by Gerald of Barry
(*c.* 1147–1220) in his *Descriptio quaedam puellae*.[11]

More poetical examples of typical beauty may be found in the Latin
poems of the so-called 'wandering scholars'.[12] In twelfth-century French
the works of Benoît de Sainte-Maure and Chrétien de Troyes bear witness
to the prevalence of the type in courtly vernacular as well as learned Latin.[13]
Of course there are minor variants. 'Grey' eyes (*vairs*) seem to be a
contribution from the French vernacular; breasts may be whiter than
hawthorn as well as snow; ladies are either tall, or 'not too tall', and they
are usually plump, but sometimes slender. Briseida alone has a blemish; her
eyebrows are separated by no 'milky way' but are joined.

The conventional description is strong in the thirteenth century,[14] and it
can be no surprise to find it in the courtly Guillaume's first part of *Le
Roman de la Rose*. Since the heroine's qualities are 'distributed' in allegory,
she cannot be described in the usual way, but there are several descriptions
of ladies. The first we meet is Idleness.[15] Her hair is yellow, her eyebrows
curved and sleek, her eyes grey—as falcon this time—her complexion
white and red, mouth small, chin cloven (perhaps the earliest occurrence of
this popular feature)[16]—in a word, she is of the usual type. Another
interesting description is the very personification of Beauty.[17] She is as
bright as moonlight, her flesh tender, face lily and rose, she is slim, her hair
is yellow and reaches to her heels.[18] All her body is well wrought.

Guillaume says she is not made up. Chaucer adds furthermore that she does not pluck her eyebrows ('No wyndred browis hadde she', l. 1018). Similarly, the lady Gladness,[19] who sings so sweetly, is like a rose for colour, of tender flesh, white unblemished forehead, dark eyebrows, eyes large in the French and grey in the English, with a small mouth (not in the English), hair yellow and shining, bound with the inevitable *fil d'or* (not in the English), and richly clad. Largesse has the usual flesh, 'whit as mylk'.[20] Fraunchyse, too, is not brown or dun, but white as new-fallen snow; her eyes are grey and laughing, eyebrows curved. She too has hair down to her heels, but only in the English, and is well clothed in 'roket'.[21] Curtesye is the only exception. Guillaume says:

> Ele fu une clere brune
> Le vis avoit cler et luisant.[22]

It is clear, however, that with this solitary and minor exception Guillaume in each of his portraits is describing precisely the same type of female beauty; there could be no clearer example of its dominance.

II. THE HARLEY LYRICS

How salutary a knowledge of governing conventions can be in the historical criticism of literature may be seen in applying the knowledge of this particular convention of beauty to the English lyrics of Harley MS 2253.[23] Several lyrics reveal the influence of the convention. The most obvious example is 'The Fair Maid of Ribblesdale'.[24] The Fair Maid's hue is bright as a sunbeam, and her forehead by day gives more light than the moon by night. She is lily and rose, and her hair is bound with a 'fyldor'

> Heo haþ browes bend an heh
> whyt bytuene ant nout to neh

and we might well guess that her brows are black, but the poet does not say so. Her breath is sweet ('speche as spices spredes'); her locks are long, her cheeks white and red as roses.

> Hire teht aren white as bon of whal.

Whalebone is presumably 'ivory'; it appears again in the same poem, and also in another lyric,

A wayle whyt ase whalles bon,
a grein in golde þat godly shon,[25]

where clearly the same white-pink-golden girl is in the poet's mind. In the present piece the long, white, full, smooth, well-set neck, like a column, of the rhetorical tradition, becomes a

swannes swyre swyþe wel ysette
a sponne lengore þen y mette.

The comparison with a swan's neck has a certain grotesque charm. It is a nice example of unrealistic idealisation which in the Elizabethan period might have been called a conceit, and may well remind us of Spenser's *Prothalamion*. The lady's whiteness is compared with paper; her lips are red to read romances. Her arms are an ell long—which again has the poetic virtue of concreteness, and a touch of almost absurd exaggeration. Her breasts are like two apples of paradise, which is a happy turn of the 'apples' and 'paradise' clichés. Her waist is slender. Her sides, 'soft as silk', call inevitably to be likened to 'milk', but it is 'morenmylk'. It may be doubted if such milk is indeed whiter than that drawn at other times of day, but the associations of morning are fresh and sweet, and the original cliché is thereby rejuvenated, though the new form soon became worn.

The comments on the lady's clothes in the last-but-one stanza are restricted to a description of the virtuous stone set within her jewelled girdle. Geoffrey of Vinsauf has a passage describing the clothes of the lady chiefly in terms of her jewels, and so this is within the learned tradition. But more particularly it appears to be a close parallel to, and probably a borrowing from, the slightly fuller description of the girdle of Rychesse in *Le Roman de la Rose*, which has a stone 'of vertu gret and mochel of myght'.[26] Harley MS 2253 is of the early fourteenth century, and this poem was perhaps written about the turn of the century. At all events it is clear that the poet is writing in what may be called a well-known if not well-worn tradition, a century and a half old at least. This is the poem of which a great medievalist said, before the texts of the rhetoricians were made available, that it depicts the 'damsel of Ribblesdale' 'with the precision of a miniature. . . . This becomes a detestable way of writing later on, with the seventeenth-century cataloguers of feminine charms, but in the fourteenth century it at any rate shows that the poet has his eye on the object.'[27] The medieval poet is quite as 'conventional' as those of the seventeenth century. Is it merely our ignorance of the perhaps thousands of lost lyrics that makes us rate the few survivors so highly? Certainly no criticism of the English medieval lyric which praises its 'freshness' can reveal anything of its contemporary quality. Their 'freshness' is our ignorance. Theories of their popular origin must also be received with caution. At least some English lyrics certainly attempt to be in the sophisticated rhetorical tradition, learned if not courtly as well. That the English lyrics have a certain rusticity, an occasional slightly absurd naivety cannot be denied, but that is another matter. This is not to question their genuine poetic charm, or deny that our ignorance enhances their poetic effect for us. They have a kind of rarity value. But it is not safe to say the poet *saw* Sir Edmund's 'damsel of Ribblesdale'. It is certain that he *imagined* her as the literary and rhetorical tradition never wearied of painting her.

The 'Fair Maid' has a few lines in common with 'Blow Northerne Wynd',[28] which also uses the descriptive convention fairly fully. Professor Brook considers 'Blow Northerne Wynd' to be a '*trouvère*-lyric' with a refrain borrowed from folksong.[29] It is certainly a learned lyric, with its formal description, comparisons with precious stones and elementary allegory. It lacks the vividness of the 'Fair Maid' and the concreteness of description which is one of the great virtues of the set-piece catalogue. The one touch of concrete imagery compares the brightness of the lady's face to a lantern shining by night. But colour of hair and eyes is not mentioned.

We should not overlook here the famous poem 'Alysoun' (Brook, iv). It is clear that Alysoun belongs to the same golden-haired dark-eyebrowed slender-waisted type.

> On heu hire her is fayr ynoh
>   hire browe broune, hire eȝe blake;
> wiþ lossum chere he on me lok,
>   wiþ middel smal ant wel ymake.

Here four characteristics out of the five mentioned are entirely typical—the fair hair, dark eyebrow, gaiety (a constant and pleasing trait) and slender waist. Her black eye, however, as Sir Edmund Chambers long ago noted, is an unusual touch. Eyes are usually 'great and grey enough', as in the 'Fair Maid'. Alysoun's neck is 'whiter than the swan'—the swan seems to be a characteristic of the English vernacular, and is a change from snow, ivory and crystal. We may feel a countryside freshness about it. Cliché as it is, it seems to distinguish vernacular poetry from that of the learned, though often grosser, tongue.

In the course of the thirteenth century (not without suggestion from the twelfth) it is possible to discern an increasing significance in the type of the beautiful woman. In the rhetoricians, and in such exercises as those of

Gerald, the description is a rhetorical adornment, a piece of beautiful virtuosity. But to some extent in Chrétien, and particularly in the lyric poets, Latin, French and English, it is not merely beauty which is being described; it is the beloved.[30] Typical beauty is harnessed to the dominant emotion of the age, to love. The rhetoricians are interested in describing various types, old and young, good and bad. They do not give special prominence to the beautiful woman even though she is more important to them than to Classical writers. But in the kind of story most favoured, a love-story, the beautiful beloved is the North Star to every wandering bark of a story. Conventionally it is her beauty which first arouses the hero's love (he is always 'smitten' through the eyes), and while her beauty thus attracts love, love itself surrounds her beauty with a special radiance, gives it a special delight and power. Since love is on the whole a moral emotion for the later medieval courtly writers, virtuous itself and encouraging virtue in the lover (the adulterous element has been over-emphasised), the heroine herself becomes more precious; her physical beauty often becomes a reflexion of moral beauty. Of course there are exceptions: the indecencies of Latin lyrics; Helen of Troy; possibly Arthur's Guinivere; and Briseida–Criseyde. Medieval writers do not neglect the corruption of the good. But it is the corruption of the good. Beauty is not in itself evil. By the late sixteenth century there must be few examples of typically beautiful heroines whose physical beauty does not reflect moral beauty.

III. CHAUCER

In the first instance, Chaucer's use of the convention[31] can best be shown by examination of his use of a specific source. *Le Roman de la Rose* has already been discussed. Chaucer's translation is so close as to give only very minor hints of his personal artistry. The earliest example of Chaucer's more independent use of the type is in *The Book of the Duchess*, where the Duchess Blanche is described. The main source for the description, as has long been known,[32] is Machaut's 'Le Jugement dou Roy de Behaingne'.[33] Machaut was both court poet and a learned man. He was therefore in both the important traditions of courtly vernacular literature and of the training of the schools. His description of the lady in 'Le Jugement dou Roy de Behaingne' occupies some 150 lines, crammed with adjectives.[34] It need hardly be said that her hair is gold, eyebrows a black thread, the nose well shaped (Machaut surpasses all exemplars by describing it also as clean and sweet-smelling). Her chin is cloven. She is in general pink and white, plump and tender with long arms and fingers, and breasts white, firm, round, high, small. Machaut also tells us her age.[35] It is fourteen and a half.

The full power of the convention in Chaucer's mind is nowhere better demonstrated than in the way he takes over this two-centuries-old picture to describe a living woman whom he had known. Nor would it be wise to assume that the Duchess had not resembled the picture drawn. The chances are that women aimed to look like the universally accepted ideal. Hair can be dyed and plucked eyebrows were not unknown in the fourteenth century.

Once one is struck by the extreme closeness of the description of Blanche to that of the lady in Machaut's poem, the interest lies in watching Chaucer enliven the traditional description. An early example of how he gives a new twist to a cliché is provided by the description of the Duchess's hair:

> For every heer on hir hed,
> Soth to seyne, hyt was not red,
> Ne nouther yelowe, ne broun hyt nas,
> Me thoghte most lyk gold hyt was.[36]
>
> (ll. 855–8)

Unexpected conclusion! Machaut has

> Car si cheveus ressambloient fil d'or
> Et n'estoient ne trop blont ne trop sor.[37]

Chaucer omits Machaut's description of forehead, eyebrows, nose, mouth, teeth, chin, haunches, thighs, legs, feet, flesh, and the statement of age. He does not say the eyes are grey and large, but he adds that Blanche had a direct glance—a good example of a physical description which points to moral qualities, and, as far as I have noticed, a unique detail. He also adds to Machaut's description that her shoulders were 'ryght faire' (l. 952) and that

> Hyr throte, as I have now memoyre,
> Semed a round tour of yvoyre,
> Of good gretnesse, and noght to gret.
>
> (ll. 945–8)

These very conventional additions show that Chaucer was by no means discontented with the rhetorical tradition. He adds also plumpness to the arms, and—a simple, vivid detail, again unique so far as I know, and very successful—red nails to the customarily white hands (l. 955). He adds also that her hips were broad, her back straight and flat (ll. 956–7), her speech goodly and soft (l. 919), her body long (l. 952); all conventional details for which no specific source need be enquired. (Suggested borrowings from Machaut's *Remède de Fortune* are unlikely, since the resemblances are very slight and general, while the known tradition is so specific.) With all this, however, it must be remembered that the chief poetic force of the description of Blanche is derived from the description (also mainly borrowed from Machaut) of her moral attributes. Chaucer entirely accepts the physical type, but he gives much less space to it than does Machaut. Chaucer's tact, human decency and, even in this diffuse poem, his relative conciseness, are striking. But we should not be eager to assume that he is attempting to describe the Duchess realistically. For a medieval writer that would be beside the point. It is her praise to describe her as the accepted ideal figure. Even her moral attributes are entirely conventional—her truth, her gaiety, etc. By the fourteenth century, moreover, these attributes, as has been pointed out, are not merely those of fashionable beauty; they are also those of the beloved. It is Chaucer's discreet use of this special warmth of description which makes his elegy so unusual and successful.

Chaucer's most notable heroine is Criseyde, in *Troilus and Criseyde*, for which, as everybody knows, the source is Boccaccio's *Il Filostrato*. *Troilus* provides an interesting example of Chaucer's use of the type, for Boccaccio does not describe *his* Criseida at all, except in a few casual remarks. She is tall (*Filostrato*, I, 27), her eyes are shining (I, 28 and a fair number of other times), her face is like a star (III, 26), was made in paradise (IV, 100); she is white (V, 19). These slender indications are certainly in accordance with the tradition, but Boccaccio, perhaps because he was more interested in representing his own sufferings through those of Troilo, is not much interested in his heroine as such.

Chaucer, however, treats his story in a fundamentally more serious way than Boccaccio. With the care of a historian he consulted the earlier accounts of Briseida and Troilus. It is not surprising, therefore, that apart from one detail he describes Criseyde as the typical heroine. In two places he uses the technique of full description, as will be shown. Elsewhere he scatters typical adjectives—her hue is bright (*TC*, IV, 663), her eyes clear (V, 566, 1338), her breast white (IV, 752; V, 219), her voice is melodious (V, 577), she is called bright (V, 1241, 1247, etc.). It is noticeable that he mentions her beauty most frequently when Troilus is longing for her after she has left Troy. An interesting point is her height. Boccaccio seems to have favoured tall women—both his Emilia and his Criseyda (against the evidence from Dares onward) are tall. Chaucer found Criseyde described as of average height in Dares, Benoît and Guido. So when Boccaccio describes her as tall, Chaucer describes her as not among the least as to stature (*TC*, I, 281), and later as 'mene' (V, 806), which means medium (not, as Robinson seems to think, short—an unthinkable quality for the aristocratic medieval heroine).

Chaucer's two formal descriptions occur at turning-points in the story, and provide a beautiful example of the right use of that rhetoric which is sometimes treated with facile contempt by modern critics. The first is when Troilus and Criseyde are at last in bed together:

> Hire armes smale, hire streghte bak and softe,
> Hire sydes longe, flesshly, smothe and white
> He gan to stroke, and good thrift bad ful ofte
> Hire snowisshe throte, hire brestes rounde and lite.[38]
>
> (*TC*, III, 1247–50)

Arms are as often praised for plumpness as slenderness (though in *The Book of the Duchess* they seem to be praised for both (ll. 953–4); 'sides', like a long body, have been praised from Ovid onwards. Throats are nearly always snowy, when they are not like ivory. There is nothing to surprise us here. Chaucer's artistry has selected those items of the formal description which are relevant to the situation and those alone. He thereby achieves the reverse of the frigid effect which such descriptions normally have. This is the 'propriety' of description advocated by Matthew of Vendôme,[39] though Chaucer betters instruction.

The other formal description of Criseyde comes at another crucial point of the story, when Chaucer describes Diomede, Criseyde and Troilus in turn, just before Criseyde gives in to Diomede. There is no hint of this in *Il Filostrato*, but a similar device is found in the *Teseida* where the rivals Palamone and Arcita are described in turn, each in a stanza (III, 49, 50). This description of Criseyde[40] is almost entirely 'moral', depending chiefly on that of Benoît, but there are some physical details, including the blemish of her joined eyebrows. Her stature is 'mene', and 'hire heres clere' are long and bound with the inevitable golden thread. Paradise stood formed within her eyes. Chaucer says he does not know her age. Thus he builds up a picture of Criseyde entirely (with the one exception of joined eyebrows) in accord with the conventionally beautiful type, with no more than a hint from his main source. And even the exception is entirely traditional.

Another important heroine whom Chaucer owes to Boccaccio is Emily of *The Knight's Tale*, which is based on the *Teseida*. The interesting thing here is to see how Chaucer, in contrast to his practice in *Troilus*, almost entirely omits the description of the heroine. Boccaccio, as is natural and usual, makes casual descriptive remarks throughout the poem. Thus Emilia is white (*Teseida*, III, 18), her hair is golden (III, 10), her eyes shining (III, 42), her hands white (III, 9). These are enough to suggest the type for us. Lest we should doubt, however, there is a full-blown 'rhetorical' description of Emilia when she is finally married to Palamone (XII, 53 ff). This takes us back to the early thirteenth century; practically every attribute is there, in the usual order from head to foot. Boccaccio is writing an epic, and so decorates it as splendidly as he knows how—and as medievally. Emilia's hair is golden, her forehead ample, white, smooth, delicate; her eyebrows are half-circles, thin and black. Her eyes are well separated by white, and are like stars; her cheeks lily and rose—not too big, not too small; her mouth as usual is small, teeth are pearls, her chin is little, pink and cloven. Neck, throat, shoulders, arms receive their accustomed meed; her breasts are firm and slightly projecting. Her hips are broad and well formed, and she is tall. Her age is fifteen, so it is no wonder that Boccaccio rather tends to emphasise her *giovinettà* early in the poem.

Chaucer does not commit such errors of taste. Although many years pass between the knights' first sight of Emily and her marriage with Palamon, he does not mention her age. Indeed, he hardly describes Emily at all. When the knights first see her in the garden early in the May morning, we learn no more than that her hair is yellow (which Boccaccio tells us) and hangs down over her back a yard long (*CT*, I, 1049–50)—a characteristically precise and concrete detail which Boccaccio does not give us. Her hue is rosy (*CT*, I, 1038), which is traditional but not in Boccaccio,

> And as an aungel hevenysshly she soong,
> (*CT*, I, 1055)

which Boccaccio tells us too, though not so concisely. Emily is bright, 'shene' (*CT*, I, 1068). Chaucer's achievement is to describe girl and garden so that it is our own imaginations which pour in all the pure and fresh associations of flowers and dewy scents and spring and dawn and girlhood. Boccaccio's three elaborate and astronomical stanzas saying that it was spring are condensed by Chaucer into three or four lines, which yet contain additions, for Boccaccio does not name the month of May, nor refer to its observances. Boccaccio does not describe Emilia as being fairer

> Than is the lylie upon his stalke grene,
> (*CT*, I, 1036)

though comparisons of a lady to a lily are frequent enough. Chaucer's triumph in the description is in his choice of the right kind of detail. Boccaccio describes Emilia

> e'n giubba e scalza gia cantando
> amorose canzon.
>
> (*Teseida*, III, 8)

Chaucer says of Emily

> Yclothed was she fressh, for to devyse.
>
> (*CT*, I, 1048)

Once it is done we can see how much better it is not to have the otiose detail of her clothes, which is anyway not particularly precise, and to have instead the simple adjective 'fresh', recalling as it does the equally simple and charming line describing Emily as

> fressher than the May with floures newe.   .
>
> (*CT*, I, 1037)

It is also an advantage not to have Emily singing love-songs, and thereby as it were inviting attention. In the *Teseida* it is her song which Arcita notices first. In Chaucer Emily is perceived by Palamon without even inadvertently drawing attention to herself. Her remoteness, her purity, her passiveness (which is part of her charm) are therefore enhanced. She is indeed like a goddess; her ideal supramundane beauty removes all worldly stain from her. It is her virtue as a heroine (as by other standards it may be a fault) that she is hardly of flesh and blood. Yet Chaucer also adds one or two precise details which sharply etch in the scene; her yard-long hair (better because a more vivid and more significant detail than Boccaccio's 'candida man', *Teseida*, III, 9, which Chaucer omits); and the flowers 'party white and rede' (*CT*, I, 1053) instead of Boccaccio's 'molti fior' (*Teseida*, III, 10).

Chaucer in fact takes only a few significant details from Boccaccio. But his brevity would not have been so successful if it were not for the ancient conventional tradition. Neither he nor Boccaccio *needed* to describe every aspect of the heroine. Everybody knew her. She was always the same. And the frequency of descriptions shows that she corresponded to a profound need and recurrent image of the mind. We have here in fact on the literary level an excellent example of a stock convention, with its stock response. We respond to Emily because of the scores of other golden-haired girls, bright, pure, gay, which literature has created—even later than the Middle Ages, but first then—which have been vehicles for so many day-dreams, secret desires, aspirations, hopes and fears. Such girls, in medieval literature at least, represent not realistic individuals, unique, never to be met with again, like Fielding's Amelia, charming as she is; they represent universals in concrete form. A convention in feeble hands loses particularity and vividness; but in capable hands, like Chaucer's, it achieves the kind of power which no mere reportage of individuals can attain. The convention both formulates and releases that 'stock response', the deliberate organisation of the mind and feelings which has been described as 'one of the first necessities of human life' if it is to be civilised life, truly human.[41] The idealised beautiful girl corresponds to a basic element in man's experience. This element was so organised in medieval literature—the physical description is but a part of it—that a great poet needed only to touch on an essential detail or two to suggest the whole and, indeed, to bring it more powerfully alive than could be done by a full description. Even Dante's Beatrice perhaps draws life from this tradition.

Apart from some minor instances, the heroine-type appears only once elsewhere in Chaucer's poetry—and here with a striking difference, which, however, still depends upon acquaintance with the convention for its full effect. The heroine is Alison of *The Miller's Tale*. Here is the furthest reach of Chaucer's art. The description is still rhetorical in origin, though it is developed in the deliberately casual manner of the portraits in the *General Prologue*. It is, indeed, partly a rhetorical joke, the point of which is the absurdity of describing a carpenter's wife, a wanton village wench, *as if* she were a heroine, a noble and ideal beauty. There is probably also some element of social satire here. Chaucer is writing for a courtly audience. He is a snob. Thus her very name is that of the lady of a famous song in the Harley Lyrics. It is also the name of the Wife of Bath. The indications are that like many once-fashionable names it had declined in the world, and was regarded in Chaucer's circle as 'middle-class' (to use a rather unhistorical term); at once vulgar and pretentious.[42] Alison's hair is not described; her forehead, however, is bright as day—but only when washed after she has finished her work (*CT*, i, 3310–11); hardly praise for a true heroine, who was always aristocratic. Her eyebrows are curved, black, and thin—very typical adjectives. They were thin because they were 'ypulled' (*CT*, i, 3245), and we may remember Chaucer's own addition of praise to Beute in *The Romaunt of the Rose* was that she did *not* pluck her eyebrows (see above, p. 33). Again, her eye, for which so many words might have been found, is 'likerous' (*CT*, i, 3244). Her hue is bright gold as any lady of romance, but it is compared to a new-minted 'noble' (*CT*, i, 3256), a gold coin worth 6s. 8d. (What is Alison's price?). Her breath is indeed sweet, not as incense, rose or honey, but as mead, 'bragot' or stored apples (*CT*, i, 3261). Chaucer never mentions the breath of his other heroines; apart from the early rhetoricians, who are not distinguished for courtliness and tact, it is mentioned only in *Le Roman de la Rose* and 'The Fair Maid of Ribblesdale'. Alison's body is noble and slender like some heroines', but also like a weasel's (*CT*, i, 3234). Her voice is hardly melodious; it is loud and eager as a swallow's (*CT*, i, 3257–8), which has no song. Alison's clothes are also part of the joke, and she could 'skip and make game' as well as any calf or kid; this is the equivalent of the comely dancing of a true courtly lady. Chaucer calls her a 'popelote', which sounds contemptuous, and 'wench', which certainly describes a low-class, loose woman in Chaucer's vocabulary.[43] Finally he remarks that she was a fine one for a lord to lie with—or a yeoman to marry.

Chaucer is not *satirising* Alison in any way, for her morals or anything else. She is not represented as pretentious (like the Miller and his wife in *The Reeve's Tale*). It is a quality of humour difficult to pin down for a modern mind which lacks the stable frame of reference in social as well as literary matters which was characteristic of medieval minds. Chaucer is not sneering at Alison; not 'sympathising' either. He has created an amusingly incongruous literary and social pattern which because of the steadiness of accepted conventions is quite without the irritability that would almost inevitably accompany it today. There is an element of parody, burlesque, which a firm literary tradition always makes possible and which by no means implies that the tradition itself is scorned.[44]

The ambivalent use of the tradition, both employing its conventions and breaking away from them, paradoxically achieves a rich poetic effect. The sweetness of Alison's mouth is the more vivid both for the long tradition of conventionally sweet comparisons and the unexpectedly down-to-earth quality, the vivid and unusual realism of the mainly attractive comparisons Chaucer uses for her. She is the brighter for being likened to a bright coin, even because such a comparison would have been odious to the bright ladies of the tradition. The quality of the humour of this portrait of Alison can only be fully realised in the light of the tradition which it employs, and subtly inverts.

In other poems Chaucer does not describe the appearance of his heroines. On the rare occasions he mentions them, the physical characteristics are the usual ones. The heroines of *The Legend of Good Women* are sometimes called bright; the only precise detail given anywhere is the colour of Lucretia's hair, which is yellow (*LGW*, 1747). In the *General Prologue*, the Prioress's appearance is also of the conventional type, but naturally description does not go very far. Her forehead is broad and fair (*CT*, i, 154), nose 'tretys' (one might say, not too big nor too small) (l. 152); her eyes are grey as glass (l. 152), her mouth small, soft and red, and she is not undergrown (l. 156). Virginia in *The Physician's Tale* is formed by the 'sovereyn diligence' of Nature herself (*CT*, vi, 9 ff) (which is a very rhetorical note), is sunlike (l. 37), and compared to the lily and the rose. Her age is fourteen, which is about the usual, not merely for the fourteenth century but as late as Shakespeare (Juliet, Miranda), though Anelida is twenty, as is the girl in *The Reeve's Tale*, and Alison is eighteen. In *The Squire's Tale* Canace is ruddy and white as the young sun (*CT*, v, 385), but Chaucer uses the rhetorical device of refusing to describe her (ll. 34 ff) and indeed, we might say he has no need. In *The Reeve's Tale* we have clearly a pretty wench, rather than a lady; she is right fair (*CT*, i, 3976), with eyes like the Prioress's, grey as glass, and with round high breasts (l. 3975). But her nose is 'kamus' (l. 3974), which is not merely too short, but, as has been recently pointed out, betrays an amorous nature.[45] She is thick and well grown (l. 3973), with buttocks broad (l. 3975) like the old woman in *Sir Gawain and the Green Knight* (l. 967), who is the antithesis of youthful beauty. In the frigid little poem 'To Rosemounde', Rosemounde shines like crystal (l. 3), her cheeks are like ruby (l. 4), and she has a seemly voice (l. 11). Chaucer, as always, is a typical man of his age.

IV. THE SURVIVAL OF THE TRADITION

It would be possible to extend the examples of medieval beauty a long way into later literature, but a few suggestions must suffice. Petrarch's Laura is of the usual type.[46] The same type also appears not merely in Lydgate and Dunbar, but also in Wyatt, and the sonnets in which Sidney and Spenser 'describe' their mistresses.[47] Shakespeare's general treatment of the heroine is too important to be fully dealt with here, but two observations may be made. First, that in his sonnets he both shows acquaintance with the tradition and reacts against it.[48] Such a reaction is seen most clearly in Donne in such poems as 'The Indifferent',[49] where the point of the phraseology, its flippancy and daring immorality, is only to be fully appreciated by a knowledge of the medieval tradition in which 'black was not counted fair', and in which purity and loyalty combined so often with the idealised description of the golden girl to create a special exaltation of love and respect.[50] The second point is that Shakespeare's heroines may be roughly divided into two types, the independent, princessly young women who take positive action, like Rosalind; and the very young, helpless and innocent, like Perdita and, above all, Miranda.

It is not unreasonable to see here the two main types of heroine; one, the 'modern', a woman fertile in resource and response, something of a help-meet (rather like Milton's Eve, a ripe woman); the other, the 'medieval' heroine, who is, even in her physical charm, a very young girl. The childlike innocence, gaiety and helplessness of the 'medieval' heroine[51] call forth a response far different from that aroused by the 'modern' heroine. The early heroine is not an equal, not a mate. She is above her worshippers and yet, in a sense, because she is passive and needs protection, she is inferior to them. Child and divinity, she links in us two sets of feelings less often combined in later literature, the feelings of both Prospero and Ferdinand: the desire to cherish and protect, the desire to reverence and worship. Although there is here no question of physical type, Miranda may well be said to represent the essential appeal of the earlier heroine, her youth, purity, gaiety—a precious symbol of an early, innocent, fresh world, and a symbol more powerful in the mind of earlier centuries than it is in ours.

5   Children in Chaucer*

To examine how a writer treats a particular topic or subject-matter is often to arrive at a fresh appreciation of his quality. So it is with Chaucer's treatment of children. He is notable among English writers of any period before the nineteenth century for the affectionate love and pity, sometimes verging on sentimentality, with which he presents babies and children. He brings them into his poetry more frequently than any other writer within several centuries of him. Nothing more clearly shows that despite his reputation as a cynical joker (which of course he is), an even more dominant characteristic is his tender pity. Considering too the normal attitude to children of his time, which he largely shares, the amount he writes about children, usually of his own invention, is another reminder of his combination of the intensely conventional and the unaffectedly independent.

Chaucer's treatment of children is also of interest in showing how, in his art, he moves between realistic and idealistic modes, from nature to supernature. And yet to say so much is to impose a false modern dichotomy on his writing. Sometimes, at least, realism and idealism are at one in Chaucer, as in his portraits of the Knight and the Clerk in the *General Prologue* to *The Canterbury Tales*. So it is with his portraits where children are concerned. Love of children is one of the orthodoxies of human nature which Chaucer takes for granted; but his feeling for children helps to suffuse his work with that glow of tenderness and bright moral idealism which gives even his most rigorous satire its balance and a touch of geniality.

Children make up a small part of the network of personal relationships that are Chaucer's chief interest in imaginative literature. His chief interest, looking at his work as a whole, is in the relationships between the sexes. He is less interested in relationships between parent and child, but they have an important if minor place. He never writes from the point of view of the

* First published in *A Review of English Literature*, 5 (1964) 52–60.

child. He writes as a father. His linguistic usages show that the father-daughter relationship is the tenderest from the father's point of view—more tender than father-mother, or father-son. But by an interesting complexity, while the verbal associations of the word 'mother', as tested by the adjectives that can be connected with the word, are always tender and sweet, the associations with 'father' are more formidable, and indeed ambivalent. The complex 'father-figure' that emerges from his work is usually authoritative, wise, and loving; but at times he is harsh, and occasionally he is hateful.[1] Such general images of family life and of the composite father- and mother-figures are partly the result of contemporary culture-patterns, and partly individual. They only indicate imaginative trends, and the hints they give must be followed up and adjusted by reference to separate writings and works of art.

The orthodox concepts of childhood in the fourteenth century are built into Chaucer's poetry, and so taken for granted as to be only lightly touched on for the most part. It is assumed by Chaucer that the proper and usual end of love between man and woman is marriage and that another good reason for marriage, and a consequence of it, is the procreation of children. The pain and weariness of child-bearing are sympathetically but very briefly mentioned a couple of times (*CT*, I, 2310; IV, 650–1). The love for children is assumed to be so natural that in *The Parson's Tale* men are merely warned against loving wife and children (among other delights) too much. There is no attempt to render the child's quality of life in itself, but the proper way to bring up children is suggested by such casual remarks as:

> The firste vertu, sone, if thou wolt leere,
> Is to restreyne and kepe wel thy tonge;
> Thus lerne children whan that they been yonge.
>
> (*CT*, IX, 332–4)

The young Griselda is praised because

> And ay she kepte hir fadres lyf on-lofte
> With everich obeisaunce and diligence
> That child may doon to fadres reverence.
>
> (*CT*, IV, 229–31)

This ideal of behaviour comes to its finest flower in the heroines of Chaucer, who in age are little more than children by our standards. It is explicit in the formal description of Virginia, the unfortunate heroine of *The Physician's Tale*, who is fourteen years old. The description is beautiful, and so, I venture to think, is the ideal. It is too disciplined and controlled to suit many people, but though we disagree with it, we should not deny its beauty, good sense and decency. Moreover, it was not a bad preparation for a hard world to have such an ideal held up before one.

Chaucer has one curious and pleasant little passage which reflects a less repressive and rigid ideal. It reminds one of those remarks in the Gospels about the wisdom of little children, which the rather Pauline Middle Ages usually ignore. The passage comes in *The Parson's Tale*, where Chaucer describes how a certain philosopher, angry with his pupil, brought a rod to beat him with. Said the child,

> 'What thenke ye do?' 'I wol bete thee', quod the maister, 'for thy correccioun.' 'For sothe', quod the child, 'ye oghten first correcte youreself, that han lost al youre pacience for the gilt of a child.' 'For sothe', quod the maister al wepynge, 'thow seyst sooth. Have thow the yerde, my deere sone, and correcte me for myn impacience.'   (*CT*, x, 669–72)

Not even Wordsworth went so far as this anecdote for teachers, but of course it is as idealised as the description of Virginia, though in a different direction. It has an especial interest because it is so unusual. The story is not known elsewhere, and one would like to think that Chaucer invented it. It shows an openness to a different ideal of childhood, which in an age more interested in children might have borne fruit.

Such a passage is an exception. Chaucer's originality is usually based on his acceptance of convention. In the case of children, one of the accepted things about them was that they usually died. Here is a side of life where in the last 50 years we in the West have happily nearly lost touch with the feelings of our quite recent forefathers. The death of children was as much a commonplace of existence in the fourteenth century as in the nineteenth. Probably three-quarters of all children born died before they were five. No complete understanding of pre-twentieth-century literature can exist without recognising that death was everywhere a commonplace, familiar experience. Up to the seventeenth century there were frequent visitations of the plague, and in the fourteenth century occured the worst epidemic plague of all, the Black Death of 1349–50. No wonder men had a different view of death. It did not seem less horrible, or cause less agony of separation than it does to us; but it was so much more familiar that it was thought about more, and more casually accepted. Where it was sentimentalised, its pain and horror were exaggerated rather than, as with us, minimised. Earlier writers—even Dickens—often seem to us at once more sentimental and more callous than we are ourselves. We must be careful how we judge them. There is deep feeling in Chaucer about the death of children, yet his passing references are surprisingly flippant. The age-old attitude of casual acceptance is well expressed in the beginning of *The Tale of Melibee*, which is mostly translation. In one of Chaucer's more personal references a child's death and mother's agony point a sort of sexual joke:

> And up he yaf a roryng and a cry,
> As dooth the mooder whan the child shal dye.
>
> (*CT*, iv, 2364–5)

Sorrow at the death of a child is noticed so casually in the relatively early *The House of Fame* (920–4) as to give an effect of bathos to the modern reader, who may well think that Chaucer is trying to be funny. In *The Summoner's Tale* one of the more amusingly odious speeches of the friar, who is satirised, exploits a mother's grief at the death of her child. Yet Chaucer makes little capital from it. All he makes the mother say is: 'My child is deed withinne thise wykes two' (*CT*, iii, 1852).

For all such apparent callousness in passing references, when Chaucer presents children more fully they are seen as pathetic victims of death or separation or hardship, objects of their parents' joy and grief, with grief predominating, and arousing in the reader sensations of tenderness and sorrow. Such must have been the typical experience of parents in his time, and Chaucer is always typical. Yet the poems themselves are also individual even in this minor aspect of his art, for in his handling of other men's stories what concerns children is often Chaucer's own personal invention.

In his rehandling of a story, Chaucer usually retains the main outline of events, but gives his own feeling and interpretation.[2] What Chaucer most obviously brings to these sometimes very ancient tales is vivid, dramatic, realistic detail and warm human feeling. When Constance in *The Man of Law's Tale* is about to be set adrift on the sea with her new-born child, Chaucer adds this stanza to the drab narrative of his source:

> Hir litel child lay wepyng in her arm,
> And knelynge, pitously to hym she seyde,
> 'Pees, litel sone, I wol do thee noon harm.'
> With that hir coverchief of hir heed she breyde,
> And over his litel eyen she it leyde,
> And in hir arm she lulleth it ful faste,
> And into hevene hire eyen up she caste.
>
> (*CT*, ii, 834–40)

There is even a touch of sentimentality here in the threefold repetition of
little, Chaucer's favourite word for a child, with its tender overtone. 'Little'
is repeated three more times in the next three stanzas. Yet a development
can be seen in the immediately succeeding narrative which is as noteworthy
as the realism of this stanza. Chaucer proceeds to put into the mouth of
Constance a moving prayer to the Virgin:

> 'Mooder', quod she, 'and mayde bright, Marie,
> Sooth is that thurgh wommanes eggement
> Mankynde was lorn, and damned ay to dye,
> For which thy child was on a croys yrent.
> Thy blisful eyen sawe al his torment;
> Thanne is ther no comparison bitwene
> Thy wo and any wo man may sustene.'
>
> (*CT*, ii, 841–7)

This and the following stanza which completes the prayer mark a change in
style to highly conventional writing. The stanza is a tissue of
commonplaces. It is none the less moving for using the familiar phrases of
Marian devotion, and the effectiveness is to a great extent based on the
preceding realism of the description of the child and the sharply visual detail
of the kerchief.

The pathos here derives from the presence of the child, but the tale has a
fairly happy ending. Others are more painful, and none makes the child a
focus for happiness. The almost unbearable story is the tragedy of Hugelino
(*CT*, vii, 2407–62), which is much more poignant, though not more terrible,
than the passage from Dante's *Inferno* from which it is translated. In this
tale Chaucer reveals a special tenderness for the suffering of the helpless
innocents and the father's dreadful predicament which Dante,
unquestionably the greater poet, has not. That Chaucer chose to translate
this particular passage is itself a sign of his feeling for children as victims,
and for the poignancy of the parent–child relationship.

The Clerk's Tale of Patient Griselda is another in which the pathos of
children is important, but here, even more than in the others, the children
are artistically used to increase the torment of their mother, and are not
interesting in themselves.

The Physician's Tale, which derives ultimately from Livy, tells how in
Rome the wicked judge Appius lusts after the beautiful fourteen-year-old
daughter of the rich and honourable knight Virginius. He arranges for one
of his men to bring a lawsuit before him, falsely claiming that the girl is not
Virginius's daughter but really an escaped slave. Appius then judges the

case against Virginius in the face of all the evidence. Virginius goes home in the deepest grief to cut off his daughter's head to preserve her honour:

> 'O mercy, deere fader!' quod this mayde,
> And with that word she bothe hir armes layde
> Aboute his nekke, as she was wont to do.
> The teeris bruste out of hir eyen two,
> And seyde, 'Goode fader, shal I dye?
> Is ther no grace, is ther no remedye?'
>
> (*CT*, vi, 231–6)

This is much the tenderest scene between father and child in Chaucer's work, and it is characteristic of the complex father–daughter relationship that this scene is the prelude to the father's killing the child. It is one of the rare occasions when a father is called 'dear'. Yet though this scene and some other passages are affecting, the poem as a whole is not up to Chaucer's usual standard, probably because, for all Chaucer's interest in the daughter, the true centre of the tale as Chaucer tells it should be the father, and Chaucer fails to bring him sufficiently to life. The conventional, idealising writing, on which Chaucer relies for his fullest effects, has not been given, in this poem, the necessary foundation of realistic, dramatic, concrete, detail.

Chaucer's great success in writing about children is *The Prioress's Tale*. It tells of a little boy, seven years old, who is the son of a widow in a great city of Asia. His mother teaches him a special reverence for the Virgin, and then

> This litel child, his litel book lernynge,
> As he sat in the scole at his prymer,
> He *Alma redemptoris* herde synge,
> As children lerned hire antiphoner;
> And as he dorste, he drough hym ner and ner,
> And herkned ay the wordes and the noote,
> Til he the firste vers koude al by rote.
>
> (*CT*, vii, 516–22)

He asks a slightly older friend what the anthem means, and then determines to learn it before Christmas. He sings it as he goes home daily through the Jews' quarter. This is the point of placing the story in Asia; there were no Jewish communities in England from the thirteenth to the seventeenth centuries, which saves the gentle Prioress from an otherwise ugly anti-

Semitism. She is talking about bogey-men. The Jews take the child's song as an insult, and murder him. The whole of the story up to here is told with remarkable realism. The dialogue between the two little boys will convince any parent with its charm. In other versions of the story, which was very popular in the Middle Ages, the boy is ten years old. By making him only seven, Chaucer increases the pathos, but also the realism, and he is extremely accurate about the child's academic schooling. All hangs together; a boy of seven is more innocent than one of ten, more docile and eager to learn. With all this, we still see the child from outside and, as it were, from above. We do not, as with nineteenth-century authors, attempt to enter into his view of the world. We do not feel with him; we feel with the mother, her joy in the child implied by her terror when he does not come home from school. A miracle follows:

> This gemme of chastite, this emeraude,
> And eek of martirdom the ruby bright,
> Ther he with throte ykorven lay upright,
> He *Alma redemptoris* gan to synge
> So loude that al the place gan to rynge.
>   (*CT*, vii, 609–13)

His miraculous singing leads to the discovery of his body, and he explains that it is a miracle of the Virgin, who will fetch his soul when he actually dies. He is given a splendid burial. The last description of his mother comes before the explanation, though after the discovery of his body, and tells how she lay swooning by his bier. There is no word of consolation for her. The Jews are put to death by torture.

There is naturally no psychological or other probability—it is, after all, a *miracle*. The poem draws its full strength from a pattern and a story which can hardly be called realistic in its *total* effect, though it employs realistic methods and materials in part. The force and beauty of the tale are based on the realistic description of the 'little clergeon', and the absence of such a base is one of the reasons for the comparative failure of *The Physician's Tale*. But on this foundation are built the walls and roof which are largely supernatural. In terms of language we move from realistic dialogue and description to the idealising and more abstract phrases 'gem of chastity', 'emerald', 'bright ruby of martyrdom'. We move from playground to altar, and each strengthens and sets off the other.

In this way Chaucer's treatment of children falls in with the general pattern of his art; his amazing juxtapositions of the comic and the pathetic, the realistic and the idealistic, the bawdy and the sincerely devout, the natural and the supernatural. The general pattern of development from nature to supernature is also found in *Troilus and Criseyde*. However puzzling the Epilogue to *Troilus* may be found by twentieth-century readers unconsciously conditioned by the naturalism and realism of the novel, it is very typical of his art.

We may go further, and suggest that though Chaucer's achievement is unique even in this respect, yet it also draws something from the general patterns of thought and feeling of the times. The poem *Pearl*, which is as great as anything Chaucer ever wrote, shares something of the same progress from nature to supernature. The poem begins with a realistic account of the father mourning his dead child. But in a vision she comes to him, no longer an imperfect human child but glorified, and instructs him and leads him to good thoughts. Here the purity and helplessness of earthly childhood are transformed. We misunderstand Chaucer and the *Pearl*-poet if we value in them only the realistic, vivid, dramatic detail, and do not recognise its place in a larger pattern, non-realistic, non-naturalistic.

6 Class-Distinction in Chaucer*

I

The social structures in Chaucer's imaginative world are more complex than is often assumed and have been little examined.[1] They are part of his literary achievement and to recognise them is part of literary criticism. Historians may also find them of interest, since Chaucer speaks directly as a witness of his own day; though the relationship between what he says and the actual situation as it was is a historical problem, which I leave to historians.

The main general points are that Chaucer portrays not one class-system operative in society but three, different though overlapping, and that none of these corresponds to the nineteenth-century concept of the upper, the middle, and the lower class. Chaucer's own courtliness, like the courtliness of his audience, is evident, but the dramatic, fictive audience in *The Canterbury Tales* is a different matter.

II

The first kind of class-distinction is that denoted by the concept of 'rank' or 'degree', familiar enough in outline, though Chaucer's own perception and use of it, and his reservations about it, are interesting. At the beginning of *The Canterbury Tales*, he says he will describe the pilgrims by telling us, among other things, 'of what degree' they are (*CT*, I, 40); that is, their social locus. The word *degree* occurs fairly frequently in describing people. There are many instances of persons being of high or low degree. Degree extends from the lowest thrall or servant (*LGW*, 1313, 2081) to the king. The fowl-royal in *The Parliament of Fowls* is above everyone in degree (*PF*, 394), and this is a comment made by Nature, who is 'the vicaire of the almighty Lord' (*PF*, 379), so that such an ordering of society in degrees is 'natural' and God-ordained. The Parson makes this clear.

* First published in *Speculum*, 43 (1968) 290–305.

God ordeyned that som folk sholde be moore heigh in estaat and in degree, and som folk moore lough, and that everich sholde be served in his estaat and in his degree . . . therefore was sovereyntee ordeyned, to kepe and mayntene. (*CT*, x, 770–5)

To maintain degree money is required. When Arcite becomes a squire of the chamber to Theseus (a rank presumably equivalent to that of squire to the king's chamber, to which Chaucer himself was appointed in 1367), Theseus gives Arcite 'gold to mayntene his degree' (*CT*, I, 1441). Chaucer's gold came to approximately £13 6s. 8d. a year, plus gifts of wine and money.[2] It might also be noted that Arcite was promoted to Theseus's chamber from being page of the chamber of Emily, just as Chaucer was promoted to the king's chamber from being page to Countess Elisabeth of Ulster, though Chaucer had to go through the intermediary stage of *valletus*.

Degree, it is generally agreed, should be kept up. When Queen Alceste describes the duties of a good king, she emphasises that he must look after the welfare of all his subjects, whether of high or low degree, but in particular, he must keep the degree of lords,

> As it ys ryght and skilful that they bee
> Enhaunced and honoured, and most dere—
> For they ben half-goddes in this world here—
> Yit mot he doon bothe ryght, to poore and ryche,
> Al be that hire estaat be nat yliche,
> And han of poore folk compassyoun.
> (*LGW, Pro.* F, 385–90)

[Estate is here much the same as degree, as appears from numerous instances, but especially *The Parson's Tale* (*CT*, x, 770–5) and *The Tale of Melibee* (*CT*, VII, 1485–90).] A king should not, of his own gentry, avenge himself even on a fly, and he should always have regard to his own degree (*LGW, Pro.* F, 399). Criseyde similarly prays Pandarus to have more regard for her 'estate', that is, degree and condition of life, than to Troilus's pleasure (*TC*, II, 132–4). In *The Legend of Good Women, Prologue* F the King of Love defends himself against the Queen's reproaches by saying that he cannot refuse her, 'If that I wol save my degree' (*LGW, Pro.* F, 447).

It is a commendation of Virginia, in *The Physician's Tale*, that she speaks according to her degree, 'ful wommanly and pleyn', without 'countrefeted termes . . . to seme wys', and that all her words were 'Sownynge in vertu and in gentillesse' (*CT*, VI, 50–4). The notion of being good 'in one's degree' is so widespread in Chaucer as to need no further annotation.

Two amusing reverse instances of the appropriateness of behaviour to degree are worth noting. One concerns May, the wife of January in *The Merchant's Tale*. Being married to a knight, she is to that extent a lady, but before he marries her she is 'of smal degree' (*CT*, IV, 1625). The semantic field of *small* is complex, but it often implies what is slight, even ridiculous, trivial, and therefore contemptible, and certainly seems to have such an implication here, the only time it qualifies 'degree'. The normal word is 'low', which is quite neutral in tone. There is something suspicious, though we are not told what, about May's 'degree', which warns us about her behaviour.

The other example of scorn is also a nonce-usage. When the foolish and dandified lover and parish clerk, Absolon, in *The Miller's Tale*, has been promised a kiss by Alison, and just before she plays her appalling trick on him, he is beside himself with joy, falls on his knees in preparation, and bursts out with

> I am a lord at alle degrees;
> For after this I hope ther cometh moore.
>
> (*CT*, I, 3724–5)

At alle degrees seems strictly nonsense: he is speaking ecstatic hyperbole. In Chaucer's hard chivalric world a man who speaks nonsense attracts a heavy penalty. But only a low-class man speaks so.

The intellectual principle behind the various subtle social perceptions and verbal formulations already quoted is made explicit in *The Parson's Tale*: 'I woot wel ther is degree above degree, as reson is; and skile is that men do hir devoir ther as it is due' (*CT*, X, 764). The various degrees, as has been suggested, depend to a large extent on the possession of wealth; Arcite needed an appropriate amount of gold, comparable, presumably, with Chaucer's £13 6s. 8d. *per annum*. It is not riches, though we do hear of 'gentil men . . . of greet estaat' (*CT*, I, 1753). Modest or great riches on their own, however, are not enough. The foolish jealous old carpenter of *The Miller's Tale* is a 'riche gnof' (*CT*, I, 3188) and all his money is not enough to save him from the contempt of this strange word, recorded only here in Middle English. As Chaucer says in his more personal poem *Gentilesse*, 'He is noght gentil, thogh he riche seme' (13). Troilus, in commenting on his financial resources, remarks: 'And *vulgarly* to speken of substaunce/Of tresour . . .' (*TC*, IV, 1513–14).

There is a moral obligation to behave as one should in one's degree both as to one's own proper behaviour, and (the only other case Chaucer mentions) in one's attitude towards one's *inferiors*. One must look after them. On the other hand, the actual attitude of Chaucer himself towards the middling ranks of society is one of condescending genial mockery (as in the *General Prologue* and in the *fabliaux*), while 'the people', to judge from one stanza in *The Clerk's Tale* (*CT*, IV, 995–1001), he despises, like Shakespeare, for their fickleness. Yet, to contrast again, in the *General Prologue* he idealises the poor Ploughman, and in *The Clerk's Tale* the product of the poorest house in the village is the beautiful, wise, good and patient Griselda. One further point; persons in authority, like Theseus (*The Knight's Tale*), Nature (*PF*), the King in the prologue to *The Legend of Good Women*, are shown usually as genial (if frightening), and anxious to behave properly. When they do not so behave, ancient wisdom advises one to swallow injury. As Chaucer the Pilgrim himself says, telling his own *Tale of Melibee*, quoting Cato's *Disticha* (fourth century):

> Catoun seith, 'If a man of hyer estaat or degree, or moore myghty than thou, do thee anoy or grevaunce, suffre hym; for he that oones hath greved thee, may another tyme releeve theee and helpe.' (*CT*, VII, 1488–90)

In all these cases we might think of degree dividing up society in layers, like a cake. This would be a mistake. The Chaucerian image, or model, traditional enough, is more complex. It conceives of degree as the rungs of a ladder. The word *degree* seems indeed sometimes to be precisely the equivalent of *ladder* (*Romaunt*, 485). This usage derives from Boethius's *Consolation of Philosophy* where we read that on the dress of the Lady Philosophy were two letters, and between these two letters 'were seyn degrees nobly ywrought in manere of laddres, by whiche degrees men myghten clymben fro the nethereste lettre to the uppereste' (*Boece*, I, 33–6). This passage refers literally to the movement from active to contemplative life, but it suggests the ladder-like way in which 'degree' was thought of, and the whole image may well be taken as a symbol of social movement. The rungs are fixed, but not the people on them. Chaucer thinks of society as spread out on the ladder, and of people going up and down. He distinguishes between persons and their status.

Social mobility is thus an important fact for Chaucer, to be set alongside the notion of proper behaviour within one's degree. It might be expected that he would regard social mobility with disfavour, but that is not always the case. The fall from high to low degree, and thus to misery, is indeed the medieval definition of tragedy, originating again with Boethius, but

repeated by Chaucer in his own verse in the Prologue to *The Monk's Tale*
(*CT*, vii, 1973–7). The Knight, however, cuts short the Monk's series of
tragedies, and says that he would very much rather hear of people
improving their position.

> As whan a man hath been in povre estaat,
> And clymbeth up and wexeth fortunat,
> And there abideth in prosperitee.
> Swich thyng is gladsom, as it thynketh me.
>   (*CT*, vii, 2775–8)

This generous sentiment is typical of the Knight, and is to some extent
general in Chaucer himself—a part of the 'moral optimism' of the general
Gothic world-view. But Chaucer is ambivalent. In the *General Prologue* to
The Canterbury Tales there is no doubt that there is some satire of the
Gildsmen's wives as social climbers, and perhaps of the Gildsmen
themselves (*CT*, i, 361–78).

The truth is that seriously as Chaucer takes the notion of degree he does
not take it too seriously. It is a worldly thing, and he is both a worldly and a
religious man. As to the worldliness of 'degree', it is evident enough. The
Franklin emphasises it in his tale when he describes the knight, who as a
husband is as humble as a lover, but who keeps the 'name of soveraynetee
. . . for shame of his degree' (*CT*, v, 751–2). Reputation (that is, *name*) and
honour (or shame) are worldly matters, and Chaucer knows the world very
well.

One can distinguish a worldly cynicism, and a more profound religious
scepticism, about the degree-structure of society in his work. The cynicism
is mainly comic and accepting; the scepticism is based on religious belief; it
is radical but not reformative. The cynicism is perhaps not unconnected
with the scepticism, and may indeed deserve the same name; but I keep the
distinction. Worldly cynicism is illustrated by the sharp words given to the
Manciple about the unfair way class-distinctions work in matters of 'love'.
Chaucer clearly shows that the Manciple speaks dramatically, but the
Manciple reiterates one of Chaucer's own favourite remarks, that words
should accord with deeds. The Manciple says

> I am a boystous man, right thus seye I,
> Ther nys no difference, trewely,
> Bitwixe a wyf that is of heigh degree,
> If of hir body dishonest she bee,
> And a povre wenche, oother than this—

> If it so be they werke bothe amys—
> But that the gentile, in estaat above,
> She shal be cleped his lady, as in love;
> And for that oother is a povre womman,
> She shal be cleped his wenche or his lemman.
> And, God it woot, myn owene deere brother,
> Men leyn that oon as lowe as lith that oother.
>
> (*CT*, ix, 211–22)

So much for *fine amour*! The Manciple goes on to make equally sarcastic remarks about 'tyrants', and about outlaws who if grand enough are called 'captains', that for a moment recall *Jonathan Wild*. A somewhat similar touch of cynicism occurs in *Troilus*, when Chaucer is describing how much ennobled Troilus is by his successful love, how virtuous, kind, gentle he is:

> And though that he be come of blood roial,
> Hym liste of pride at no wight for to chace.
>
> (*TC*, iii, 1800–1)

Although he was of royal blood, he behaved really very decently. The remark has that poker-faced ambivalence so characteristic of Chaucer, so much part of his personal style, and so personally baffling. It hardly seems polite to royalty, yet the Balade *Lak of Stedfastnesse*, in which Richard II is exhorted to 'shew forth thy swerd of castigacioun' and govern strongly, shows once again that Chaucer is no revolutionary.

A more comic exercise in cynical class-distinction is the whole *fabliau*, *The Miller's Tale*, put in the Miller's mouth, of course, but really a courtly joke against old-fashioned provincial love-language, and against petty low-class folk who in their animal lusts ape the refined manners of their betters. It is the counterpart of the Manciple's sour comment, coming (paradoxically and non-realistically in the Miller's mouth) from the point of view of the upper classes.[3] The 'heroine', the carpenter's wife, Alison, is described in a way that parodies the formal description of the beautiful court lady, but the parody, though splendid comic poetry, does not mock the formal ideal; it mocks its lower-class subject, Alison, who is finally described, in the amusing, and snobbish, lines,

> She was a prymerole, a piggesnye,
> For any lord to leggen in his bedde,
> Or yet for any good yeman to wedde.
>
> (*CT*, i, 3268–70)

This is obviously meant for an audience of lords, not yeomen.

Chaucer's actual audience here, as elsewhere in *The Canterbury Tales*, must be distinguished from the dramatic audience of the tales, who are the pilgrims. Chaucer's *actual* audience, as appears from the remark here, from similar deductions to be made elsewhere in the *Tales*, and from his addresses to the audience in other poems, clearly consists of lords, ladies, knights, well-to-do gentry-folk like 'moral Gower', and upper-class scholars and lawyers like the 'philosophical Strode'. All the fifteenth-century manuscripts of *The Canterbury Tales* were owned by such people, apart from the odd monastery owning a copy of the Parson's sermon. But within the dramatic structure of *The Canterbury Tales* a number of the pilgrims address the *dramatic* audience as *lordings*—a mode of address familiar in the English romances, but *never* used by Chaucer towards his own audience.

The views expressed dramatically by the Manciple and the Miller are not really inconsistent with other views of degree: they simply indicate a partial cynicism in Chaucer, and in his general culture, which is not incompatible with a belief that degree, for what it is worth, ought to be kept up. Naturally, the pressure of such cynicism suggests a considerable detachment from the system, which we may find confirmed in Chaucer's deliberate 'first person' refusal to classify his pilgrims according to degree, for which he apologises, not very seriously, at the end of the *General Prologue*: 'My wit is short, ye may wel understonde' (*CT*, I, 746).

Behind the cynicism, and rather different from it, lies a deeper scepticism. Chaucer's scepticism is not the product of an embittered, rebellious or anarchic mind, nor of simple selfishness. It is part of a general religious theory of the nature of man, society and existence—namely, that they are contingent on eternal values, which according to fourteenth-century Christian thought would be realised after death, in heaven and hell. Naturally, these views are expressed in *The Parson's Tale*, and here is not the place for a detailed exposition of the ambivalent attitude maintained by historical Christianity towards worldly values. The ambivalence is fully present in *The Parson's Tale*. The Parson, as has already been shown, upholds degree, which, 'sith the time of grace cam', has been necessary to restrain sin, which can easily enthrall even royal blood (*CT*, x, 765–70). Here we have a potent, but confusing, mingling of moral with social standards. The Parson also asserts that our common humanity is the reason why lords should treat their inferiors properly. To ill-treat inferiors is a damnable sin, and 'as seith Seint Peter', 'whoso that dooth synne is thral of synne' (*CT*, x, 140–5)—a recurrent theme of the sermon. This uses the class-system to classify the moral system, thereby making the eternal dependent on the temporal and worldly.[4] The Parson condemns worldly honours, delights and riches, indeed, but only in hell. He supposes that people now possessed of honours, delights and riches will have behaved badly in this world and so will be compensated not only by losing such goods but by receiving their opposite. There is no honour or reverence in hell. No more reverence shall be done there to a king than to a knave.

> Honour is eek cleped greet lordshipe; ther shall no wight serven other, but of harm and torment. Honour is eek cleped great dignytee and heighnesse, but in helle shul they been al fortroden of develes. (*CT*, x, 189)

For honour they shall receive shame and confusion. Similarly with other worldly delights. Where shall be in hell the gay robes, and the soft sheets, and the small shirts? Sinners shall have moths as a mattress and their covertures shall be of worms of hell! (*CT*, x, 195–200).

This might as first glance seem a condemnation of worldly values; in fact it is a validation of them. To proclaim that there shall be no honour or service in hell is to praise honour. Those who *have* honour, etc., in this world may be condemned, but this is not to condemn honour itself. And honour is what degree extends to. The distinction is again made here between people and their social status and attributes. What it amounts to here is a proper scepticism about people.

One would wish that the Parson (and other preachers) had given us as trenchant a comment on heaven as on hell. One knows that heaven, which has certainly its Lord and King and ranks of angels, was thought to have also degree, though the contemplation of it would be purged of both Christian scepticism and worldly cynicism.[5]

There is also a more thorough-going scepticism, a deep *contemptus mundi*, in Chaucer, as we might expect, coexisting with, and perhaps making possible, his other, more limited, cynicism and scepticism. It occurs chiefly among those short poems mainly of Chaucer's maturity which are often both humorous and disillusioned, and which bring us as near as we are ever likely to come to a direct personal statement, though the content is derived from the general tradition of Christian thought, and especially from Boethius.

In *The Former Age* Chaucer contrasts the moral decay of his own day with the purity of 'the former age', complaining about war, commerce, tyrants, vices, lords, etc.—voicing the normal comprehensive complaints about life-as-it-is of the eternal literary intellectual. The spendid poem *Truth* contains a thorough-going condemnation of the world, and of trying either to succeed in it or to improve it: 'The wrastling for this world axeth a fal' (16). From a worldly point of view the poem looks pessimistic; it is not, because it invokes a sphere of reality wider than ordinary worldly experience. Take what comes in the world, do not kick against the pricks, do not be anxious; know where and what you are; 'thank God of al'; control yourself, pray, 'And trouthe thee shal delivere, it is no drede' (28). Along with the world and society the class-system of degree is thus here both accepted and denied in the name of a thorough-going mentalism. That this poem, and the other-worldly sentiments expressed in it and elsewhere, can coexist with the different sentiments expressed, for example, in *Lak of Stedfastnesse*, calling for strong, just, this-worldly government from Richard II, may be attributed to a subtle perception of the multifold nature of reality; or to Gothic 'dualism'; or to human inconsistency; or to characteristic English upper-class hypocrisy; according to the taste and fancy of the critic. At least it prevents the notion of degree in Chaucer attracting such a passionate commitment as appears in the famous speech on degree by Ulysses in Shakespeare's *Troilus and Cressida*. For Ulysses it is 'degree' that holds the world and society from chaos: for Chaucer, following Boethius, it is love.

'Degree' or 'rank' would seem to be the normal dominant English idea of the divisions of society. One may sum up briefly in noting that it allows social mobility, since it conceives of people apart from their position in society, and they may move up or down the ladder. It carries no inherent concept of class-conflict, though it allows that you may fall off the ladder, or tread on the fingers of those beneath you. Though it has a close relationship to economic fact, it does not admit of broad mass groupings whose economic interests are identical within the group and opposed to other groups. Never closely schematised, it is capable of complex overlaps and continual subdivision within a generally cohesive society, in whose stability all individuals have some, though maybe unequal, interest. It is more like a whole lot of ladders than one, linking all members of society. The nineteenth-century concept of three main classes, an upper (aristocratic) class, a middle (bourgeois) class, and a lower class (the 'workers'), does not exist for Chaucer and cannot be applied to his society. Instead, we must speak, as English people still naturally do, of the upper classes, middle classes, lower classes. The plurals are important.

The ladder of degree, though the most comprehensive and realistic model of social distinctions in Chaucer, is not the only one. His work shows that a society may maintain several coexisting systems of class-distinction, overlapping but not quite coinciding, matching differing human demands and different aspects of society in the classifications they offer. In Chaucer, besides the 'ladder', which is primarily social, economic and pragmatic, there is a binary system which tends to become moral, though it may be legal in origin, and a triple system which is functional though largely theoretical.

III

What I have called the binary system was until recently still perfectly familiar to the English: it concerns the difference between being, and not being, a gentleman (or a lady). In Chaucer's formulation it is the difference between gentles and churls, which is several times referred to, especially by the Parson.

The distinction is apparently in origin social and perhaps legal. The OE *ceorl* meant simply 'a common man'. The cognate form from Old Norse, surviving in Middle English as *carl*, is used four times by Chaucer in a casual, neutral, non-moral way to signify a rough man of low class, as, for example, the Miller (*CT*, I, 545). *Churl*, meaning simply 'man', occurs in *Troilus* (*TC*, I, 1024) referring to 'the man in the moon', and is incidentally the latest recorded instance of such neutral usage. This simple usage only occurs elsewhere in Chaucer when the Parson refers to 'lords and churls' saying, for example, that both spring from the same seed (*CT*, X, 760–5). The Parson means 'high and low', that is 'everybody', and it might well be argued that he is merely instancing the top and bottom of the social ladder of degree. But he also occasionally uses the distinction between *bond* and *free*, and it looks as if this distinction may underlie the general feeling in Chaucer of difference between churls and gentry, especially as the Parson closely associates *churl* with *thrall*. The notions of bondage and freedom are potent in Chaucer, and the semantic fields of both words and their associates are widespread and complex. But the interesting thing here is that the basic legal distinction they imply is present in only a shadowy way in Chaucer, here in *The Parson's Tale*. As far as I know there is no way of telling whether Chaucer's Ploughman or Griselda were bond or free. The *churl* of *The Summoner's Tale* is a well-to-do yeoman. Chaucer's silence on bondage and freedom as a social and economic fact when it was a matter of great importance to at least some of his contemporaries may itself be significant of upper-class disregard.

Chaucer's interest in the gentry/churl antithesis was not legal nor social, but moral. The Parson develops the association between churls and thralls, because even lords can become thralls to sin—one of the dominant themes of his sermon. Sin is thraldom. Here as earlier a social division is used to articulate a moral structure, though in this case as we shall see the moral structure eventually undermines the social.

The Parson also associates servitude (*servage*) of sin with ribaldry (*CT*, x, 460–5). And when that obvious scoundrel, the Pardoner, offers to tell a tale, the *gentils* all cry out

> Nay, lat hym telle us of no ribaudye!
> Telle us som moral thyng, that we may leere
> Som wit, and thanne wol we gladly heere.
>
> (*CT*, vi, 324–6)

The Miller is not merely a 'stout carl', he is a churl. The word *churl* is used for several shades of opprobrium in Chaucer, and when the poet warns us that the Miller is a churl, and tells a 'churl's tale', we know what to expect. Chaucer makes a mock apology to every 'gentil wight'—he claims the poet has to report accurately what his pilgrims said, however bad it may be—but if the reader does not like the 'harlotry' of the tales by the Miller and Reeve, says the poet, he can turn over the leaf and choose plenty of stories that 'toucheth gentillesse', and also morality and holiness (*CT*, i, 3167–86). On the one hand, therefore, we have *churls, ribaldry, harlotry*; on the other, in opposition, *gentils, gentilesse, morality, holiness*.

Who are the *gentils* who cried out on the Canterbury pilgrimage? The actual social distinctions are not quite clear. The *gentils* must include the Knight and his son the Squire, the Prioress, the Franklin; and probably too the Physician, Merchant, Man of Law, Gildsmen, and their wives. But what of the Wife of Bath? The Parson, to judge from his general high standards, must be included; and why not the Ploughman, his equally high-minded brother? But what kind of *gentil* is he? It is noteworthy, too, that Chaucer expresses a secular, not a clerical, condemnation of the Pardoner's expected ribaldry. Here as elsewhere Chaucer absorbs the clerical into the lay element and entirely disregards enclosed religion—all his monks are 'outriders'—and mystical spirituality. *Gentil* includes a wide range of kinds and degrees of persons.

The *gentils* can thus hardly be determined by external social standards. Although we hear of 'gentil men of greet estaat' (*CT*, i, 1753), and people can be 'gentil' by speech (*Romaunt*, 1987) (though this may not be by Chaucer), there is a very strong tendency to make the *gentils* elect themselves. Dido says 'I am a gentil woman and a queen' (*LGW*, 1306). May, making the most of her 'small degree', says 'I am a gentil womman and no wenche' (*CT*, iv, 2202). It is how you *choose* to behave that, very largely, and in theory, makes you *gentil*. Chaucer seems to have become more and more interested in *gentilesse*, and following a line of thought he learnt from Boethius, but which also appears in Dante and Jean de Meun, *gentilesse* becomes less and less associated with wealth and social status. Both *The Franklin's Tale* and *The Wife of Bath's Tale* centre on the problem of *gentilesse* and the topic arises elsewhere.

The Wife of Bath's tale is a paradox in *her* mouth,[6] as the Miller's is in his, but that need not affect our conclusions. The essential point is that in her tale Chaucer most explicitly dissociates *gentilesse* from rank or degree. If a man does not do 'gentil' deeds,

> He nys nat gentil, be he duc or erl.
> (*CT*, iii, 1157)

Gentilesse has become a moral ideal, a virtuous nobility of character independent of external social rank. It is personally chosen, and evinced in personal behaviour.

> Thanne am I gentil, whan that I bigynne
> To lyven vertuously and weyve synne.
> (*CT*, iii, 1175–6)

Such sentiments are directly reinforced by the short, more personal poem, *Gentilesse*, quoted above (p. 56), which says that worldly dignities belong to virtue, not virtue to dignities. If a man does not love virtue

> He is noght gentil, thogh he riche seme.   (13)

Or, as the Franklin says,

> Fy on possessioun,
> But if a man be vertuous withal!
> (*CT*, v, 686–7)

Though *gentilesse* thus becomes dissociated from economic or social status in one respect, in another it is brought sharply into conflict with the present economic and social *status quo*, for *gentilesse* may deny that present society is properly based, and may claim to organise social superiority on the basis of virtue—which would be revolutionary indeed! In this instance there seems no risk of the interesting confusion between virtue and noble rank noted earlier, when virtues appeared to have been unconsciously subordinated to rank.

There is no doubt that Chaucer takes *gentilesse* seriously as a civilising moral ideal, and many of his worthiest characters are warmly described as *gentil*. Yet in practice the moral concept as shown in Chaucer does not, except in *The Parson's Tale*, become fully detached from its class-base. In *The Parliament of Fowls*, the birds though classified on the literal level in a biological system that Chaucer found in his favourite encyclopaedia[7] also have some symbolic relation to the classes of society. The hawks represent the knightly class, and are *gentil*; the goose, duck, cuckoo are *churls*. Yet here again we see that one can choose to be *gentil*. The turtle-dove, though one of the lower birds in a sense (perhaps the notion of 'degree' is faintly in the background), aligns her sentiments about true love and faithfulness with the hawks. So to this extent a class-basis is denied, or one may say that upward social mobility of a special moral kind is shown to be possible. But the general situation aligns hawks with *gentilesse*, and the most vociferous, insubordinate, 'lewd' (*PF*, 520), imperceptive and unrefined of the others with churlishness. The general tone may be summed up in the line ' "Now fy, cherl!" quod the gentil tercelet' (*PF*, 956) addressing the duck. In this poem more clearly than any of the others we begin to discern the image of class-conflict, though presented in the form of 'the strong antipathy of good to bad'.

Even the rightly most famous evocation of a 'gentil wight' does not deny a class-basis, though he himself shows no class-feeling. This is the description of the Knight in the *General Prologue*, where the moral beauty of the ideal is so finely portrayed in a personal and class portrait whose power endures today, summed up for ever in Chaucer's best-known line: 'He was a verray, parfit gentil knyght' (*CT*, I, 72). There is no questioning the serious moral elevation of *gentil* here.

Yet Chaucer would not be Chaucer if, while giving the word *gentil* such an aura of moral approbation and an appealing warmth, he did not also often use the word mockingly or ironically. The fraudulent Manciple, the unwholesome 'harlot' the Summoner, the hypocritical swindling Pardoner, the Tabard Inn itself, Roger the dishonest and ulcerous cook, Chantecleer the cock, the lecherous May and untrustworthy Fame are all called *gentil*. This does not invalidate the distinction *gentil/churl*. So far from doing that, it depends on the distinction for humorous effect. But one needs to make sure when the usage is serious, and when ironic.

If *gentil* when not ironic implies the good, then *churl* must, with the rare morally neutral exceptions already noted, imply the bad. There is no ironical use of *churl* signifying approbation, though it has a touch of ironic humour in *The Summoner's Tale*. The Wife of Bath says 'For vileyns synful dedes make a cherl' (*CT*, III, 1158). *Cherl* does not here imply an actual class-status. The knight who commits a rape in the *Wife's Tale* is both knight and *cherl* until he learns better and chooses aright, yielding 'sovereignty' to his wife. (Insubordination towards properly constituted authority is the mark of the churl, and a proper obedience is the mark of the *gentil*). Incidentally we may note here too that the Wife associates the word *vileyn* with the churl's sinful deeds. *Vileyn* and *vileynye* are always used by Chaucer in a moral, never in a neutrally technical legal or social sense. Nevertheless, *churl* does not quite escape the implications of its social origin for Chaucer. There is a notable instance where he *seems* to be using it to describe the characteristics of a social class, but is in fact using it morally, with an effect of irony which, for once, he seems unconscious of, and which turns back on his own class; the courtiers become the true churls. This happens when Chaucer calls the Miller a churl and says he tells a churl's tale. Here, as when he makes the *gentils* cry out against the Pardoner's expected ribaldry, he appears to be asserting that *fabliaux*, 'dirty stories', of the kind told by the Miller and Reeve, are low-class forms of literature. This is a misleading class libel. No doubt the lower classes did tell rough and crude jokes, but the implication that the upper classes did not is self-evidently untrue or what is Chaucer himself doing? The origins of the *fabliaux* are not very clear, and Chaucer's own *fabliaux* are a late and complex development of the genre, but their authors and audience are plainly upper-class, courtly, clerical.[8] Chaucer was a courtier whose own audience was composed of the members of the king's court, and of similar gentry-folk and 'professional' men. His own *fabliaux* are the most courtly poems he ever wrote. *The Miller's Tale*, in especial, as I have already noted, is rich in literary and social mockery of the lower classes; it is not harsh or savage, but it is unquestionably written from an upper-class point of view. The *fabliaux* are attributed to 'churls' because of their somewhat indecent subject-matter. This is not a true social placing but a moral comment, part of that general movement in human society, or at least in European society, to impute vice to lower classes and virtue to upper classes. This movement, if we consider the semantic fields and general developments of such English words as *noble, vulgar, common, low*, is not limited to Chaucer. Most of these words, like *gentil* itself, whatever their social origin, gravitate towards the either/or antithesis of *gentil/churl* which is, we may say, the natural rough-and-ready classification, good/bad, of the moral aspects of society, not meant to be socially analytical, and never closely worked out.

Some of the general implications of this moral binary view of, or comment on, society as it appears in Chaucer's work, have already been briefly suggested. Others that occur readily to mind suggest that it is powerful and not quite so crude in some respects as might be expected. In so far as it attributes virtue to *gentils*, that is, to the upper, or dominant, section of society, it makes for acceptance of the social order; in so far as it suggests that only the good should be considered *gentil*, it makes for revolution. As it emphasises virtue, so it encourages that 'internalisation' of values which is so notable a development in fourteenth-century English literature; such mentalistic self-sufficiency works *against* the pressures of society, though not necessarily in a revolutionary way. It encourages the individual to think and choose for himself. On the other hand, the formation of broad groupings of like-minded people is also encouraged by the simple antithesis. The *gentils* are conspicuously co-operative, though *churls* argue amongst themselves. As far as the *gentils* are concerned, at least, their *gentilesse* modifies some of the competitiveness of the 'ladder' of degree. Yet, paradoxically, it is only in this moralising view of society that we get any real sense of class-conflict, which is imaged in *The Parliament of Fowls*, and hinted at more vaguely in the outcry of the *gentils* in *The Canterbury Tales* against the Pardoner. There is a touch of aggressiveness in *gentilesse* which suggests an underlying insecurity: we may suppose it was difficult to be *gentil* in the rough-and-tumble of fourteenth-century life, while the misery of the oppressed churls made them dangerous and insurrectionary. A further paradox appears. Though *gentilesse* implies due obedience to properly constituted authority, it is also, within its charmed circle, a great leveller. The king himself can be no more than a gentleman, like an untitled subject, and the queen herself no more than a lady; while, on the other hand, a great lord may become a churl if he submits to the thraldom of sin. This binary division more subtly articulates society, motivates and controls its members, judges both individual and general behaviour, is more free and fluid, than may at first appear.

IV

As well as the binary system, which is socio-moral, and as well as the system of degree, which is pragmatic and concerned with status, we can detect yet another system, which is functional, though it is also highly theoretical. The functional system is the familiar threefold division of medieval society into Knights, Clergy and Ploughmen, often referred to by some medieval vernacular writers of the fourteenth century in England. Knights defend society and maintain law and order; clergy defend men's souls and feed their minds; ploughmen provide food to maintain men's bodies. Langland is the author who perhaps takes this system the most seriously. It would seem to be the only class-system known to medieval theory. Langland, with his yearning for ideal absolutes (which he conquered, indeed, in the end), seems to be much attached to this attractive and simple scheme, while the pragmatic, tough-minded, sceptical, historically interested Chaucer never explicitly refers to it, even in *The Parson's Tale*. Nevertheless, even Chaucer uses it, as it seems, unconsciously, in the *General Prologue* to *The Canterbury Tales*. If it was unconsciously used, we have here an illustration of the familiar proposition that ideas held subconsciously may mould our minds and feelings much more radically than the more anti-intellectual are likely to conceive. The series of portraits in the *General Prologue* is one of the most fascinating blends of the formal and the 'realistic' ever composed, and it presents several detailed observations on fourteenth-century class-distinctions which cannot be pursued here. All the portraits are 'idealised' in the literary sense; that is, each person is presented as the best, or the quintessential, example of his kind. Some, not all, of the portraits are also morally idealised (though to say so does not prejudice the possibility of real-life counterparts almost as good). Those who are morally idealised are the Knight and his son the Squire; the Clerk of Oxford and the Parson; and the Ploughman and Yeoman. We obviously have here the threefold functional division of society, with Chaucer's characteristically courtly and secular bias. The Ploughman, for all the literary and moral beauty of the description, is the least realistic of the portraits, and enclosed religion is not represented. Anyone who, like the burgess, does not fit into the scheme of the three functions, or who, like most of the clergy, being a member of one of the functional groups, divagates from its theoretical ideal, is, to say the least, taken not quite seriously. Some are savagely satirised. Since those who do not fulfil the functional ideal include most people in the national society of the fourteenth century, who were both interesting to Chaucer and safe to comment on, the great majority of the characters presented in the *General Prologue* are satirised in varying degrees of severity. It is hard to feel that Chaucer did not notice some shortcomings in the knightly class of England: but he never mentions them. On the other hand, he also leaves the poor alone, except for the highly idealised Griselda, a few incidental characters, and a few comments, usually sympathetic. Chaucer's point of view is essentially courtly and learned.

The functional system of class-division is not concerned with the status or wealth of individuals. It is probably because the Knight and the Parson fulfil so well their *functional* ideal, rather than for any *gentilesse*, that they seem to have no class-feeling, and are no respecters of persons. The functional system thus treats all persons as potentially equal in one sense, whatever their actual occupation, but condemns all those who do not fulfil any of the three functions. It is therefore an essential part of Chaucer's social satire in the *General Prologue*. Its presence may also account for some apparent puzzles. The status of the Franklin, for example, has long been a subject of controversy. He is clearly a gentleman, as Gerould[9] long ago showed, but critics have felt some degree of uneasiness about his Epicureanism and his insistence on *gentilesse*. The answer is surely that he is well enough up the ladder of degree to be safely equivalent in *that kind* of status to the Knight; secondly, that he is anxious to elect himself into *gentilesse*, and avoid churlishness, according to the binary system, though keeping open house may not be quite the right way of going about it, and his position is just a little equivocal; while thirdly, since he is not a fighting man, not a 'proper' knight, and is obviously neither cleric nor ploughman, he can find no place in the functional triple system and is therefore lightly mocked or satirised.

There is another character in *The Canterbury Tales* whose social situation is closely analogous to that of the Franklin.[10] This is Chaucer himself, or rather, that image or character of himself that he gives both in the *General Prologue* and in the prologues to his two tales. Little is said of Chaucer the pilgrim in the *General Prologue* that directly serves my purpose here, and the impression we receive is as usual a little ambivalent. Since Chaucer is named in *The Canterbury Tales*, the work certainly makes reference to his known character outside the poem, as it equally certainly refers to the actual contemporary Host of the Tabard Inn, Harry Bailly, and probably several others. Chaucer the pilgrim, who both is and is not Chaucer the poet, is obviously some way up the ladder of degree; he chooses *gentilesse* and explicitly dissociates himself from such churlishness as *The Miller's Tale* (but of course ambivalently); but he is not a Knight. He is lightly mocked. His tales, as was the case with the Franklin's, are a rather different matter. One, *The Tale of Melibee*, is a serious moral treatise. The other, *Sir Thopas*, is a brilliant mockery of old-fashioned English romances and of Flemish knighthood. Within these two tales the courtly, learned, secular point of view is confident in its own superiority. Yet the pilgrim Chaucer is clearly somewhat insecure, and everywhere, as I have suggested, there is finally in Chaucer the poet a certain detachment from *all* class-systems, as well as an acceptance of them.

It may be that this remarkable witness from the fourteenth century, with his strong sense of complex social reality, was more affected than he could have realised by his failure to fit into the most theoretical, the most simple, the least practical and realistic of the class-systems he knew or sensed, that is, the functional. He was the son and grandson of rich merchants and a trusted courtier in a brilliant court; he was without question well up the ladder of degree. Though of relatively inferior status, there were many others of similar status in the court, and he can hardly have felt himself to have been an isolated social climber, nor a bourgeois among aristocrats, a 'middle-class' man pushing into the upper class. He was a kind man, says Lydgate, and certainly, to some extent, of a tender, sympathetic cast of feelings, to judge from his poems; he would seem to have wished to be *gentil*, not a churl; his adherence, in general, to the *gentil* side of the binary system seems clear. He could thus fit the first two systems I have distinguished. But he could not, or at any rate did not, fit into the functional system. He did not choose religious poverty, nor even the life of a university clerk; he could not dig, neither did he sow; he was not a knight. He admired clergy, ploughmen, knights, in theory, yet closely as he was associated with knights (when on his early expedition to France, and in the court continuously throughout his life), and with learned clerks (Strode and perhaps others from Merton), there was in theory no place for him among their ranks. He was the new man, the literate layman who was not a clerk, the courtier who was not a knight; he was not poor (like Langland), but not rich; a salaried man, not landed gentry (like Gower); he was not even a merchant like his father and grandfather. The literate layman, as Tout long ago observed of Chaucer himself, was a very important person to emerge in the latter part of the fourteenth century.[11] To be such a new man may have created in him a sense of insecurity, strain, loss, even desertion. Here, possibly, is a root for that recurrent symbol in his writings, to which he devotes such sympathy, the betrayed and deserted woman.[12] The division between old and new, present in everyone, remarkably wide and deep for Chaucer, may well have divided his own feelings, and be a root cause of his remarkable, perhaps uniquely pervasive irony, and his notable ambivalence towards his own culture and values. It is a commonplace observation today that social fluidity creates personal insecurity and ambiguity.

It is also a commonplace that social fluidity creates greater awareness of what social structures there are. Such might well have been the case with Chaucer. In any event, he shows a rich awareness in his historical context of class-distinctions, class-feelings, and social matters generally; I am very conscious of how much more might be said on this. The social implications of vocabulary,[13] especially in the 'socialised' language of love and marriage (*sovereignty, man*, to *serve* (meaning to *love*)); the implications of grammar (for example, his use of the second person singular); his use of nouns and pronouns of address and personal names (the name 'Alison' is obviously *déclassé*); a number of individual comments, like the flippancy about Jack

Straw (*CT*, vii, 3394–7); all these suggest themselves as worth investigation. The imaginative world of Chaucer's work is rich in social structures and implications.

7 *The Reeve's Tale* and the King's Hall, Cambridge*

The appearance of Dr A. B. Cobban's remarkably learned and detailed study, *The King's Hall within the University of Cambridge in the Later Middle Ages* (Cambridge, 1969), enables us to reconsider and take further the generally accepted reference to the King's Hall as Soler Hall in *The Reeve's Tale* (*CT*, I, 3990).

There is little doubt that the King's Hall is meant, though earlier accounts by Chaucerian scholars have been misled in some details, owing to the absence of an accurate history. After consideration of the evidence that the King's Hall was much the largest of Cambridge colleges, having 32 or more fellows; that Garret Hostel (sometimes mentioned as a possibility) was not even a college; and that University (later Clare) Hall, which has also been mentioned, never had more than 13 fellows at most; Dr Cobban considers that the King's Hall is by far the most likely to be indicated as the 'greet collegge' (*CT*, I, 3989). He concludes:

> The designation 'Soler Halle' is not found anywhere in the King's Hall records [which extend in a detailed, unbroken series from 1337 to 1546] and, apart from the *Reeve's Tale*, I am unaware of its occurrence in any other contemporary source. 'Soler' is most certainly derived from *solarium* meaning an upper room or sun-chamber of a house. It is beyond dispute that every upper chamber of the King's Hall was called a solar (*solarium*) and every first floor room a celar (*celarium*). But as this contemporary terminology was a common one, it does not by itself afford conclusive proof of the identification with Chaucer's 'greet collegge'. Nevertheless, if the identification cannot be definitely proven from the existing evidence, it is assuredly the most probable hypothesis. (Cobban, *King's Hall*, p. 17)

---

*First published in *The Chaucer Review*, 5 (1971) 311–17.

This is sufficient encouragement for the moment, though it may later be possible to prove the hypothesis.

It is certain that Chaucer must have known the King's Hall and a number of its fellows well, not only because of an entertainment of parliament at the college in 1388, which has been referred to, but also because of the peculiar nature of the institution itself. As Cobban many times makes clear, the King's Hall had a specially close relation to the king's court. It had been founded by Edward II, was maintained by royal endowment (in the first place specifically to provide further education for children of the Chapel Royal), and seems always to have been intended to provide a supply of graduates in both ecclesiastical and secular spheres particularly for the king's service. Such service was very notably given by such men as Richard de Medford and Richard Ronhale, exact contemporaries of Chaucer.[1] Medford in particular, who was a fellow of the King's Hall from 1352 to 1378, is several times associated with Chaucer, both being members of the king's *familia*, and receiving grants, in 1369.[2] It is worth noticing, too, that both Medford and Ronhale were of the 'court' or the 'king's' party, as Chaucer probably was.[3] Medford was deprived of his position as king's secretary by the Lords Appellant in 1388, but after Richard's assertion of his own power on 3 May 1389 Medford was consecrated Bishop of Chichester in 1390, a little later than Chaucer was given his own more modest job in July 1389.

Besides the intimacy of the college's connection with the court, and their interchange of personnel, the King's Hall also enjoyed a certain notoriety in the 1370s and 80s because of bad management. For example, the warden, Simon Neyland, had to be expelled, along with six offending fellows, in 1385, consequent to complaints by the other fellows to the king and a visitation, as royal agent, of the Bishop of Ely. The college was run by the warden and a committee of six elected fellows, called seneschals, and Cobban notes that 'in the rather exceptional circumstances which prevailed for a number of years during the latter part of the fourteenth century a handful of young, inexperienced Scholars without degrees were, out of necessity, appointed seneschals of the college with detrimental and perhaps even disastrous consequences' (p. 178). The situation improved in 1386, but notoriety for bad management can hardly have quickly evaporated if modern experience is anything to go by.

It is clear then that the King's Hall, the biggest college in Cambridge, intimately linked to the royal court, notorious in various ways, was an excellent subject for a pointed joke with Chaucer's courtly and university-educated audience, and a splendid setting for a *fabliau* about two rowdy clerks. As Chaucer's own affiliations seem to have been with Oxford,[4] it is hard not to feel also something of an inter-university mockery of a very traditional kind—Oxford men laughing at that big notorious Cambridge college. It is noticeable that Chaucer is not nearly so specific in his references to Oxford university or colleges in *The Miller's Tale*, though he must have known Oxford quite as well as Cambridge.

What is suggested by Chaucer in *The Reeve's Tale* of college organisation fits in exactly with what is now known of the arrangements of the King's Hall. The head was called the warden, as in Chaucer (*CT*, I, 4006), and was a crown appointment. Although at first he had absolute control, by the second half of the fourteenth century, as already mentioned, he shared this control with the committee of seneschals, as far as day to day management of the society went, in a manner quite similar to the modern administration of a Cambridge college: i.e. certain fellows had specific responsibility for the various departments. The chief of the college servants was the manciple, as he was first called in the college accounts, and as he is called in Chaucer, though by the second half of the fourteenth century he is normally called *pincerna*, 'butler' (Cobban, *King's Hall*, p. 165). It would naturally have been the manciple's or butler's job to get the wheat and malt ground, not that of the scholars. But the manciple in *The Reeve's Tale* was sick. There were a few other regular servants—probably cook, baker/brewer, kitchen knave, barber, book-bearer, laundress—at this period, together with some casual labour (Cobban, *King's Hall*, pp. 231–42). Some interchange of function was occasionally necessary, caused perhaps by illness or absence. Among examples given by Cobban, the barber in 1505–6 was sent to buy wheat for the college in place of one of the contracting seneschals (Cobban, *King's Hall*, p. 240). The bakehouse/brewhouse was the most efficiently run of the domestic departments, with careful accounts being kept. Cobban does not, alas, record any instance of contracting with a miller for grinding wheat and barley, but dishonesty in a miller would be easily recognised in this department and the more readily resented. If the manciple was sick, and the other servants occupied, it would be natural enough for two high-spirited young scholars to undertake the job of supervising the milling, even though, as appears from *CT*, I, 4027, the manciple is a servant and Alan and John are not.

The status of Chaucer's Alan and John is 'young, poor clerks'. They could nevertheless be King's scholars, that is, fellows, and the reference to 'oure felawes alle' (*CT*, I, 4112) may be specific in this sense. The terms *scholaris* and *socius* are interchangeable in the fourteenth century. All new entrants to the King's Hall were (with rare exceptions) full fellows from the start (Cobban, *King's Hall*, pp. 184–5). According to the statutes they might be as young as fourteen (Cobban, *King's Hall*, p. 58) though many were mature men, especially in the later days. A fellow, therefore, might be either undergraduate or graduate, though whether young or old he was supposed to be sufficiently instructed in elementary grammar. Exceptionally in 1383 one John Rauf was nominated from the Chapel Royal though he had to go to grammar school when appointed; he left in 1383, and in the same year no less than three boys were nominated from the Chapel Royal though weak in grammar.[5]

Though there must therefore have been plenty of young King's scholars in the early 1380s, neither well schooled nor perhaps well behaved, even though in positions of some importance in the college, it does not seem that they were likely to be particularly poor. There was a requirement, usual in colleges, that scholars should relinquish their fellowships if they received benefices yielding more than a certain sum, but this was apparently often neglected. The general standard of living in the college seems to have been rather higher than average, while many if not all of the fellows must have had some sort of influence in high places to be appointed at all. At this stage, therefore, we may suspect that the *fabliau* stereotype of the *poor*, but lusty and headstrong (*testif*, *CT*, I, 4004) clerks begins to take over. Even so, in the story they carry enough silver to pay for an unexpected dinner out (*CT*, I, 4135). They are not apparently like those poor scholars whom the King's Hall sometimes employed as casual labour in the garden (Cobban, *King's Hall*, p. 233, n. 2).

Alan and John also wear swords (*CT*, I, 4085). This is not a detail in any way required by the internal economy of the plot, and has all the appearance of empirical realism reflecting actual life, though I do not mean that I believe that the events of the plot (a 'folk-tale' for which there are enough analogies) actually took place! It was illegal by both university and college statutes for clerks to carry offensive weapons (Cobban, *King's Hall*, p. 89). Here is simply another, and probably authentic, instance of bad discipline among clerks in general, perhaps also of a certain 'young gentleman' element, borne out by Alan's and John's later behaviour. In one respect, however, which is crucial to the plot, the clerks are well-disciplined, namely, in not returning after nightfall. This is not because it was too dangerous (Malin could go into the 'toun', no doubt Trumpington village, for ale and bread (*CT*, I, 4136–7) in the dark), but because, according to the statutes, when the doors of the King's Hall were locked and bolted at night after the curfew was sounded from Great St Mary's, all the scholars should be within doors.[6]

Before considering the question of the possible identities of John and Alan two other points in which *The Reeve's Tale* tallies with what we now know of the King's Hall may be mentioned. First, the careful system of accounts kept by the college shows how important was precisely the management of wheat and malt barley, which is the college's concern in the poem (*CT*, I, 3988), and also, for what it is worth, that Trumpington was one of the many parishes where the college dealt in both (Cobban, *King's Hall*, pp. 126 ff). Second, Alan makes some use, at a crucial moment, of a legal maxim (*CT*, I, 4179–82), and the King's Hall was particularly notable, above all other Cambridge colleges, for the study of civil law, especially *c*. 1350–*c*. 1450 (Cobban, *King's Hall*, pp. 254–6).

Without for a moment indulging in the absurd notion that an actual adventure of two particular scholars is recorded in *The Reeve's Tale*, it is tempting to speculate, with so much clear evidence of an 'in-joke', whether there is not an imputation cast on recognisable persons. After all, there were not so very many scholars at the King's Hall in the 1380s, and most, if not all, must have been known at court (though the court included an enormous number of people apart from the favoured inner circle—or circles—to which Chaucer belonged). Emden (*Register of Cambridge*) includes an index of the Christian names of all Cambridge University men up to 1400. There are approximately 650 Johns, but only 13 Alans (the last instance given of the 14 names in the index is an error). Unfortunately, no Alan is recorded in the King's Hall after Alan le Mareschal who left in 1343 until Alan Pyke who came in 1399–1400. Alan Acon was a priest of York diocese in 1399, but his college is unknown. There was an Alan de Tylney who was fellow of Gonville Hall in 1371, but there seems no reason to blacken his faint memory with our speculations. Alan, however, was perhaps a northern name, and as editors have pointed out, occurs in the Strother family (cf. *CT*, I, 4014). It is also noticeable that in Emden's equivalent list of Christian names for Oxford, where about 700 Johns appear to 16 Alans, eight of the Alans have some kind of northern (mainly Yorkshire) association.[7] The presumed places of origin of the fellows of the King's Hall reveals a decided bias towards fellows from East Anglia and Yorkshire (Cobban, *King's Hall*, pp. 157–61, 275). So, though no individual appears, the poem's general consonance of northern clerks speaking the perennially comical dialect of the north, with membership of the King's Hall, is very close. As so often in Chaucer's work, fundamental fantasy is penetrated in a remarkable way by local supporting realism.

Such a series of closely realistic parallels, besides practically confirming that the King's Hall is indeed satirically if passingly aimed at in the name of Soler Hall, also makes one wonder about that name, accepted by all the editors. Most of the documents call the King's Hall *collegium scolarium*, and refer to the scholars as *scolares aule regis*, *scolares aule nostr' Cantebr'*, or *scolares collegii nostri* (Cobban, *King's Hall*, pp. 88–9). The statutes name the hall *Aulam Scolarium Regis*. The name Soler Hall is not found except in the poem, and there seems no special significance in calling the upper rooms 'solars', which was a perfectly usual name for an upper room. They merely happen to be referred to in the account books. Nor does it seem distinctive to have upper rooms. There were surely plenty of two-storey houses in Cambridge. In other words, there seems no reason to distinguish the college as Soler Hall. In French it is *la Salle des Escoliers*.[8] Clearly what would be a more natural, yet less usual, and therefore more distinctive name for the college, would be a translation of part of the Latin name, which would be Scoler(s') Hall. Names and customs at Oxford and Cambridge are often so esoteric, not to say idiosyncratic, that it is hardly surprising if fifteenth-century workshop scribes preferred the superficially more expectable collocation of *soler* with *hall*, in preference to a university title, perhaps almost university slang, which makes better sense, but of which they were quite ignorant. This argument from the principle of *lectio difficilior* is not quite cast-iron, but it does seem on balance more likely that *scoler* in collocation with *hall*, for non-university scribes, would generate the error *soler hall*, rather than the other way round. If we now consult the manuscripts through the Manly–Rickert edition we find that four unrelated manuscripts do indeed read *Scoler*; viz. Bodley 414, Holkham 667, Manchester English 113, New College D 314. Bodley 414 is of the fifteenth century and belonged to one of the Pastons. It even increases the northern dialect of the clerks in *The Reeve's Tale*.[9] The Norfolk affiliation might suggest some special knowledge of Cambridge which led to a restoration of the form *Scoler*, not shared by the closely cognate Phillips 8136, Holkham 667 is of the mid-fifteenth century, and was probably a Suffolk manu-script[10]—and again the relative closeness to Cambridge may be noted. Manly and Rickert write 'Hk is somewhat carelessly copied but edits scarcely at all, and is valuable as representing a line almost independent, coming off near the top of the large composite group' (pp. 286–7). Manchester English 113 is dated 1483–5. The dialect is East Midland with some Norfolk forms, though the manuscript was in the west of England by the early sixteenth century at latest.[11] New College D 134, of the mid-fifteenth century, is in the East Midland dialect, though with more both northern and southern forms. In the early sixteenth century it is firmly located in East Anglia, with a strong probability of earlier owners and also scribes being East Anglian. It is quite likely that the text descends from texts which had belonged to the family of Chaucer's friend Henry Scogan.[12] The strong East Anglian associations of these four manuscripts in, so to say, the hinterland of Cambridge and the King's Hall may well have caused the scribes either to preserve or to restore the reading *Scoler* if it was indeed original.

Certainty cannot be hoped for in such *minutiae*, but the majority of manuscripts (including the 'best') against the reading *Scoler* can no longer be argued as conclusive evidence against it since G. Kane's exposition of editorial method.[13] It would be quite possible for a few generally 'bad' or edited manuscripts to preserve an original reading and for the majority to err. Now that certainty in the genealogical descent of manuscripts has been shown, in the case of the heavily contaminated fourteenth- and fifteenth-century English manuscripts, to be impossible to attain, each line, and each reading, must be looked at in its own right. The very existence of the variant *Soler/Scoler* questions *either* reading. The familiarity of what we may well call Scoler Hall among specific court and university circles, and new textual theories, makes a strong presumption in favour of *Scoler* as original.

8   The Ages of Troilus, Criseyde and Pandarus*

How old are the protagonists of Chaucer's *Troilus and Criseyde*? We have to make assumptions because we are never told, and indeed Chaucer explicitly disclaims knowledge of Criseyde's age (*TC*, v, 826). Such an ostentatious disclaimer itself invites speculation; but we may also ask ourselves, if the poet disclaims knowledge, can we properly seek it in his poem? We strike immediately on the ambivalence which characterises the poem. The ambivalence tells us that none of the assumptions we may make is quite safe. For example, it is usual to assume that Criseyde herself, since she is so beautiful, is also young. But if Chaucer wants us to realise that, why does he not say so, why does he leave the question of her age open? The poet *never* describes Criseyde as young. She thinks of herself as young, once (*TC*, II, 752), but at what age does a woman cease to think of herself as young? And is she not older than Troilus? Troilus is certainly young ('so yong', *TC*, II, 636) and if we think of him as younger than Criseyde our understanding of the relationship will certainly differ from that based on the assumption that he is older. And how old is Pandarus, uncle of Criseyde and seeming so much more experienced than either of the other two, who is yet constantly with Troilus, and classes himself with 'us yonge' (*TC*, III, 293)? A careful reading of the poem itself in the context of Chaucer's general usages and attitudes, and of the long tradition in literature of Troilus's youth, may not come to any firm conclusion, but can clarify the areas of doubt and illustrate the nature of the poem, poised as it is between romance, novel and tragedy.

The earliest reference to Troilus available to Chaucer is in Virgil's *Aeneid*, certainly read by Chaucer as a school-book, and partially summarised in *The House of Fame*. Virgil's one brief reference strikingly establishes Troilus's military prowess, his death at the hand of Achilles, his extreme

*First published in *Studies in English Literature* (Tokyo), English number (1972) 3–15.

youth and his bad luck, the last two summed up in the phrase *infelix puer* (*Aeneid*, I, 475):

> Parte alia fugiens amissis Troilus armis
> Infelix puer atque impar congressus Achilli,
> Fertur equis, curruque haeret resupinus inani,
> Lora tenens tamen.
>
> (*Aeneid*, I, 474–7)

According to Lewis and Short's *Latin Dictionary*, *puer* is up to fifteen years old, when *adolescentia* begins.

Servius, the late-fourth-century commentator on Virgil, or at least the extensive commentary going under his name that was well known in the Middle Ages, gives us nothing to the point here, though he remarks that Troilus, while killed by Achilles, was also beloved by him—a suggestion happily not taken up by subsequent writers. Dares and Dictys, referred to by Chaucer (*TC*, I, 146), are more explicit, clearly indicating Troilus's extreme youth. When Troilus is shamefully killed, Dictys Cretensis writes of the Trojans

> recordati aetatem ejus admodum
> immaturam, qui in primis pueritiae annis, cum
> verecundia ac probitate, tum praecipue forma
> corporis amabilis, atque acceptus popularibus adolescebat.
>
> (*De Bello Troiano*, IV, cap. IX)

His extreme youth, modesty, integrity, beauty and popularity are thus emphasised. Dares Phrygius repeats the pattern in his briefer description: 'Troilum magnum, pulcherrimum, pro aetate valentem, fortem, cupidum virtutis' (*De Excidio Troiae Historia*, cap. XII).

About the ninth century the first of the so-called Vatican Mythographers makes a passing comment that Troilus was father of Ganymede (!) but in his principal reference remarks, after briefly recounting the death of Troilus, 'Cui dictum erat, quod, si ad annos xx pervenisset, Troia everti non potuisset.'[1] Praise indeed that had he attained the age of twenty Troy would not have been destroyed! There is no evidence that Chaucer knew this obscure mythographer's work, as he knew the texts cited so far, but the tradition is here made very explicit.

When Joseph of Exeter, whom Chaucer occasionally consulted, according to the editors of *Troilus*, takes up the tale his interpretation is the same, mentioning specifically among other hyperbolical praises that Troilus was a boy in age, *aetate puer* (*De Bello Troiano*, IV, 61).

Up to this point the youth of Troilus is emphasised. When Benoît tells the story in the twelfth century he accepts the youthfulness but makes no special point of it, seeing Troilus rather as an exemplification of the ideal of masculine beauty (which in medieval times was surprisingly girlish). However, Troilus is described as 'still a young man, the fairest of the youths of Troy' after Hector.[2]

> Bachelers est e jovenceaus,
> De ceus de Troie li plus beaus
> E li plus proz, fors que sis frere
> Hector . . .[3]

Chaucer also seems to have consulted the *Historia Destructionis Troiae*, by Guido delle Colonne, largely based on Benoît. Guido describes Troilus as the fifth and youngest legitimate son of Priam, 'iuuenis quam plurimam virtuosus in bello'; whereas the other sons are called 'filius' or 'vir'.[4] But though *iuvenis* could mean 'a youth', it could extend to the age of thirty. Troilus's war-like qualities are greatly emphasised, but in the scene when his beloved Briseida laments that she must be sent to the Greeks, Troilus is qualified as *iuuenilis* or *iuueniliter*, weeping for love, and so foolishly believing a woman's word. He is a *fatuus iuuenis*.[5] Women are by nature inconstant.

Boccaccio has told the story of Troilus, he claims, in order to mirror his own griefs, and though his Troilo is 'young'[6] he need be thought of as little younger than Boccaccio, who was probably twenty-three when he wrote the poem. Nevertheless, when he describes Troilo as *valoroso giovane* and especially *figliuolo* of Priam,[7] Troilo is perhaps thought of as especially young.

Boccaccio's Troilo is a cynical young man who knows all about the pains and pleasures of love at the very beginning of the poem, but who happens at that moment to be fancy-free, contemptuous of his own previous and other young men's present painful infatuations.

Chaucer therefore had a certain freedom of choice in his presentation of Troilus. The earlier tradition, dominated by Virgil, whose *Aeneid* was a school-book known to every educated man, emphasised Troilus's extreme youth, in connection with his prowess, worth and misfortune. The later treatments are less interested in his youth.

Chaucer seems, as so often, to keep his options open, and to preserve a deliberate vagueness which modern readers, conditioned by the realism of the naturalistic novel, often find disturbing. His Troilus is more innocent than Boccaccio's Troilo, without sexual experience before, as he is without bitter anti-feminism after, he has loved and lost. Troilus's innocence is perhaps some indication of youthfulness. Another indication may be the obvious distance that Chaucer the poet preserves between him and his hero. The distance is not unsympathetic, but it allows a detachment very similar to the sympathetic detachment of the middle-aged Theseus from the young Arcite and Palamon in *The Knight's Tale*, and very different from the explicit (though partial) identification by Boccaccio of himself with his hero. Neither Boccaccio nor Chaucer is interested in the beauty of young men. Troilus is 'proportionate' (*TC*, v, 827) and of a nobly martial appearance, but his conformity to the medieval masculine ideal is at most implicit.

If we accept the usual chronology and speculations of the editors we may suppose that Chaucer read *Troilus and Criseyde* to the court about 1386. It seems reasonable to suppose that the compliment to Queen Anne (*TC*, i, 171) and also the singular pronoun of address, 'sire' (*TC*, iii, 83), which has so far escaped comment, suggest the presence of Anne and Richard in the audience. They had been married in 1382 when Richard was fifteen.

Troilus might well therefore be thought to be about the age of Richard when the poem was completed and read, if the date of 1386 is accepted—nineteen years old. (And one may add that the violence of Troilus's grief at losing Criseyde was more than matched by Richard's when Anne died in 1394, and Richard ordered the destruction of the palace at Sheen.) Troilus's love-affair lasted for three years (*TC*, v, 8–13). J. D. North dates the action and composition of the poem April 1385–May 1388.[8] Troilus might have fallen in love at sixteen, hardly older than Richard when he was married.

Yet it is apparently not Chaucer's purpose to emphasise Troilus's youthfulness. His youth is part of his exemplary nature:

> So fressh, so yong, so weldy semed he,
> It was an heven upon hym for to see
> > (*TC*, ii, 636–7)

and again

> Yong, fressh, strong, and hardy as lyoun.
> > (*TC*, v, 830)

But 'young' as applied to a man is not particularly definitive. For example, in *The Book of the Duchess*, the man in black was

> Of good mochel, and ryght yong therto,
> Of the age of foure and twenty yer;

Upon hys berd but lytel her.
(454–6)

This is a little strange. Young men nowadays, in British universities, appear to be able to produce great facial bushes (only to be compared with that of the Green Knight in *Sir Gawain and the Green Knight*) at an age much less than twenty-four. On the other hand there seems no reason to suspect irony here. In *The Legend of Good Women* Theseus is 'yong, but of a twenty yer and thre' (l. 2075). Up to twenty-four must be considered to be for Chaucer 'right young' for men. The 'young' Squire in the *General Prologue*, who has already considerable battle-experience, is twenty (*CT*, i, 79, 82), as was Jankin 'oure clerk' when the Wife of Bath, elderly at forty, married him (*CT*, iii, 595–600). Emetreus, champion of Arcite, is twenty-five and not described as young:

Of fyve and twenty yeer his age I caste.
His berd was wel bigonne for to sprynge.
(*CT*, i, 2172–3)

Perhaps men may be still young at twenty-three and twenty-four; mature and well bearded at twenty-five. Distinctions in Chaucer are, however, not so objective. The monk in *The Shipman's Tale* is thirty but described as 'This yonge monk' (*CT*, vii, 26–8) and comes to seduce his friend's wife 'With crowne and berd al fressh and newe yshave' (*CT*, vii, 309). The category of youth is vague and to some extent depends on context. In the light of the context of the tradition the conclusion may well be that Troilus, in the light of the tradition and Chaucer's general usages, should be thought of as twenty or less. At such an age his emotionalism, and even his bravery, may be regarded as quite natural; and surely the poem is very much about (in the words of an old popular song) 'doing what comes naturally'.

How old is Criseyde? Chaucer deliberately introduces notes of uncertainty whenever he writes of Criseyde, and on the topic of age, on which women are traditionally mysterious, he is not likely to make an exception. As already noted he emphasises his ignorance of her age: 'But trewely, I kan nat telle hire age' (*TC*, v, 826). Criseyde, however, 'thought that love, *al come it late*' (*TC*, iii, 468) had opened the gate of joy, when Troilus loves her. Clearly she had not loved, in this sense, or been loved by, her late husband—her remark to Diomede that her husband was the only person she had loved in Troy is a lie to preserve her reputation (*TC*, v, 975–6). But how old does a girl have to be to think that love has come 'late'. Eighteen? Yet Chaucer never describes Criseyde explicitly as 'young'.

Criseyde herself, it is true, describes herself as 'right yong' (*TC*, ii, 752)—which, at least as far as men are concerned, we have seen may mean as old as twenty-four. January, in *The Merchant's Tale*, thinks a thirty-year-old woman no better than 'bene-straw' and will have a wife no older than twenty (*CT*, iv, 1417–22), but women might not agree. 'Young' for women in Chaucer seems to be about twenty. Of Anelida the poet says 'Yong was this quene, of twenty yer of elde' (*Anelida and Arcite*, 78). Alison in *The Miller's Tale* is eighteen (*CT*, i, 3223) and the daughter in *The Reeve's Tale* is twenty (*CT*, i, 3970). Women might marry young; the Wife of Bath was twelve at her first marriage—no wonder she hated her old husband (*CT*, iii, 4)—and the daughter whom Walter in *The Clerk's Tale* pretends to be about to marry is only twelve (*CT*, iv, 736). Virginia, heroine of *The Physician's Tale*, is fourteen (*CT*, vi, 30). Criseyde *might* have been married to her husband when she was twelve and widowed the next year. She *could* have been thirteen when Troilus fell in love with her! It would be extravagant to think so, nevertheless. She has nieces and a household to manage, even if she likes Pandarus to advise her (*TC*, ii, 213–19). She is conscious of her independence and she is self-confident enough. (The fearfulness that has been attributed to her is only one of her charmingly womanly characteristics and by no means always affects her.) To be 'slydynge of corage' (*TC*, v, 825) does not mean, as seems occasionally to be assumed, to be weak in *courage*, but to be *unstable*, which is also traditionally attributed to women, but which Benoît and Guido specially attribute to Criseyde, under the name Briseida, which Boccaccio changed. Briseida is not mentioned by Virgil, but Servius and the First and Second Vatican Mythographers mention her in passing in connection with the story of Achilles, not Troilus. She is formally described by Dares, Dictys, Benoît, Guido and Joseph, as the editors note, but no mention is made of her age. In commenting on his ignorance of her age Chaucer exactly reflects the absence of earlier comment, but of course in *mentioning* his ignorance he draws attention to the problem, with his customary baffling absence of tone, that may equally well be registered as naivety or profoundly sophisticated ambivalence. However the comment be understood, its effect is to draw the reader into as it were complicity with the poet in recreating the imagined sequence of events, yet without giving much guidance. In the end, if Troilus is to be thought of as around nineteen, one might think of Criseyde as several years older, perhaps, since she manages herself and her own affairs apparently without too much difficulty, and with only occasional advice or help.

For Pandarus, there is no verbal evidence. All we have are his personal relationships, the sequence of events, and his own speeches. As so often in

Chaucer there is ambiguity. He is Criseyde's uncle and advises her about the management of her estate, as already noted. We can hardly suppose him the brother of her father Calkas (if he were he would surely be more closely implicated in his treachery), so he is presumably Criseyde's deceased mother's brother. (Criseyde's nieces, by the way, must be the children of yet another aunt and uncle of Criseyde, presumably also deceased.) As uncle, and adviser, Pandarus is presumably older than Criseyde, though he need not be if Criseyde's grandparents on the mother's side had a widely spaced family. It is Chaucer's invention to make Pandarus the uncle of Criseyde, rather than cousin, as in Boccaccio's poem, and this suggests strongly that Pandarus is intended to seem older. We may also note that Pandarus as adviser to Troilus inevitably has the appearance of being older: he is more learned; for example he understands astrology (*TC*, II, 74–5), and the art of letter-writing (*TC*, II, 1023 ff). His use of proverbs contributes to our sense of his experience of life. His cynicism makes us feel he is older. It is also very noticeable that he is no soldier. Nowhere in the poem is there a word of his military deeds, in a city under desperate siege, and in a culture (ancient or medieval) where to be a noble was practically synonymous with being a soldier, and where Troilus himself is so outstanding a warrior. True, Pandarus tells Criseyde that on an occasion he was discussing military tactics with Troilus (*TC*, II, 510), and this must have been plausible, but the episode he is relating is apparently a string of lies anyway. All this makes him seem decidedly middle-aged.

Yet, except on the battle-field, Pandarus is Troilus's daily companion, in his sports, like casting of the spear (*TC*, II, 513), as in familiar conversation in his chamber. Pandarus is also a lover, and a very unsuccessful one, who is as miserable and sleepless on occasion for love as ever Troilus was (*TC*, II, 57–63, 98). To this extent, Pandarus seems to be of the same age as Troilus in Chaucer's poem, just as in Boccaccio's poem Pandaro seems to be of the same age as Troilo. Chaucer's Pandarus certainly numbers himself among 'us yonge' (*TC*, III, 293), but then, so does Shakespeare's sixty-year-old Falstaff, who refers to 'us youth'.[9] (The character of Pandarus does not exist, though the name does, in the earlier authorities on the Troy story.)

How then are we to imagine Pandarus? The only reconciliation of the evidence that seems possible is to think of him as one of those people not unfamiliar in large communities where youth predominates (or, as in medieval courtly society, where at least youthful ideas (such as love and fighting) predominate): he seems to be the sort of energetic man who refuses to grow up. In early middle age such men are physically active, wearing youthful styles, following youthful habits, consorting with the young on apparently equal terms, yet always advising, always being consulted and listened to, often guiding and even leading, because in fact they are not as young as their companions, and because age and the accumulated learning and experience that age brings to an intelligent man inevitably give him advantages over them, even if such advantages can only be bought by moral inferiority to those he consorts with; just as Pandarus, the easy collaborating worldling, is morally inferior to, though perhaps more sensible than, the intransigent and idealistic young Troilus.

It is quite possible then, to see Pandarus, in terms of our modern jargon, as a middle-aged trendy. Although this would be quite acceptable, the realistic and naturalistic description has many gaps, as for example in the implicit structure of Criseyde's family background, of a kind that, if the poem were really a novel, would constitute serious weaknesses, raising questions without an answer. The poem is not quite to be read as a novel, though it has novel-like characteristics. The poem as a whole is not truly 'organic', though this is not a fault. Actions and characteristics may be juxtaposed in Chaucer's art in a lively representation of life, but not without some possible inconsistency, as in Criseyde's family, or in the young–old Pandarus, and not without vagueness in the presentation of details, such as the age of Criseyde, which could be known, or guessed at, fairly definitely in what we call 'real' life.

APPENDIX: IDEAS OF AGE IN THE MIDDLE AGES

Classical Latin usages of the words for the ages of man are subject to some confusion. *Iuvenis* tended to mean 'mature', but could also be confused with *adolescentia*. This confused Classical background should be borne in mind, but the standard encyclopaedic summary for the Middle Ages is found in Isidore, *Etymologiarum Libri, XX* (ed. W. M. Lindsay, 1911) xi, ii. He gives six ages of man: *infantia* (up to seven); *pueritia* (up to fourteen); *adolescentia* (fourteen to twenty-eight); *iuventus* ('the most stable of all ages', twenty-eight to fifty); *gravitas* (fifty to seventy); *senectus* (any remaining years).

Isidore's account is repeated in the thirteenth-century encyclopaedia by Bartholomeus Anglicus, which was translated into English by Chaucer's contemporary, John of Trevisa, whose translation was added to and published by Stephen Batman as *Batman vppon Bartholome* (1582), which is the edition cited here. Lib. vi, cap. 1 treats of age, of which the passage on *adolescentia* may be quoted:

Adolescentia, the age of a young striplyng, & dureth the thirde

seaventh yeare, that is, to the ende of one and twentie yeares, as it is said
in Viatico: but Isidore sayth that it endureth to the fourth seaven yeares
. . . [but physicians say up to thirty or thirty-five].

In national life, as opposed to encyclopaedias, in the fourteenth century,
all men between sixteen and sixty were liable for military service. There
would be nothing unusual in a soldier under the age of twenty, and many
infantry officers throughout the centuries in the British Army have been
under twenty (including the unwarlike writer of the present article).
Edward of Woodstock, the 'Black Prince', born in 1333, commanded the
right wing at the battle of Crécy (1346) and took his part bravely in the
fighting, as Froissart records. Chaucer himself took part in the French
campaign of 1359–60, and may then have been no older than fourteen if he
was born as late as 1345; though even if as is more likely he was born as
early as 1340 he would still be hardly twenty when he was ransomed on
1 March. Mention of Chaucer also reminds us finally not to take this question of age too seriously. In an age without birth-certificates, newspapers
and all the other regular time-paraphernalia and time-mementoes of
modern urban life, who, apart from princes, could have any certain record
of his own age? Certainly not Chaucer. When he gave evidence at the
Scrope-Grosvenor trial in 1386,[10] he is recorded as of age 'xl ans et plus
armeez par xxvii ans'. He knew he had carried arms for 27 years, but not
exactly how old he had been when he began—presumably in the very
campaign of 1359–60. Then, he could well have been of the same age as
Troilus—whatever that was.

9   Honour in Chaucer*

The vagaries of the notion of honour are complex in English, different from
Continental notions, and of great human importance and literary interest.
Chaucer mentions honour frequently and creates a characteristically rich
and subtle concept, which it is essential to understand for appreciation
especially of *Troilus and Criseyde*, but also of several other poems, and of
Chaucer's own literary personality.[1]

   Chaucer's notion of honour does not seem to change as he grows older,
but to become more finely developed. It is signified by a range of words
with overlapping semantic fields, of which the noun *honour* itself is the
chief. With it are associated in varying degrees of closeness *worship*, the
older English word for the same thing which Malory so much prefers,
worthynesse, *renoun*, *loos*, and more remotely *preisynges* and
commendacioun, *laude*, *reverence*, as well as more frequently *name* and
fame which so conveniently rhyme with the antonym *shame*. *Shame* itself
may in certain contexts be honourable. With these nouns go other
corresponding parts of speech. It is not my purpose to analyse all these
variants and their relationships in this present essay, which offers rather a
more general analysis of the notion in Chaucer's works. As such, I have
also accepted particular instances of the use of the concept as valid
contributions to the general notion, whoever the speaker in the poem or
work may be, except where a specifically dramatic or ironic meaning may
be detected. Thus a character in a poem, or Boethius, or the Lady
Philosophy, or the poet, are taken as valid contributors, since nowhere, as
far as I can recall, is an offered idea of honour denied, though it may be
qualified. My aim, in other words, is to elucidate the structure of a general
'socio-literary concept', if I may be forgiven the expression, to which not
every dramatic character in the work, could he be consulted, might agree—

*First published (in an abridged form) in *Essays and Studies of the English
Association, 1973*, ed. J. Lawlor (London, 1973) pp. 1–19.

not even the poet himself as a person, nor, certainly, myself. The concept is a product of Chaucer's historical culture, as well as of his own individual mind. A poet is a spokesman before he is, even if he ever is, an unacknowledged legislator. What I have to say depends on its empirical validity rather than on its method, and any reader who feels uneasy about the latter may look for justification or its reverse to the former. I use the noun 'honour' for the general concept but italicise when the verbal form itself is significant.

The duality of honour strikes any reader of Chaucer, or of earlier English literature, rather more strongly than readers of Continental literature.[2] In English, and notably in Chaucer, honour is Janus-faced. On the one side honour looks towards goodness, virtue, an inner personal quality; on the other side looks towards social or external reputation, to marks of dignity, like giving generous feasts, or making honorific gestures like kneeling. Honour in terms of virtue perhaps reaches its highest expression when the Virgin herself is described as *honour*, and root of goodness after Christ (*CT*, VII, 463–5). She is also described as the *honour of mankynde* (*CT*, VII, 619). Such expressions are not reducible to any clear scheme in their own terms, though they are based on the association of female honour with chastity. Each aspect of the expression, the Virgin, and honour, is conceived of as the highest value, and each reflects glory on the other. To be honourable or worshipped is always to be approved. More clearly in a schematic way, Chaucer's translation of *The Consolation of Philosophy* of Boethius (henceforth referred to as *Boece*) makes *propre honour* synonomous with intrinsic personal virtue (*Boece*, IV, 3, 27).

At the other extreme, that of social reputation, *Boece* makes equally clear in Book III, proses 2 and 4, which particularly discuss honour, that 'to be holden honourable or reverent ne cometh nat to folk of hir propre strengthe of nature, but oonly of the false opynyoun of folk' (III, 73), which Criseyde would have done well to remember. Honour may consist only of the externals, of *dignytees*, which are good in themselves, it is assumed (and certainly many people are said by Lady Philosophy to believe), but which are trivial, and are 'yyven ofte to wikkide men' (II, 4, 10). Honour, therefore, of this kind, is an earthly good, and like all such goods is for Boethius a real good, but also really bad, in that such earthly goods are only a sort of parody of the divine goodness, and may deflect us from achieving that; they are appearance rather than reality. This double stage of goodness is an essential element of the *Boece*, as I believe it is of *Troilus*. It inheres in the vocabulary and confuses discussion because such a word as *dignyte* (e.g. *Boece*, III, 4, 102) may mean either '*dignyte* as normally and erroneously conceived in the world of appearances' or 'true *dignyte*', which may often appear to the worldly eye as no *dignyte* at all. But in the case of honour the confusing but not necessarily confused or mistaken duality of appearance and reality is built deep into Chaucer's and our culture, and as a general concept cannot be divided. External reputation would be nothing if it did not impute and by intention confirm internal virtue, however often mistakenly. Internal virtue would not have the power and implications essential to it if it did not in some ways appear, and be honoured for what it was when it did appear. Yet external honour may be even a danger to internal worth, as *Boece* makes clear, and as becomes explicit in religious terms when Melibeus is told by his admirable wife Prudence that he has so much enjoyed, among other delights, *honours of this world*, that he has forgotten Jesus Christ his creator (*CT*, VII, 1411).

Nevertheless the continuum of meaning between intrinsic worth and external reputation, dignity and reward, is not hard to understand. Appearance *ought* to coincide with reality, and though we know that often or usually it does not, we ought to try to make it do so. Prudence tells Melibeus that 'he sholde not be called a gentil man that after God and good conscience, alle thynges left, ne dooth his diligence and bisynesse to kepen his goode name'. And she quotes Solomon for support on the value of a good name as being above great riches (*CT*, VII, 1635–41). 'Good name' is not so loaded a term as 'honour', but numerous passages and collocations show that it is a near synonym. Prudence goes on to quote, quite correctly, a sermon by St Augustine which says, with supporting quotations from 2 Corinthians 8:21 and 2 Titus 2:7, that we have a duty to preserve both good conscience and good name, Latin *fama*.[3] St Thomas Aquinas expresses the duality in a more unified form, though this does not appear explicitly in Chaucer.[4] Honour is by no means necessarily un-Christian in its full formulation. As it faces internally, it supports virtue; as it faces externally, it respects virtue in others and reports, for the respect of others, the inner virtue of the bearer.

Honour, therefore, is not so much a virtue as an activity, perhaps like courage, which should support virtue, but does not always do so. The verbs *honour, worship* are always used in a good sense in Chaucer and may be both religious and secular. Similarly, *to honour*, or *do honour*, or *reverence* can be used of quite general morally neutral social activities, especially giving a feast and not hurrying people away, as January does in *The Merchant's Tale* (*CT*, IV, 1766); or by paying a courtesy, as the Sowdan in *The Man of Law's Tale* asks his mother 'The honour of his regne to susteene' (*CT*, II, 392) by riding out to meet his bride.

The activity of honouring, whether internal or external, indicates paying respect to, and therefore being loyal to, a person or a moral ideal. Thus it develops, as will be shown, towards *trouthe*, and one breach of honour is treachery, that greatest of medieval vices and crimes. Criseyde's father Calkas is dishonoured by his treachery in leaving Troy: a traitor cannot have honour, and this applies to both men and women, for whom otherwise honour is so different.

Within the honour-system an authoritarian and hierarchical pattern of personal relationships between superiors and inferiors is established, reflected in terms of gesture often by kneeling, as in prayer to God (*TC*, iii, 183–4), or as Troilus would do to Criseyde, were he not lying in bed shamming sickness:

> 'allas, I may nought rise,
> To knele and do yow honour in som wyse'.
> (*TC*, iii, 69–70)

The typical movement of psychic energy is thus from inferior to superior. John Donne, with characteristic hyperbole two centuries later, in a poetic letter to the Countess of Bedford beginning 'Honour is so sublime perfection', remarks: 'So from low persons doth all honour flow.'[5] But Chaucer in the same scene between Troilus and Criseyde makes Troilus ask Criseyde

> And that ye deigne me so muche honoure
> Me to comanden aught in any houre.
> (*TC*, iii, 139–40)

Honour may flow from superior to inferior, but in terms of command, not of service. However, this seems to be the only clear example in Chaucer, though apparent equals may also honour each other, as nobles do Jason (*LGW*, 1408). It would of course be dishonourable for an inferior to command a superior. Such situations do not much interest Chaucer. The characteristic movement that attracts his imaginative interest is 'upward' aspiration and desire, and it is clear that for Chaucer and his whole culture there are deep satisfactions in that movement of the spirit of love and admiration and desire of the good, so unfamiliar in the present phase of our literary culture, but which we still call 'worship'.

Self-forgetful yet deeply satisfying as this human quality of paying honour is in itself, it has a further important component easily overlooked today; that of belonging to a group, to some extent self-selected, of which the members have something fundamental in common. To pay honour to someone is to associate oneself with him or her, and of course with other worshippers too, so that in some senses, to pay honour is also to receive it, provided your honouring is accepted. If you do not pay honour, or if it is not accepted, you are outside the honour-group. The religious aspect of this is clear enough but Chaucer develops it on the secular side, following traditional concepts. In what I take to be his section of the translation of *Le Roman de la Rose* Vileynie is foul and churlish: she knows too little of nurture, that is, she is too lacking in good upbringing 'to worshipe any creature' (*Romaunt*, 180). From this, and from the quotation above from *The Tale of Melibee* we may assume that in order to pay honour you also have to be *gentil*. This again is a word like *honour* itself which has a range of meanings in Chaucer from inner virtue to social rank, with, as I have shown elsewhere, a predominantly moral implication,[6] as is no doubt the case when Prudence speaks. Nevertheless the social ranking is important in practice, and we may see how it works in the career of Arcite in *The Knight's Tale* which gives such an interesting glimpse of social mobility in Chaucer's favourite upward direction. The noble Arcite comes secretly in disguise and with a false name to the court of Theseus, from which he has been banished on pain of death, and takes employment as a hewer of wood and drawer of water. He is so charming at these menial tasks, 'so gentil of condicion', that everyone thinks he should be promoted to some

> worshipful servyse,
> Ther as he myghte his vertu exercise.
> (*CT*, i, 1435–6)

That is, he can only exercise his virtue in a worshipful, an honourable, way, at a higher social level. We may also note in passing the close association of honour with service. Then Arcite's *name* is sprung so wide (a phrase found as early as *Beowulf*, l. 18), that is, he wins fame, which is a form of honour, that he is promoted again to squire. This illustrates the fourteenth-century acceptance of mobility within, and perhaps even out of, a social class, though the illustration is the less striking in that Arcite is actually of royal lineage and moreover has a secret private income.

The use of the word *name* and even more particularly Arcite's own secret complaints about his own changed name illustrate another general aspect of honour. Arcite sorrowfully exclaims that after all he is serving his mortal enemy, Theseus;

> And yet dooth Juno me wel moore shame,
> For I dar noght biknowe myn owene name.
> (*CT*, i, 1555–6)

Not to be able to answer to one's own name is shameful. Honour
contributes to the sense of personal identity which is a product of both
internal and social forces. A man must be able to answer for himself and be
recognisable as what he is, in order to be approved. If one loses one's name,
one loses honour, one's place in the honour-group and thus in society.
One's function becomes uncertain. In the end, honour comes close to
identity, particularly when that is conceived in terms of social relationships.

The nature of the identity sought in Chaucer's own culture, or rather, in
the selective view of it that he gives us in his writings, is revealed in broad
terms by the types of what is honourable. The Virgin as the highest concept
of honour has already been mentioned, but the references are few, and this
is the place to recognise that they are placed in the mouth of the Prioress, for
whom they are dramatically suitable. They must therefore be regarded as
possible in Chaucer's culture but not necessarily completely accepted. They
are both religious and feminine. More important from our present point of
view, because more casual and not dramatically orientated, are incidental
references to the king as the type of honour, as in *Anelida*: 'And dide him
honour as he were a kyng' (l. 130). It is normally granted to a king by God
that he should be honourable (*CT*, v, 21; vii, 2210), which gives special
force to Chaucer's adjuration to Richard II in *Lak of Stedfastnesse* 'O
prince, desyre to be honourable' (l. 22). The stanza fills out the duties of an
honourable king; his obligations are downward in the social scale, and
'external', i.e. to love and cherish and also discipline his people; they are
also internal and upwards on the moral scale, personal in relation to God,
but also in relation to high abstract ideals:

> Dred God, do law, love trouthe and worthinesse,
> And wed thy folk agein to stedfastnesse.   (ll. 27–8)

The stability of the social fabric depends on honour as incarnate in
honourable individuals, supremely the king. It is important to notice that to
be honourable is to love *trouthe*, not to love *honour*, and again honour if
analysed is not exactly a virtue but a maintenance of virtue. The possible
divergence between honour and virtue becomes of great importance in
certain contexts. Here we may note, what has been extremely important for
English culture far beyond the bounds of literature, that the king in
England is not presented as the fount of honour, as Wilson points out he is
in Spanish literature, any more than he is above the law, as according to
Pitt-Rivers he also is in Spanish literature. Therefore, though he should be a
type of honour, he is not in any way above the honour-system, as he is in
Spanish. Wilson notes that in English Renaissance drama, too, honour does

not derive from the king but is a perquisite of noblemen. In Chaucer, it seems, honour derives from the public recognition of virtue, as in Arcite's case when under the name of Philostrate he achieves honour in the court of Theseus. Honour therefore arises as a tacit understanding in the honour-group, *gentils of honour* according to the expression in *The Wife of Bath's Tale* (*CT*, III, 1209). But the honour-group may exclude the regular clergy on the one hand, and, to judge from the absence of reference to honour and the positive evidence of their activities, it excludes on the other hand millers, carpenters, manciples, university men and *swich rascaille*.

The edges of the group are blurred as so often in English society, for among the pilgrims in *The Canterbury Tales* the honour-group perhaps includes the Pardoner, since he, with his superficial social morality, in his bogus sermon, condemns drunkenness and gambling not as vices, but as dishonour, as shame (*CT*, VI, 580, 595), and commends the Ten Commandments as *honurable* (*CT*, VI, 640) which the Parson does not. However, the Parson himself condemns lechery as depriving both man and woman of good fame and *al hire honour* which enables the devil to win 'the mooste partie of this world' (*CT*, X, 847–50). Although the Parson attributes to 'the prophete' this fairly comprehensive denial of true honour, the source has not been traced and the sentiment could be Chaucer's own. It may still be dramatically suited to the Parson. The same sentiment about lechery is attributed to Cenobia in *The Monk's Tale* (*CT*, VII, 2293), even in marriage. Whether it represents the secularisation of religious values or the sanctification of a secular concept of honour I leave it to others to decide. What we may well think is that, as with the Prioress, this religious notion of lechery as dishonour is only partially applicable to the general honour-system, and is probably more religious and female than male.

Honour also can be inherited from ancestors (*CT*, VII, 2197–8, 2643) and this concept is never attacked as the closely connected notion of inheriting *gentillesse* is attacked in *The Wife of Bath's Tale*. Honour is a more social concept than *gentillesse* and it holds the group together not only at the present moment but also in time, from ancestor to descendant. Inheritance of honour also firmly establishes the existence of the sub-group of the family within the larger honour-group.

Within an honour-group the concept of sharing honour is important, which is why a person has to be accepted in the group, or have, as in a family, an inherent biological right to be a member of it, and not merely wish to be a member. Individual persons' relationships with each other sustain honour to each other; but, because of their mutual bonds, they also divide each other's honour. If our king is honourable we not only benefit from his honour as activity, we share in his honour as glory. Association means participation. To be accepted as an associate of honourable men is one way to gain honour. And you can lose honour if another member of your group loses honour. So that the honour-group is defensive and judicial: and to damage its honour by one's dishonourable behaviour is to risk being thrown into outer darkness, which for those who value honour highly, like Criseyde, is the ultimate horror, and the grim irony of her fate. Such a fate is not the result of legal or of moral judgments but of social, though all three necessarily overlap to some extent, and the Parson does indeed say it is a sin to deprive one's neighbour of his good name (*CT*, x, 795). This mixture of liabilities makes honour a rather tense business. Honour may be attacked by envy (*Romaunt*, 260 ff; *CT*, I, 907–8); or it may apparently just fade away, since Prudence says you have to work constantly to keep it up (*CT*, VII, 1842); or it may be lost by old age (*CT*, I, 3051–6). This all refers to personal reputation of course. Poverty may lose honour and so shame one's family; and of course one's family may bring shame on one. Sub-groups exist within the larger honour-group, and yet the individual always has an indivisible identity, and may even have to act against the most intimate members of his dearest sub-group because of the pressure of the larger group. Paradoxically it is the relation with the larger group that enforces individual self-sufficiency within the smaller group. The individual's existence is guaranteed by society through the concept of honour.

Within the large honour-group of the *gentils* are two very important major sub-groups, for whom the practice of honour, so far discussed in general terms, is very different. They are, naturally, men and women, or rather, knights and ladies. We become vividly aware of the biological base of what has so far been discussed in social and moral terms. The honour of knights rests on the dominant biological characteristic of most young men, their aggressiveness. Honour institutionalises a vital but unruly and often destructive element in young men, and so to some extent controls and directs it into socially useful channels, that is, the defence of the group against external aggression, or at least into socially if not physically harmless activities like sport, such as jousting. This is how honour not only cements the group together but offers social approval for the biological masculine role, and contributes to the knight's sense of identity and social function. A knight acquires *honour and worship* essentially by fighting bravely, by the exercise of arms, which is his predominant duty. In Arveragus's case in *The Franklin's Tale* it takes him away from the wife to whom he is utterly devoted for two years and there is no suggestion within the poem that he ought to do otherwise. His absence is the measure of his devotion. 'I could not love thee, dear, so much, Lov'd I not honour more.'

Arcite's acquisition of honour is more vague and more civilian (his career as a courtier is curiously parallel to Chaucer's own), but though he wins honour partly by 'his good tongue' (eloquence being important in Chaucer's knightly ideal), he also wins honour by 'dedes' (*CT*, I, 1438). Honour for a man is primarily based on military prowess, which is often the meaning of *worthynesse* (*LGW*, 1648; cf. *CT*, I, 3060). There is nothing surprising in all this. Until weakened by the machine-gun and high explosive, to say nothing of atom bombs, such a concept prevailed in even advanced societies, let alone traditional ones. Dr Johnson considered that every man thought the worse of himself if he had not been a soldier (and the predilection of many youths in Western societies today for fancy soldier's uniform suggests that the uninstitutionalised feeling is far from dead). What is notable about Chaucer is that he, in that chivalric fourteenth-century court, shows practically no interest in military prowess. Nevertheless he accepts it unequivocally as a high moral ideal and this most ironic and satirical poet never mocks bravery. To be called a coward is intolerable in Chaucer, though oddly enough most of the occurrences of the world occur in marital or sexual contexts, except for the Parson, who is unexceptionably martial—it is a 'coward champioun recreant, that seith "creant" withoute nede' (*CT*, x, 695–700). According to Pandarus, too, it is no honour for a man to weep (*TC*, v, 408–9), though Pandarus, that man of action not of feeling, is usually impatient of weeping anyway (*TC*, I, 697–702).

Except by Pandarus, who can hardly be called a man of honour (amongst other reasons, he never does any fighting), it seems generally agreed that in one situation timidity on the part of a knight is a virtue—that is, when he falls in love. In *The Book of the Duchess* the Knight's boldness when he meets his lady is turned to *shame* (ll. 617, 1213) and so is Troilus's. *Shame* comes to mean modesty, Shakespeare's 'maiden shame' more usually attributed to ladies. In Chaucer we have here an extension of that ancient European concept, which has strong Christian connotations, of the knight who is a lion in the field, and a lamb in hall among ladies. (It is not absolutely gone. An obituary, published in *The Times* of August 1972, of a winner of the Victoria Cross in the war of 1939–45 records an identical pattern.) Chaucer's young men are in sexual matters paradoxically the less aggressive the more honourable they are, and the extreme instance is Arveragus who rejects honour for *trouthe*.

One must not make this too moralistic. Although it is admirable and even usual for good and brave young men to be shy with ladies, seduction and adultery are not described as dishonourable, except in so far as they would come under the Parson's description of lechery as dishonourable, already mentioned. Aurelius and Damian, squires who are respectively unsuccessful and successful seducers of the ladies married to the knights they serve, are not regarded as dishonourable. And the Monk, admittedly even less of a dramatically characterised teller of his tale than most, describes Alexander as

> of knyghthod and of fredom flour;
> Fortune hym made the heir of hire honour.
> Save wyn and wommen, no thing myghte aswage
> Hig hye entente in armes and labour.
>
> (*CT*, vii, 2642–5)

In other words, though sex and drink (soldiers' vices, after all) were a distraction from his activities, he was still the height of honour. There is absolutely no signal for an ironic interpretation of the text here. It may incidentally be noticed that Pandarus says almost outright that it would be no shame to Troilus for him to keep Criseyde as his mistress (*TC*, iv, 596–7). It is not entirely clear that even rape is dishonourable to a knight. Tereus, is indeed described as *this traytour*, *this false thef*, and does Philomela further harm after raping her by cutting out her tongue 'For fere lest she shulde his shame crye' (*LGW*, 2332). One cannot be certain whether the shame is his, or the shame that he has wickedly inflicted on her. The rape committed by the hero of *The Wife of Bath's Tale* is never described as dishonourable, only as *oppressioun* (*CT*, iii, 889). Rape is of course both a sin and a crime, but, as already noted, dishonour is not always or exactly correspondent with either or both. To be false, a traitor, is to break *trouthe*, which is closely connected with honour but again not exactly the same thing. Calkas 'has lost so foule his name' (*TC*, iv, 466–7) that he dare not return. Falseness and dishonour are also closely equated between Palamon and Arcite, when Palamon says, with angry understatement,

> It nere ... to thee no greet honour
> For to be fals, ne for to be traitour
> To me, that am thy cosyn and thy brother
> Ysworn ful depe ...
>
> (*CT*, i, 1129–32)

Treachery in a man's world is clearly dishonourable. It is less clearly condemned by men when women are concerned. Anelida reproaches her false beloved:

> And thenke ye that furthered be your name
> My swete foo, why do ye so, for shame?

To love a newe, and ben untrewe? Nay!
And putte yow in sclaunder now and blame . . .
(*Anelida*, 272–5)

But this is the woman's point of view, which may have limitations similar to the Parson's. It cannot be said that it is *generally* accepted in Chaucer's poetry, any more than in the Western tradition as a whole, that to debauch and destroy a woman is regarded as dishonourable. Honour here diverges from virtue and justice and of course from the teachings of Christianity, and perhaps the most that can be said is that Chaucer more nearly associates honour with virtue in this respect than do Continental writers.

Nevertheless love in Chaucer is a very different matter from sex, especially for women, as will be shown, but also for men. A knight may be shy with ladies, and yet passionately in love, like the Black Knight in *The Book of the Duchess*, and Troilus. Troilus seems to be sexually innocent. A knight will grow in honour simply by being in love, as the poet suggests (*TC*, I, 251) that Troilus tells himself hopefully at the beginning of his love (*TC*, I, 374–6); and as seems to be borne out when successful though secret love so increases his honour that it rings to the very gate of heaven (*TC*, III, 1723–5)—though a knight has to be in an honourable state to start with for his honour to increase by love.

On the whole, however, honour does not seem much involved in a young bachelor's love-life. The emphasis, especially in *Troilus*, is so much on Troilus's inner life that references to his honour are few, whereas references to Criseyde's honour are numerous. She herself makes a characteristically cool and worldly-wise distinction. At a moment of crisis she suggests that she will so manage matters 'That I honour may have, and he plesaunce' (*TC*, III, 944). This is when Pandarus suggests that Troilus shall visit her in bed. Criseyde feels it is a question of honour for her, but not for Troilus. A cynic might feel, and think himself justified by the story, that female honour and male pleasance are incompatible. In another place Criseyde says that if Troilus's plan to elope were known, her life and his honour would be jeopardised, but here she is thinking, as he is not, of Troilus's military and therefore social responsibilities and obligations. She says he would be ashamed to return to Troy if peace came, and he must not 'juparten so youre name'. People would say that he was driven not by love but by 'lust voluptuous and coward drede' (*TC*, IV, 1560–75).

But it is striking that whereas Criseyde shows intense concern for what people will say, and for social and indeed moral obligations (in this respect typical of all Chaucer's ladies, though she is a significantly extreme example), Troilus is quite ready for Criseyde's sake to desert the Trojan cause, to which he is so necessary, without a moment's thought. Arcite also in *The Knight's Tale* says he will gladly forgo his honour if only he can please Emily (*CT*, I, 711). There is apparently no great clash between love and honour in Chaucer as there is in Spanish and perhaps other Continental literature, because love, not honour, is taken by young men as the supreme value. Indeed, just as Troilus's honour is increased with his successful love, Troilus, when he hears that Criseyde must go to the Greeks, says that he has fallen out of honour into misery (*TC*, IV, 271–2). Troilus equates successful love with his good fortune and both with honour; his ill-fortune in love is to him loss of honour. This view of honour as secondary to love, yet attached to it, sets Chaucer apart from many European writers who have used the concept of honour, and no doubt sets him apart also from the normal social concepts of his own time outside literature. For Troilus the association of love with honour may perhaps be regarded as a sort of serious parody of marriage. Troilus in his absolute fidelity to Criseyde, as also in his invocation of Hymen (*TC*, III, 1258) and his address to Criseyde as 'fresshe wommanliche wif' (*TC*, III, 1296), imaginatively, but of course erroneously, constantly identifies himself with the married state, as Criseyde rarely does. If Troilus had truly married Criseyde he would have saved himself a lot of trouble in one respect, though he might have found more of a different kind. But the poignancy of the story is precisely that it is *not* about marriage: it is about a love which is largely unsupported by social institutions. The evasion of social institutions of a legitimate kind of course involves the employment of a well-known social institution that is illegitimate, the bawd or pimp, a function to which Pandarus has given his name in English. Chaucer makes Pandarus confess or hint three times how shameful a role this is (*TC*, II, 355–7; III, 249; V, 1734). In Mediterranean culture and literature, it is pointed out by Pitt-Rivers, the pander is the prototype of male dishonour (*Honour and Shame*, p. 46). Chaucer here softens the harsh Mediterranean clarity, but there is no reason to think that he thought Pandarus's actions other than shameful. A simple modernistic view of the poem may too easily overlook this point, as it may Troilus's consoling remark to his friend that of course he hasn't done it for money and he is very decent, and to prove it he, Troilus, will readily procure his own sister or any other woman to Pandarus's taste. Troilus may be ultimately excused by the ignorance and enthusiasm of youth, and by the depth and loyalty of his love, but Pandarus has less excuse and the poet as it were deliberately holds them over a moral abyss (*TC*, III, 239–420). Whether he lets them drop in may be disputed.

Though Troilus may behave morally as if married he naturally cannot take part in the full honour-structure of the married man. In this the wife shares honour with her husband, and married couples may be said to constitute honour-groups partially within such other honour-groups as the family, and knights, or ladies (*CT*, III, 961–4). A *good* wife confers honour on her husband (*CT*, IV, 133) so that with this qualification marriage itself confers honour on a man. It is specifically the faithfulness of a wife which is an honour to the husband (*CT*, IV, 2171; cf. v, 1358 ff), but a well-dressed wife is also an honour to her husband (*CT*, VII, 13; *LGW*, 2473), though this of course needs money (*CT*, VII, 408).

The emphasis being on faithfulness, dishonour comes to both husband and wife if *she* commits adultery. An unfaithful wife is described by Hypermnestra as 'a traytour lyvynge in my shame' (*LGW*, 2702). This is, or rather was until very recently, so completely accepted in all advanced Western and Eastern cultures, perhaps universally, that it hardly needs illustrating. However, a number of modern criticisms of *The Franklin's Tale* underestimate this deep and powerful notion. When Dorigen makes her 'complaint' in her dilemma between death and dishonour, giving a long list of those wives who have chosen death rather than commit even forced adultery, the deliberate artificiality of the passage, which allows us to contemplate the situation with detachment, and even a touch of amusement, rather than with inappropriately tragic expectations, is surely not calculated, as some critics think, to satirise or raise a trivial snigger. Chaucer in his serious poetry, however, is not much interested in adultery, notwithstanding the astonishing prevalence of the modern notion that medieval love is always adulterous. Troilus and Criseyde are not in a position to commit adultery, and Chaucer mainly writes about adultery as a joke amongst those who have little or no honour, as part of the effect of some of his comic poems, including the Wife of Bath's *Prologue*, though not her *Tale*. Part also of the comedy of the Wife of Bath's reversal of values is that her cowed fifth husband allows her to keep the marital honour (*CT*, III, 821) and that in her tale the wife is allowed to choose what course of action will be most honour to both her and her husband (*CT*, III, 1232–3). Once given this choice the wife in the tale chooses to be both fair and good, that is, faithful, and to *obey* her husband in everything he wants. Honour is interchanged. In the comic poems proper January of course loses honour when cuckolded, but that is his own fault and serves him right for being a lecherous as well as a silly old man. May is also dishonoured, but she is hardly within the honour-group, being of *smal degree* (*CT*, IV, 1625), not quite a lady. The merchant in *The Shipman's Tale* is only doubtfully a man of honour, since he is not in any way a fighting man, nor associated with men of honour, and his cuckolding is part of other social and moral systems, like the goings-on in *The Miller's Tale* and *The Reeve's Tale*

Adultery within the honour-group therefore hardly arises in Chaucer.

The family as an honour-group may be briefly mentioned here as arising out of marriage. The extended family share their honour, of course, and a man may easily lose honour by the conduct of his unmarried female relatives, even when this is not by their own choice. The outstanding instance is *The Physician's Tale*, where the father kills his daughter to preserve her virginity against tyrannical oppression, thereby preserving her, and consequently his, honour. 'I could not love thee, dear, so much . . .'. That this story derives from Roman antiquity reminds us again that these concepts are ancient and widespread. Yet a certain mechanical quality in Chaucer's telling of this story suggests that his imagination was not fully engaged in so simple and traditional a representation of the concept, however completely he may have accepted it.

More interestingly, Pandarus feels dishonoured by Criseyde's behaviour. He perhaps ought to have felt dishonoured by her lechery with Troilus, and perhaps he would have done it had it been socially known. What actually troubles him is not her unchastity but her falseness, that other aspect of honour (*TC*, v, 1727).

There is a puzzling relationship between honour and responsibility. It seems that in the case of a knight responsibility for another person means that a knight's honour is concerned in the other person's actions. Incidentally we hear only of responsibility for women—daughter or niece or wife. Chaucer is not interested in sons. Responsibility evidently requires authority. Authority, or sovereignty, is clear in Virginius's case, as he is father of Virginia; it is uncertain in Pandarus's relation to Criseyde, and highly questionable in husbands. But it seems that in marriage honour goes with whoever is in charge, so to speak, with sovereignty. Whoever holds the sovereignty overtly holds the honour overtly. This creates the dilemma of Troilus's parodic marriage. Criseyde is of course not married in the eyes of the world, nor indeed (by contrast with Troilus) in her own eyes, so she is responsible for her own honour. But since she has taken a lover the inner truth is different from the outer appearance: she has to share her honour— secretly—with her lover; he therefore has in a sense control over her honour because he may cause her to lose it by publishing the affair; he has some degree of responsibility. In a love-affair the lady has sovereignty and Criseyde at first goes out of her way to emphasise this, while Troilus always in his humility firmly subscribes to her sovereignty. He has thus no sovereignty, but some responsibility. Hence the painful dilemma. He must preserve her honour even at the cost of his own life, but has to leave all decision to her. In a comparable dilemma Arveragus, who is truly married, makes the decision himself. Since Troilus is not married the overt social situation, leaving Criseyde independent, being at variance with the true inner personal situation of intimate relationship, forces the lovers apart. Society and the individual are at odds, and honour is the knife which separates Troilus and Criseyde.

We come at last to the honour of ladies, which is much the most interesting in Chaucer. He is notably more orientated towards feminine interests (and indeed superiority) than any other author until Richardson. Honour for ladies resides primarily in their chastity, the biologically determined defensive or recessive virtue that characterises, or used to characterise, women, to complement the biologically natural aggressive virtue of men. One may here briefly mention what often seems to modern notions unjust, that men may commit adultery, or be sexually promiscuous, without losing honour, while women may not. The reason lies simply with the traditionally accepted truth that men and women are different, and that therefore their honour and identity and virtue have a different base. This also explains the apparent paradox that honourable men may try to seduce honourable women, yet despise them when they succeed. In the process women—not men—lose honour, and so drop out of the honour-group, though they may retain or even increase their attractiveness. Conversely, a woman was not dishonoured by being a coward. The classic comic treatment of the difference in that respect is the 'duel' between Viola and Sir Andrew Aguecheek in *Twelfth Night*. Both are arrant cowards, but Viola only gains in femininity and lovableness with our recognition of her charming cowardice, while we despise, however genially, Sir Andrew. (That Shakespeare also accepted the ideals of other traditional distinctions in honour, including chastity for women, is amply clear, for example in Posthumus Leonatus's praise of Imogen for often rejecting his advances even when they were married.) The Church has always partially accepted and partially rejected these very ancient traditional notions.

The reason why the Virgin *is* honour is that she is the supreme exemplar of feminine chastity. For more ordinary ladies their honour is chiefly interesting for its relation to their love of a man. The constant note for Chaucer's heroines from Blanche the Duchess onwards is that they love entirely, always 'saving their honour'. Of Blanche, the Black Knight tells us that she gave him her *mercy*, when she understood his woe and when she understood

> That I ne wilned thyng but god,
> And worship, and to kepe hir name
> Over alle thyng, and drede hir shame.
> (*The Book of the Duchess*, 1262–4)

It is Blanche's virtue that no one might do her shame because she loved so well her own name (ll. 1017–18), that is, her honour, her very identity, founded upon her chastity (cf. *LGW, Pro.* G, 300; 1812; 2586). The close relationship between being truly known to others and being self-sufficient in one's own integrity is well illustrated here. Chastity, after all, may well concern more than one person, yet is an individualising concept. The honour-system builds sexuality much more significantly into the role of the integrated female personality than into the male, with good biological reason, it may be thought, though all this is strange to modern literary culture.

Sex and love are differentiated for ladies as for knights, but in a different way. Men's sexuality is accepted; it may become love, with its self-sacrifice, ultimately even sacrificing sexuality and life itself, as in the case of Troilus. But there is never any suggestion that Troilus's or any other young knight's love is not sexual and aiming at sexual possession. For ladies, on the contrary, sexuality at most comes after love, if it comes at all. It comes even for Criseyde *after* love, though perhaps somewhat precipitately. The Wife of Bath is not a lady, and, for her, sex is what she chiefly means by love; which is why she is something of a comic man-eating monster, and why the joke of her tale is partly on her.

The Wife of Bath's obsession with sex is nowhere better illustrated than in the tiny detail where she quotes the Apostle's injunction to women to dress modestly:

> 'In habit maad with chastitee and shame
> Ye wommen shul apparaille yow', quod he
>   (*CT*, iii, 342–3)

according to her. It is a *misquotation*. The text (1 Timothy 2:9), in all the versions I have seen, reads not *chastity* but *sobriety*. The minute dramatic artistry of Chaucer is here most remarkable and shows the Wife of Bath as bad a case of sex in the head as D. H. Lawrence himself. However, the general association between female clothing, chastity and honour is well illustrated by the coarse popular proverb, which the Wife also quotes, that a woman puts off her shame with her smock (*CT*, iii, 782–3). Here, by a common inversion remarked earlier, *shame*, the antonym of *honour*, takes over part of the meaning of honour itself. In Chaucer, as often traditionally, sexuality is always shameful for women, even in marriage, and though wives are holy things they have to put up with it, as he says in *The Man of Law's Tale* (*CT*, ii, 708–14). Following the same line of thought, January, a good conservative, judges that he must offend May on their marriage night with his 'corage . . . sharp and keene' (*CT*, iv, 1756–9).

Ladies naturally do not exactly acquire honour any more than they acquire virginity (whereas a knight has to earn his), but they may increase in honour by going up the social scale as Griselda does, and by marrying and being faithful to their husbands. They can lose honour no doubt through poverty or old age or envy, like a man, but the interesting way to lose it is by being known to have a lover, if unmarried, or if married by committing adultery, which is represented as treachery, the height of medieval vice which absorbs other delinquencies into it. 'Falseness' is both sin and shame.

Death should be preferable to dishonour for both knight and lady but as it was a normal occupational hazard for knights it seems more significant, perhaps because usually more volitional, for ladies, as *The Physician's Tale* shows in the death of Virginia, and as Dorigen represents in her long list of examples of the death of virtuous wronged ladies. Troilus says he himself would rather die than cause *disclaundre* to Criseyde's name, though Criseyde herself does not express such heroic sentiment.

The consideration of Criseyde's honour weighs more heavily with both Troilus and Criseyde than anything else, even their love, as Book IV frequently shows. Ladies have a very high degree of responsibility for their own honour, even when married, and for a widow in Criseyde's position, and with her temperament, it may well be—ironically—her chief concern. Criseyde looks after her own honour very assiduously (e.g. *TC*, II, 468; III, 944). She is always talking about it, and it is far more crucial to the story and the poem than is often realised. A word-count illustrates this in a crude but effective fashion. There are 47 occurrences of the word *honour* in *Troilus and Criseyde*. No less than 26 occur in connection with Criseyde, and seven of these are references by herself to her own honour. By contrast only nine occurrences of the word refer to Troilus, and not one of these is a reference made by himself. The remaining 12 occurrences are a miscellaneous scatter, four of them in reference to the gods. Of eight references by a person to 'my honour' seven are those by Criseyde as already mentioned, and the eighth by whom but Pandarus. In whichever way one analyses the totality of references in the poem to honour, Criseyde dominates them. It is after all in some respects a poem about her honour, or rather, her dishonour.

Since honour must be shared, and a lady's honour is sexual, she shares her honour with the man with whom she has sexual intercourse. In the case of marriage this is socially recognised and the source of increased honour to them both. If the lady is not married the sharing is secret and therefore more complex. She is in her lover's power, since if he boasts of his conquest she loses her honour, as Criseyde tells Troilus (*TC*, III, 165; cf. V,

1077). Criseyde anxiously and absurdly talks of her own *honeste* which elsewhere means chastity (as in *LGW*, 1673), when the context shows that she really has in mind, as usual, what people will think of her. How foully my *honeste* will be spotted, she says, if I go away with you. I should never regain my *name*—and *name* clearly here means honour and the reputation for chastity (as in *LGW, Pro.* G, 301; 1812; 2587). Criseyde argues that if she eloped with Troilus, as his mistress—and no alternative status is ever envisaged by either—she would lose her honour, that is, her place in society, her very identity. She is a very conventional young woman, and she is quite right. Would they pass their lives in some Black Sea holiday resort? Benjamin Constant's *Adolphe* and Tolstoy's *Anna Karenina* are both parables, set in societies whose values differed astonishingly little from those of fourteenth-century England in this respect, of what happens to lovers who are unsupported by the institutions of society and where the man's—like Othello's—occupation's gone. Criseyde has no need to doubt Troilus's entire devotion to her, but that is not the only point for her. Because she has always found him true she says that she will always behave 'That ay honour to me-ward shal rebounde' (*TC*, IV, 1666). She seems self-regarding, but in a sense she has to be. She needs social support and a social contract. Pandarus has betrayed her, and even Troilus's devotion is based on a relationship which if known would dishonour her though not him. It is true that later she regrets not eloping with Troilus (*TC*, V, 739–40) and remarks that one should not pay attention to what people say, but she is already by this time on the downward path, and anyway under no risk of having to do anything. When she is told she must leave Troy the poor girl is in a cleft stick and honour is the source of the profound irony of her fate as a literary figure. She who is more interested in her own honour than any other character in Chaucer, or in English literature except Richardson's heroines, is represented in the poem as *the* person in history who has lost her honour. She has put external social worldly reputation before the internal value of *trouthe* to Troilus and has ironically lost the external reputation just because she preferred it. To prefer appearance to reality is to lose both. But the reason that she is in a cleft stick is more complex still, because she has become confused about the nature of honour. She has applied, in a sense, the wrong sort of honour to herself. She has constantly retained the view that her honour consists in her chastity, as an unmarried woman. But her relationship with Troilus has changed her status in practice if not overtly and socially. She is judged in the poem *as if she were married*, though she is never represented during the poem as being quite as devoted to Troilus as he to her. Still, she has twice made vows of unending fidelity to Troilus (*TC*, III, 1492 ff; IV, 1534 ff), and she is judged according to her own expressed intention. A married woman's honour is judged by her loyalty to her husband, and Criseyde, who is not married, is yet judged not for her lack of chastity, but for her falseness, her lack of *trouthe*.

> She seyde, 'Allas for now is clene ago
> My name of trouthe in love, for everemo!
> (*TC*, v, 1054–5)

One might say that if she goes away with Troilus she is dishonoured in the eyes of society for her unchastity; and if she abandons Troilus she is dishonoured in the eyes of the poet and his readers for her lack of *trouthe*. The poem curiously and in a way inconsistently bridges two worlds here, Criseyde's public world, and her private one. Within the public world of the poem Criseyde's loss of honour could only occur in relation to her seduction by Diomede, as a loss of chastity which—her dead husband apart—she had already secretly lost to Troilus. But poet and readers may think they perceive the inner value, the personal loyalty, *trouthe*, based on, but transcending, physical relationship, which Criseyde has broken.

As we hear in *The Franklin's Tale*, 'Trouthe is the hyeste thyng that man may kepe' (*CT*, v, 1479), or woman either, we must add. *The Franklin's Tale* is explicitly about *trouthe*'s superiority to honour. The poem is of course artificial in the same way that a folk-tale or a parable is artificial: it is not an illusionist transcript of ordinary life but a narrated series of events and characters put together to make a specific point about life, often the more penetrating because of the primary limitations in literary convention. Once these have been accepted, however, as any ordinarily experienced reader, who does not have to make a living by publishing critical essays, normally does accept them, the poem has plenty of witty observation of ordinary life, and a strong sense of reality.

At the beginning Arveragus in his happy marriage keeps the appearance of sovereignty in marriage because of his honour as a knight—'for shame of his degree' (*CT*, v, 752) as we are told by the poet (and here as so often in *The Canterbury Tales* we are justified in disregarding in such details the 'dramatic narrator', in this case the Franklin, whose function has for the moment ceased). Arveragus like a proper knight values his honour and in order to acquire more (*CT*, v, 811–12) goes abroad. As with the false knight in *The Squire's Tale*, but without reference to falseness,

> resoun wolde eek that he moste go
> For his honour, as ofte it happeth so.
> (*CT*, v, 591–2)

Dorigen then, pestered by the squire Aurelius, to soften her absolute refusal of love with a sophisticated joke which she rightly later regrets, says she will give herself to Aurelius if he removes the rocks on the coast which threaten her beloved husband's safe return. Once this is apparently done she is trapped, having promised dishonour for honourable reasons; promised treachery out of faith. There are many rich implications here which must be left aside. In the matter of honour, when Arveragus returns safely and the squire's bargain is apparently fulfilled, the first point to note is that Dorigen at last gives to her husband the reality, not just the appearance, of sovereignty when she asks him what to do about Aurelius. Honour rightly undertakes responsibility and receives sovereignty in marriage. When Arveragus decides, with grief, that Dorigen ought to keep her promise, her *trouthe* to Aurelius, he is thus ironically and paradoxically forced to resign that honour, so important to him, which he now truly possesses, and which resides in his wife's faithfulness to him, just now so touchingly demonstrated, in order that she, on behalf of both of them, shall keep her paradoxical *trouthe*, her promise to commit adultery with Aurelius. She has to accept her own dishonour because it would be dishonourable not to: it is a shame to a woman to trick a man, it is said (admittedly by Pandarus, *TC*, III, 777). *Trouthe* is loyalty, and in the cluster of notions that compose the sentiment of honour, the keeping of *trouthe* must be isolated as so much the superior inner moral value as to be, as on this occasion, positively hostile to social relationship and reputation. It was this complexity that poor Criseyde failed to observe. But the exquisite delicacy of the sacrifice cannot be appreciated if we forget or deny the other elements of honour, bravery and chastity, the shame of cuckoldry and of panderism (for does not Arveragus *send* his wife to Aurelius?), the shame of sex for women, the pain of loss of social reputation. Indeed Arveragus shows no exaggerated heroism, for he hopes that the whole business can be kept as quiet as possible, though the true inner situation is what appals him, not the appearance only (*CT*, V, 1481–6). The interest lies in the way that the ironic paradox of dishonour rooted in honour is poetically incarnate in a living culture. Honour as social virtue, and honour as chastity or possession, are subordinated to honour as obedience to a high moral ideal, perforce an inner, indeed, a spiritual value. The story of course is given a happy ending. In Chaucer's fundamentally optimistic Christian culture goodness brings forth goodness. The story shows how sacrifice creates happiness. Sexual jealousy and possessiveness, personal domination, narrow legalism, are all rejected in favour of openness, truth, loyalty, trust, toleration and love.

Of course we must accept the primary conventions. In actual life, we might ask that the long-term promise given by Dorigen to her husband when she married him take precedence over the short-term and obviously joking promise made to Aurelius. But that would be to judge the poem by the totally inappropriate premises of the realistic novel, which are never even accidentally invoked by Chaucer, for all his realism.

This spiritualisation of honour was not a late development in Chaucer. It was inherent in the complex religious and secular tradition of many centuries, though Chaucer creates his own individual and characteristic forms. He had earlier, in *The House of Fame*, taken to himself as poet the internalised stability and confidence that his greatest heroine so clearly lacks, showing in his own self something of that carelessness of honour as reputation that his heroes possess, or perhaps indicating that he himself, for all his interest, is really outside the honour-system, being no knight, no fighting-man. If so, it may be one reason for his modernity, for the honour-system in England, never so strong as on the Continent, has surely now collapsed. Yet modernity cannot be too easily claimed, for the Church had in certain respects for many centuries denied the value of honour. Lydgate the monk has a dreary little poem (founded, as Skeat noted, on an earlier Latin line) which says that four things make a man a fool: age, women, wine—and honour.[7] Yet even Lydgate may well be more modern than he looks.

In that strange poem *The House of Fame*, the poet (and I call him the poet, not that man of straw, the so-called Narrator of many modern critics) is asked, Don't you care what people think of you? He replies:

> Sufficeth me, as I were ded,
> That no wight have my name in honde.
>
> (*HF*, 1876–7)

It rings very true; and when we consider that his name is more than ever in hand, nearly six centuries after his death, it constitutes the most delightful of Chaucerian paradoxes.

10   Gothic Chaucer*

Lo here the forme of olde clerkis speche
In poetrie, if ye hire bokes seche.

What is the general nature of Chaucer's works and its relation to his times?
The Canterbury pilgrims know what *they* want: entertaining stories giving
sentence (or *doctrine*) and *solaas* (or *mirth*). For them, story-telling is an
agreeable *game*, or it conveys serious information—not both at the same
time. The Knight and Harry Bailly the innkeeper, good representative men,
express these common-sense ideas (*CT*, I, 788–801). Like many such ideas,
on examination they appear less clear. The first testing comes in *The
Miller's Prologue*. All pilgrims, but especially, says Chaucer, the *gentils*,
think *The Knight's Tale* 'noble'. Then the Miller also proposes to tell what
he too describes as a 'noble' tale. It will be, he says, 'a legende and a lyf',
that is, a saint's life—probably the most generally popular fourteenth-
century genre—but his 'legend' will be of a carpenter and his wife.
Everyone assumes that the Miller's tale will be a 'lewed dronken harlotrye',
so we can expect parody, at least, and the literal-minded Reeve expects
slander. Despite the protests, we may assume that as a tale it is *solaas*. Yet
most of the audience oppose it and we can assume no such organic
relationship between *sentence* and *solaas* as that suggested by the Horatian
dulce et utile, or by the Neoclassical 'instruction by delighting', which has
been familiar since the Renaissance and is often urged, if in perverse ways,
even in the twentieth century. Chaucer himself emphasises that the tale the
Miller will tell has nothing to do with *gentilesse*, *moralitee* or *hoolynesse*: a
cherles tale, told by a *cherl*, of *harlotrie*, as the Reeve's tale also will be. A
blunt warning. We shall need a subtle argument for the improving effect of
the study of literature if we accept the poet's own clear description and

* First published in *Writers and their Backgrounds: Geoffrey Chaucer*, ed. Derek
Brewer (London, 1974) pp. 1–32.

interpretation of it. The subject-matter is immoral; and it is not hypocritically offered as a cautionary tale. We may well disapprove. The poet, however, turns the tables on us if we disapprove. He writes (and we may notice the inconsistent abandonment of the illusion of oral delivery): 'Turne over·the leef and chese another tale' (*CT*, I, 3177)—which receives an echo in modern controversies over the presentation of obscene television shows—you can always switch off. Such an argument can of course also be used in defence of public hanging, drawing and quartering (no one *has* to look). This fourteenth-century poet, like a modern artist, adopts a morally neutral stance in judgment of his subject-matter: again, like the modern artist, his only obligation, he says, is to the way things are; as he puts it, he feels he must not 'falsen' his 'mateere'.

There are some differences from modern times. Chaucer is joking, and is satirising his audience. His matter is a story, not 'reality'. You know, he implies, that you want to hear this dirty story, and don't in the least care about *sentence* in this case, even if you did think *The Knight's Tale* 'noble'. He will satisfy us, but take no responsibility. Nevertheless, at this point he remains within the fictional plane. That is, we do not for a moment believe that he is really reporting the actual courtly words in rhyme of a real peasant Miller on a specific pilgrimage; it would obviously be impossible, indeed ridiculous, and is therefore amusing. We may similarly expect, for the same literary reason, not actually to be told of real immorality in the tale. On the other hand, Chaucer truly is disclaiming responsibility for telling immoral tales. He is denying the instructions of the dominant, or 'official' culture, essentially ecclesiastical in literary matters, which (quoting St Paul, Romans 15:4) required that all that is written should be written for our doctrine; should be morally improving. He also amused himself over that same requirement at the end of *The Nun's Priest's Tale*, though the free play of mind in that poem has not always been observed by critics intent on making too earnest of his game.

Chaucer ultimately repented his revolt against the official culture, as we know from the 'Retracciouns' at the end of *The Canterbury Tales* (not present in all the manuscripts), in which he repudiated not only the obviously immoral tales like *The Miller's Tale*, but *all* his secular writing. Moreover, the 'Retracciouns' deny the possibility of purely self-enclosed fiction. They assert that literature has an effect on us. In them the poet breaks out of the mainly self-enclosed fictional frame of *The Canterbury Tales* to address us directly, a real man speaking to men, no narrative pose or irony, no jokes, but in real sincere earnest. This major inconsistency in *The Canterbury Tales* has been somewhat neglected, but it is only one of many inconsistencies, of different kinds, in Chaucer's works.

The range of inconsistencies and internal incompatibilities within *The Canterbury Tales* is formidable and deserves recognition for what it is, which is a historical and cultural general *style*. Much criticism has been devoted to arguing round or through such difficulties in a local way, or in condemning them as artistic flaws, but we might do better to follow our intuitions: that is, to accept the dislocations first as natural enough, then to see that they imply important differences from what we usually expect in art and culture which are worth our while to recognise. The recognition of difference will increase our enjoyment and understanding. We shall see what it is to be a Gothic poet, rather than a Neoclassical or Romantic or modern poet. We shall become more conscious of Chaucer's immense, though not unlimited, variety, and of the problem of unity, or at least, of whatever is the opposite of disintegration, in his work. We shall learn to meet in Chaucer's work a frequent ambivalence at all levels, and to find an art that ebbs and flows into life like the tide on an indented coast, with no clear demarcations.

In the subject-matter of *The Canterbury Tales sentence* and *solaas* may be distinct and incompatible. *The Miller's Tale* has plenty of *solaas*, but no *sentence* even in mockery. The very notion of *sentence* may be mocked, as it is explicitly in *The Nun's Priest's Tale*. *The Parson's Tale* has only *sentence* and the Parson quotes St Paul to deny the value of all fiction (*CT*, x, 33–4). He himself aims at truth, though what he calls his 'meditation' (it is not the sermon it is often called) turns out after all to be typical old-fashioned layman's moralising. The Parson disdains *solaas* and *mirth*. Such *sentence* opposes *solaas*, as Chaucer's 'Retracciouns', already referred to, condemn all his secular works. Apparently incompatible subject-matter is contained within *The Canterbury Tales*.

There are also many inconsistencies of form in Chaucer's works. The 'Retracciouns', apart from its subject-matter, is a glaring example of the author breaking the fictional frame and speaking to us directly and sincerely. It is not surprising that many scribes omitted it. More scrupulous modern editors and readers cannot so easily disregard it, because Chaucer clearly makes it run straight on from *The Parson's Tale*, and because it is fully consonant with the Parson's remarks in his Prologue. We find similar breaking of the fictional frame in one way or another elsewhere: for example in *The Prologue to The Man of Law's Tale*, where there are references to the real-life Chaucer himself; the ending of *The Clerk's Tale* in the so-called 'Lenvoy de Chaucer', whose fictional status, and compatibility with the tale it follows, are very dubious; and in *The Merchant's Tale*, where a character inside the tale refers to the Wife of Bath who exists outside the tale on a different fictional level altogether (*CT*, iv, 1685). When to these examples are added addresses to both the real and fictional audiences; comments by the poet himself and meant literally about his own narrative art; and such self-description by the ostensible narrator as being himself a dull man in the middle of *The Squire's Tale*, supposedly told by a very sprightly young man (*CT*, v, 278–90); then we have a formidable list of inconsistencies and discontinuities of various kinds. Yet there are more; for example there are major inconsistencies in the presentations of character, as in the learned references made by the unlearned Harry Bailly and the Wife of Bath, or in the extraordinary changes in the Pardoner's attitudes at the end of his tale. There are also varying inconsistencies between the pilgrims and the tales they tell. There are further inconsistencies of narrative level and point of view within the tale; and local inconsistencies of tone. The varieties of tone themselves may constitute an inconsistency best described as indecorum; yet they are quite deliberate, like the jumble of religious references with gross improprieties.

To sum up, it is as if we have to do with a picture that does not obey our laws of perspective, though our natural enjoyment leads us to reject the notion of the poet's mere clumsiness, and suggests that other, unfamiliar, shaping principles may be at work. The analogy between Chaucer's works in this respect and the quality of the Gothic visual arts contemporary with him, with their disregard for perspective and their discontinuities of naturalistic representation, is close and fruitful. It has been argued by several critics. We are justified in adopting the term 'Gothic' to denote by analogy the literature contemporary with Gothic art.[1] Chaucer is therefore part of 'English Gothic Literature'.

Chaucer was aware of the problem of inconsistency. In *Troilus and Criseyde* he quotes Geoffrey of Vinsauf's recommendation of the need for overall planning of a work (*TC*, I, 1065–71), though with reference to conducting love-intrigues, not poems. Again, Pandarus advises Troilus not to mingle in a letter: 'Ne jompre ek no discordant thyng yfeere' (*TC*, II, 1037). There was a well-known medieval doctrine of decorum of style to subject-matter. But this limited stylistic decorum does not govern subject-matter, nor changes of style and subject-matter within a work. Inconsistencies and discontinuities are unquestionably present in Chaucer's work.[2] In any case Chaucer would not be the only poet who practised something different from what he preached, even if Pandarus's instructions to Troilus on writing love-letters were to represent Chaucer's general views on art.

Our problems with form are matched by our puzzles over Chaucer's status as a poet. He is both irresponsible and responsible as an artist, and in neither way quite fits a modern reader's prepossessions. His disclaimer of responsibility for retailing improper fictions has already been quoted. On many other occasions, even where no question of impropriety is involved, he is apparently anxious to shift responsibility to his 'auctor', his 'authority'; for example,

> Wherfore I nyl have neither thank ne blame
> Of al this werk . . .
> For as myn auctour seyde, so sey I.
>   (*TC*, ii, 15–18)

But Chaucer is artistically even more irresponsible, because he has apparently no concept of the inviolability of artistic form, of the impossibility or indeed the heresy of paraphrase, of the enormous importance of the *mot juste*. He does not, as Sidney and Neoclassical and Romantic critics do, proclaim the sheer *importance* of literature, its supremacy over all other forms of human discourse and activity, and consequently the supreme calling of the poet as artist. At a high point in *Troilus and Criseyde* when the lovers are at last brought to the point of consummation, not only does he indulge in a touch of indecorous levity, but he actually invites the reader or hearer to increase or diminish his language according to preference and personal experience (*TC*, iii, 1335–6).

This is a licence that we modern critics, in so far as it concerns his *meaning*, have not hesitated to take up, but on the part of the poet it implies a wonderfully fluid, easy-going attitude to artistic integrity. At the end of the same poem Chaucer invites Gower and Strode to correct it where need is. Like his Manciple and Parson he seems not to claim to be 'textueel' (*CT*, ix, 235; x, 57; cf. vii, 959–61). Words are slippery things. On the other hand, even because of their slipperiness, in actual practice he is most anxious—no problem of sincerity here!—that scribes should get his words exactly right (*Chaucer's Wordes unto Adam, His Owne Scriveyn*; *TC*, v, 1795; *CT*, i, 2062–3; more amusingly:

> What was comaunded unto Lamuel—
> Nat Samuel, but Lamuel, seye I.
>   (*CT*, vi, 584–5)

even with this, one scribe muddled the second Lamuel). But that anxiety is the great craftsman's concern, not a literary concept of the perfect unparaphrasibility of poetry and the high status of poets. He is entirely casual about his own reputation or posthumous fame (*HF*, 1876–7). He constantly adopts a deferential attitude towards his audience. He is an entertainer; almost, we may think, the last of those minstrels who did not turn to musical instruments. He mocks his own achievement through his Man of Law, who knows no stories but those

> That Chaucer thogh he kan but lewedly
> On metres and on ryming craftily,
> Hath seyd hem in swich Englissh as he kan.
>
> (*CT*, ii, 47–9)

It is as if he regards them as not well done, but is surprised to find them done at all. He worked hard when he was young, he writes, but as an old man he reflects, with a sincerity hard to doubt, that 'al shal passe that men prose or ryme' (*Scogan*, 41). Chaucer has in the end no more care for literature than had Shakespeare.

Quite different ideas were available to him. Contrast with Chaucer's Gothic disengagement towards literature the views of Petrarch expressed in Italy about the time of Chaucer's birth. Petrarch had an exalted, almost Neoclassical, view of the poet's superiority, of which a concise statement is available in the oration he delivered when crowned Laureate at Rome on 8 April 1341. Petrarch writes, in part:

> poets under the veil of fictions have set forth truths, physical, moral and historical—thus bearing out a statement I often make, that the difference between a poet on the one hand and a historian or a moral or physical philosopher on the other is the same as the difference between a clouded sky and a clear sky, since in each case the same light exists in the object of vision, but is perceived in different degrees according to the capacity of the observers. Poetry, furthermore, is all the sweeter since a truth that must be sought out with some care gives all the more delight when it is discovered. Let this suffice as a statement not so much about myself as about the poetic profession. For while poets are wont to find pleasure in a certain playfulness, I should not wish to appear to be a poet and nothing more. . . .
>
> The poet's reward is beyond question multiple, for it consists, firstly, in the charm of personal glory, of which enough has been said already, and secondly, in the immortality of one's name.[3]

The similarity of these views to those of Sidney, who, in his *An Apology for Poetry* (1595) creamed off the works of European scholars of literature in the sixteenth century, is obvious. But they also represent a medieval tradition, expressed for example by Alanus de Insulis[4] in the twelfth century and by many commentators on Virgil. It is natural for men with powerful minds who devote themselves to literature, whether creatively or (especially) critically, to exalt its importance. It certainly happens today. And they are not entirely wrong. But how different from Chaucer.

The kind of responsibility Chaucer feels towards literature complements his irresponsibility. When taking a responsible view he cites the Pauline view already referred to in his 'Retracciouns', 'Al that is writen is writen for oure doctrine', and appears to understand it to mean that 'anything that is written ought to be written in order to improve us'. He comes down to the narrowest interpretation of *doctrine*; in his own work, as he mentions, to the translation of Boethius, legends of saints, homilies, morality, devotion. All other writings are 'enditynges of worldly vanitees' and to be recalled. They are worthless; it was irresponsible to produce them; serious literary responsibility condemns fictions, even if they are products of high literary art.

We are therefore in a curious position with regard to Chaucer's works. Our own responses, and six centuries of mature readers, including all our greatest poets but Tennyson, encourage us to believe that here is great poetry, and that great poetry is of high human value. Yet the poet himself did not share his view and the poems seem by our usual standards of form to be as fragmented as a shattered mirror, which the poet cannot be bothered to pick up. This must be wrong. We had better shatter and reconstitute our own ideas.

In fact this has already been done for us in modern literature and art. The drama nowadays has broken away from its self-contained Neoclassical unity that lasted from the seventeenth century till as late as the 1920s and has spilt over the proscenium arch to involve the real audience in its fictions. Illusion and reality are no longer clearly divided. A variety of dramatic forms abandons the fixity of a rigid printed text. Again, poetry has become oral to enthusiastic audiences and also frequently abandons fixed forms of metre, syntax, logic, meaning itself. Chaucer's inconsistencies and discontinuities are not remarkable by comparison with those of many modern poets. The novel now frequently abandons its original eighteenth-century concern with realistic representation of the natural social world.

Music offers us another useful analogy. The harmonic scales that underlie both 'Classical' and 'Romantic' music, with their strong emotional and imaginative associations, were developed first about the sixteenth century in Europe and came to dominate high musical culture. Medieval music was modal, whether the Gregorian chant, courtly song or folk-song. Under the triumph of the harmonic scale (and who would wish it away?) from among traditional forms only folk-song survived, largely unrecognised by high art until towards the end of the nineteenth century. The twentieth century has seen a revolution in music from Stravinsky onwards which has quite altered our understanding of earlier music. Folksong has been recovered especially by the ballad scholars, and our ears are open again to the still strange, but now marvellously attractive cadences of medieval musicians once entirely forgotten or derided. The principles of unity and fixity of note, of tonal compatibilities, of dominance and subordination, of associations of feeling, in this music are quite different from what Europeans and North Americans learnt from the seventeenth century onwards. Having been emancipated by modern music we can now hear and enjoy medieval music in its own right, fortunately without having to abandon the subsequent great classics.

It need hardly be added that the visual arts in our time have seen a similar destruction of once-accepted absolute standards. Since the fifteenth century in painting Europeans became accustomed to the framed picture constituting its own self-enclosed world, dominated by a single visual point of view, giving a regular perspective of receding depth and consonant proportion, aiming with homogeneous materials to present an idealised naturalistic image. At the end of the nineteenth century began a process explosively developed in the twentieth century that destroyed the frame, scattered the single point of view and perspective, portrayed what could never be naturally seen by one pair of eyes at one moment, used miscellaneous materials, denied representationalism its supreme value, and exalted the casual and accidental, the crude, rough, the non-ideal. Once again it was possible to turn back to medieval art, in this case especially to manuscript illumination, and see it afresh in something like its own terms. The art of the thirteenth to the fifteenth centuries, the Gothic period, has attracted interest in its mixture of realistic and non-realistic forms, of partially disregarded frames and varied levels of representation, of multiple points of view, its indecorous mixture of serious and comic, religious and grotesque. Such a work as the famous Beatus Page of the St Omer Psalter in the British Museum (Add. MS 39810, fol. 7) with its almost incredibly rich mixture of various elements offers a real analogy to such a work as *The Canterbury Tales*, and can, by being compared with later types of picture following different conventions, really clarify the nature of Chaucer's work, and of our response. It is by such analogies that we are justified in referring to English Gothic literature, and to Gothic Chaucer.

The history of criticism reinforces our sense of radical changes in forms of artistic culture which first changed away from the medieval and then, in the twentieth century, if not turned towards the medieval, nevertheless moved as it were in a parallel direction.[5] The great changes in English

literature are in the seventeenth and twentieth centuries, but the first period
of change was heralded by a New Criticism, the Neoclassical, whose first
theoretical spokesman in England was Sir Philip Sidney in his *An Apology
for Poetry*. Here is the insistence on decorum, on an idealised nature, on
simplicity of genre (e.g. not to mix comedy and tragedy), on a single
dominant point of view, with exaltation of the status of the poet, already
foreshadowed by Alanus, and emphasised by Petrarch. Poetry becomes
fully the instrument, in some ways the highest expression, of the official
culture, conveying the official moral system, the official philosophy. What
was once only the possession of Latin has now become the attribute of the
fully-fledged vernacular. The formal Neoclassical ideal was stretched, not
broken, by Romanticism and it remained dominant until the middle of the
twentieth century. Nor is it, we may hope, utterly defeated: yet its
weakening allows us to see medieval literature more in its own terms, as
they now appear more nearly parallel with ours.

We live today in a time of the breaking of forms, and social institutions
experience a turmoil which also offers some parallels, if remote ones, with
the situation in the fourteenth century in England. It seems likely that
universities, for example, those characteristically medieval inventions, are
today becoming more like their medieval counterparts. They had taken on a
new shape, at least in England, in the sixteenth century, and were designed
as educational institutions for an elite, quite as much as institutions for
research and the advancement of learning. Few readers of this book will
need to be reminded that nowadays the forms and functions of universities
are rapidly changing away from such hierarchical patterns and that in the
late 1960s and 1970s they rather more resemble the disorderly congeries of
the fourteenth century. In each case central authority is weak, though in
different ways. In the fourteenth century it was the means of control in a
technologically primitive society with a high level of illiteracy which caused
weakness, though authority made absolute claims. Nowadays authority is
weak for other reasons. The parallel of the medieval situation with *The
Canterbury Tales*, in terms of authoritative *doctrine* and rebellious or
unconforming *solaas*, is clear. One aspect of this is the development of
individualism. By the end of the fourteenth century the historical
development of the sense of the individual as someone potentially apart
from and even hostile to the social frame had proceeded a very long way.[6]

Different choices between varieties of life in the world and in religion
were becoming open to many men. Even within each way of life either
conformity and social cohesion or independence and alienation were
possible. When at the same time traditional social constrictions and the
claims of older authority were immense, the resulting tensions issued in

open rebellion, like the Peasants' Revolt of 1381, or in deeply dissident religious movements like Lollardy (associated by many at the time with the Peasants' Revolt). I am not arguing for a strong similarity between the changing social structures of today and the fourteenth century, only for a distant analogy which allows us some degree of sympathetic insight into those earlier social and artistic forms. It is now a commonplace that late twentieth-century advanced Western national societies, and certainly that of England, are pluralist in culture; fourteenth-century English society may be described as unintentionally or reluctantly pluralist. There is enough similarity, for all the obvious differences between the modern and the ancient period, to enable us, in our day, to respond with particular sympathy to the extraordinary variety, and to the tensions, which seem to be reflected in the art of the fourteenth century, and specifically in Chaucer's work.[7]

Chaucer's genius is more versatile than that of any other major English writer. Although much of this versatility must be due to personal causes, it could not have flourished as it did except in a culture which favoured pluralism. The fourteenth century was peculiarly favourable to variety and miscellaneity, to sustaining simultaneously incompatible or conflicting cultural elements. Of course all human culture does this: no culture, no person, is a completely harmonious self-consistent whole. But some periods seem notably more tense than others, just as the Gothic style, more than most styles, accepts conflicting elements. To be able to speak of a certain style, even of a culture, implies some containment of fissiparous elements, a kind of unity such as certainly existed in the fourteenth century in England, and in the Gothic style. But within the containment may be differing degrees of inconsistency, and consequent variety or multiplicity, and a versatile genius has consequently much scope. The fourteenth century offered Chaucer this scope, particularly in his specially favoured environment around Westminster and London. Even Gower makes use of it. Westminster was becoming the permanent centre of the king's court, and was also important in religion. London was only two miles away and was the centre of the nation's commercial life, and of legal, perhaps liberal, learning at the Inns of Court. Within this small area between city and court were gathered remarkably varied possibilities, and the experience of severe strains.

If, in the light of modern experience and a contemplation of fourteenth-century culture, we therefore abandon the attempt to discover a relatively simple, unified, non-Gothic, dominant pattern in the literary culture represented by Chaucer's works and their social circumstances, we can allow ourselves to distinguish several competing centres of power. I have already referred to one of these, the dominant ecclesiastical official culture, represented most effectively for our interests by *The Parson's Tale* and the 'Retracciouns', but found elsewhere in many places in Chaucer's work. Another centre of power was the courtly vernacular. The courtly element was itself also partly an official culture, but was secular not ecclesiastical, orientated towards this-worldly personal human relationships, activities and enjoyments. These two official cultures were in close but uneasy relationship. They were allied in many respects. For example, they shared a hierarchical view of society, and the court and the kingdom were largely administered by clerics. But they were hostile in other respects, for example in some (not all) of the notions about love and sexuality, or the value placed on personal armed combat. Moreover, Lollardy, in origin as much courtly as anything else, and certainly lay rather than ecclesiastical, as the Lollard knights witness, shows how the lay courtly culture could attack the ecclesiastical on its own moral grounds as well, probably, as on grounds of financial greed.[8]

Both ecclesiastical and courtly official cultures were complex in themselves as well as being both allies and rivals. The official ecclesiastical culture comprised, but did not exactly control, the purely intellectual culture represented by philosophy and science, and it developed with intellectual discovery. Moreover, the central Christian teaching has always been based on paradox and irony, of divinity that is human, of power that is not ordinary power, of losing one's life to gain it, of life that is death and death life. The Synoptic Gospels are perhaps the most variously paradoxical and ironic documents in the world's writings. Christianity itself began with that status of an unofficial culture to which in the latter part of the twentieth century it seems rapidly to be returning, and even when the medieval Church's version of Christianity was dominant it necessarily contained within itself the ironic seeds of self-criticism and change, even of destruction and renewal. For the moment, however, our consideration must be limited to the more dominating aspects of the official ecclesiastical culture as represented in Chaucer.

All rationalisations, literal interpretations and institutional embodiments of the Gospels tend to rigidify their fluidity, to choose a dominant version that ossifies in the process of time, to simplify. A prime example of such simplification occurs at the end of *The Parson's Tale* with the evocation of the eternal delights of heaven, and the need to live a miserable life in this world in order to achieve the delights and avoid the horrors of the next.

Heaven is the official ecclesiastical culture's view of the good life. Since all official cultures become so by repudiating certain areas of experience and kinds of behaviour, which may then be called unofficial counter-cultures, hell is the official ecclesiastical culture's view of unofficial counter-cultures. When the official culture is narrowly ecclesiastical, hell tends to be equated with the secular, and that is no doubt partly what the Parson is doing, in a way very typical of the Gothic period. Since the courtly was also secular we easily arrive at the famous joke in the thirteenth-century French poem *Aucassin et Nicolette* where the hero wishes to go to hell when he dies, for there are all the courtly lovers and the beautiful people.[9]

The Parson's concept of heaven is rather static. There is more movement in hell. Hell is presented in his meditation as a horrible pit down into which a soul damned at judgment shall be drawn by a multitude of devils. It is a place of mental and bodily pain, burning and darkness, crowding and confusion of people, without respect for rank or sex, with poverty and mutual hatred; a general anarchy of misery. Similarly, the Deadly Sins are all represented as of demonic energy, unloving, greedy, grasping, selfish, divisive, competitive and individualistic, taking always short-term gratifications instead of long-term benefits. The Parson has a regrettable, entirely human, interest in hell, and hardly describes heaven. If heaven is the opposite of hell it is calm, bright, joyous, comfortable. There is an accepted hierarchy and distinction where each has his justified place, but co-operation and mutual love allow the individual to sink his sense of himself in the whole. Virtue, similarly, is co-operation, self-sacrifice, postponement of personal gratifications in a long perspective.

The pattern of heaven and hell, official culture and unofficial culture, is repeated in Chaucer's poetry. What is approved of tends to be static, aiming at serenity, unmoved, or detached from the world, like Chaucer's heroines, or the quietist longings expressed in the short moral Boethian personal poems, or the views expressed by Theseus in *The Knight's Tale*. The competitive, quarrelsome, active elements are contrasted with heavenly serenity, and tend to be secular (like the young men in *The Knight's Tale*) as opposed to ecclesiastical or philosophical; or, within the secular world, they are the ribald, unruly lower-class elements, contrasted with the upper-class. In passing, it may be remarked that there is a striking dearth of references in Chaucer's work to purgatory: of a mere total of five, two refer to wives being their husbands' purgatory on earth: another is Arcite's denial that he is in purgatory when in prison—he is in hell. Of the remaining two references, both by the Parson, one is merely casual and assimilates purgatory effectively to hell (*CT*, x, 715–20); the other is the briefest passing reference (*CT*, x, 805–10). Chaucer's imagination prefers the either/or, the *pro* or *con*. Genial he may be, but not compromising.

In so far as the official ecclesiastical culture recognised hell, it was inclusive; in so far as it repudiated hell, it was exclusive. In a sense it was both, as was Chaucer's poetry; illogical but natural. An acceptance paradoxically encloses a rejection. The official culture is inevitably in contact, because in conflict, with the unofficial. Each needs the other to maintain its sense of its own identity. The recalcitrant, relaxed, evasive, amorphous or rebellious nature of unofficial counter-cultures means that they take on meaning largely in opposition to the dynamics of effort, will and control of the official culture (though unofficial cultures also have some important positive qualities of their own). And also, of course, the official culture necessarily works on the unofficial cultures and is itself affected by their responses. The two kinds of culture are defined in related opposition to each other. Each is denied complete victory or defeat, and sometimes they change places, as seems to be happening in the late twentieth century. Mutual definition in conflict appears in the fourteenth century when official and unofficial cultures are seen in the form either as ecclesiastical versus secular, or as courtly secular versus low-class secular. Chaucer's poetry represents these conflicts of embrace: ecclesiastical versus secular conflict appears most vividly in the 'Retracciouns' with almost total victory going to the ecclesiastical. The courtly secular versus the low-class secular conflict appears in the derisive term *cherles tale*, imputing to the lower classes the vulgarity of what is after all a courtly *fabliau* such as *The Miller's Tale*. Courtly versus lower-class contempt appears in the presentation of the vulgar behaviour of the lower classes in the same *fabliaux*, in the competitive quarrelsome behaviour of the lower classes on the Canterbury pilgrimage, and in a number of casual references, for example, 'O stormy peple! unsad and evere untrewe!' (*CT*, IV, 995). Yet Chaucer's poetry is also notable for the hospitality it offers to the unofficial cultures; to secular and lower-class elements, to folk-tale, folk-humour even of a coarse kind (as in some of the *fabliaux*), and in the laughter he raises often enough against the official culture, by satirising clerics, for example. The benefit comes from the failure in Chaucer's poetry of the official culture to crush its opposite, and therefore from the fact of coexistence, the almost-balance of *pro* and *con*.[10]

The relative weakness of the official ecclesiastical culture in many places is nowhere more apparent than in its treatment of sexual love and of women, where the courtly secular is both unofficial and at its best. The sentiment of love is plainly rooted in biological sexual desire which is not a cultural phenomenon but a given condition of life. Nevertheless, our feelings are also culturally conditioned. The Middle Ages, as is well known, developed the sentiment of sexual love with an elaboration far beyond anything previously or even subsequently known and has influenced culture since then throughout the world. Now, when all qualifications are made about the inter-reactions of secular with religious influences in the medieval elaboration of the sentiment of love, it can hardly be disputed that the incapacity of the Church to recognise much medieval treatment of sexual love as a genuine attempt to control, stabilise, humanise and even sanctify sexual desire was a great failure and a great disaster, equivalent to the split caused by the Reformation, with which it was closely connected (Luther's marriage may be recalled). In the case both of love and of the Reformation we see the triumph of the logic of the official culture in excluding what it disapproved of (or alternatively we find incompatibilities within the total pluralistic culture so developed as to produce absolute divisions between elements that had previously coexisted). It is as if there were an attempt by heaven not only to repudiate hell but to banish it by logic from the cosmos: in other words, since this is not possible, to deny coexistence and plurality, to pretend that hell does not exist. Such concealment is always dangerous to heaven itself. In practice this situation did not arise in the fourteenth century because of the weakness of ecclesiastical prohibitions against the semi-official strength of the courtly culture which was devoted to the love of ladies, and because, after all, the Church recognised love in a more general sense as the root of all being. The relative weakness of the Church as an authoritarian body which had only come to insist on priestly celibacy in the eleventh century allowed many priests to have unofficial wives, and many respectable clerics to write, in holiday moments, less respectable love-songs, even in Latin.

Nevertheless, another strange aspect of the dichotomy between official and unofficial cultures was that it was also a sexual dichotomy; since the official culture was exclusively masculine most of the feminine element in life must be unofficial—an extraordinary state of affairs, however much mitigated by qualifications in theory and practice. The dichotomy was reinforced, in an age when physical strength was very important in every sphere of life, by the greater physical weakness of women worn out by unlimited child-bearing. It was further reinforced by their deprivation of education. Even so, it was not completely inevitable. The Anglo-Saxons had given much greater equality to women than did later medieval men, who seem to have had a great desire for much greater specialisation of human roles. (And English women have always had notoriously greater freedom than their Continental sisters.) The fact remains that in the Middle Ages women were largely identified with the unofficial culture, with temptation to sin, distraction of the ongoing masculine intellect, disorderliness. Abelard's love for Heloise is the tragic emblem.

One must not exaggerate, simply because no culture could obliterate the most vital element in the human condition. Since men need women, the official Gothic ecclesiastical culture adopted with passionate intensity one supreme feminine element, that represented by Mary the Mother of Christ, Mother and Virgin. Heaven was full of women. A curious sidelight on the developing 'feminism' in fourteenth-century England is that apparently the 'sex' of angels in general came to be represented as feminine about the middle of the century.[11] So the feminine image split, and as far as Chaucer's poetry goes we may say that he has broadly two positive images of the feminine to each of which he gives full, if apparently contradictory, assent: that of the official culture, represented by the Virgin-Mother, by St Cecilia, perhaps Emily in *The Knight's Tale* as courtly, official, and so on; and that of the unofficial culture, or cultures, an image represented by Venus on the courtly mythological level, by Criseyde, and on a lower social and moral level by Alison and the Wife of Bath (Venus's daughter).

Chaucer is the most notably feminist author in English until Richardson, and has had few rivals since. Both the official and unofficial feminine images are important in his works, and it is characteristic that both should be so. We may well feel, however, that less interest attaches to his *positive* presentation of the official image, for though it is not weak, it is less artistically worked, and far less extensive. More interest attaches to his presentation of the official but *negative* image of women, that is, of the long tradition of fiercely jocular clerical Latin anti-feminist satire. This is the unofficial image of woman seen from the official side—hell from heaven. (And it must be remembered that images of hell were also often comic, at the same time as horrific, in medieval culture.) Admittedly a man need not be a celibate cleric in order to mock women, wives and marriage, as extremely secular modern vaudeville comics and newspaper strip-cartoonists know. Anti-feminism is quite natural in societies which to any extent specialise the roles of the sexes: but the satire that Chaucer enjoyed was mainly formulated in official Latin clerical writings from St Jerome onwards, and although it appears elsewhere in Chaucer's work is brought to climax in *The Wife of Bath's Prologue*. This Prologue is a confession designed to make her appear as a comic, man-eating monster, embodying in part that ancient masculine fear of sex and of women that is less often recognised today than it should be. But as we should expect in Chaucer, he is equivocal. In his dramatically expressive portrait of the Wife in her Prologue, though he uses Latin material, he transposes it into the language of broad vulgar English free-wheeling feminine humanity. The Wife of Bath is triumphantly human and sympathetic, gloriously selfish and materialistic, always sacrificing long-term benefits in heaven for short-term gratification on earth.[12] There are some inconsistencies in her presentation, including the uncertain impression we have that her fifth husband is alive at the beginning of her 'confession' and dead at the end—but that, though inconsistent, is very fitting, as reflecting the sense of flux, the absence of a fixed point of view. No sensible reader worries. The incompatibilities can live together. As a result, the satire against women of the official culture is joined by the laughter by and about women and also against the would-be dominant male, of an unofficial culture with a powerfully aggressive feminine element. Yet the official culture's hierarchical scale of values is even accepted. The Wife gladly agrees that virginity is superior to marriage, that she is barley-bread in comparison to wheat. She is no revolutionary. But she has 'had her world as in her time', which is more than monks have had. The advantage of short-term gratifications is that you have at least made sure of them. A bird in the hand is worth a bird of paradise after death. Fundamentally the Wife of Bath is satisfied, though far from sated.

We also have a useful pointer here to the nature of laughter in Chaucer. It arises, as is generally the case, from the juxtaposition of incongruous elements; in particular in Chaucer from juxtapositions of official and unofficial aspects of culture. Such juxtapositions are so extraordinarily frequent in Chaucer, by contrast with his contemporaries, as to be a principal defining quality of his work.

First we may note how he presents himself. Laughter was traditionally associated with satire, and the classical justification of satire is that it is corrective. Certainly there is less kindliness in laughter than the rather sentimental English view usually assumes. It is painful to be laughed at and probably most people go out of their way to avoid it. Therefore clowns, and all those who for professional or other reasons attract laughter against themselves, almost always promote a double vision of themselves, whereby they dissociate their 'true' personality from that part that deliberately invites laughter. Comic actors can frequently be seen creating such a double image of the self. Chaucer does the same thing when he projects a comic image of himself in his poems. Such apparently self-mocking self-description inevitably implies a superior part of himself which is associated with the audience, like them being later in time than the events being described, and it is this superior part of himself which tells us about his earlier, foolish, lesser, less essential self. Who could *really* take Chaucer to be the 'dul man' he so often represents himself to be? This division between superior and inferior selves, in those poems in which he presents his own self as actually one of the *dramatis personae* (e.g. the love-visions, the *General Prologue* to *The Canterbury Tales*, but *not Troilus and Criseyde*) in itself corresponds to a division between higher and lower cultures, in this case between the official aspects of the courtly secular culture, and the ignorant, consequently rejected, therefore unofficial, aspects.

On the other hand, though to be laughed at is painful, it is less painful than exclusion or assault. Laughter on the part of those who laugh is a substitute for more hostile action. If we laugh we do not fear, even if we usually do not love either. While we laugh we do not attempt to remove the object or cause of laughter. We tolerate it if it is superior to us, or patronise it if inferior, and we may even feel in part kindly towards the object, attribute to it some value, because we get enjoyment from laughing at it. Partly for this reason we like the Wife of Bath. Laughter therefore has a unitive function between those who laugh and those who are laughed at, though a unity arising from difference. In Chaucer most laughter is superior; either of the official culture against the unofficial, as with the official antifeminism of *The Wife of Bath's Prologue* against her crudeness, or of the courtly against the inferior uncourtly, most obviously in *The Miller's Tale* and *The Tale of Sir Thopas*, or the learned against the ignorant, as in *The Reeve's Tale*. But the laughter is by definition not simple condemnation; it implies acceptance, even pleasure. Furthermore, a certain amount of laughter in Chaucer's poetry is of the unofficial against the official. The Wife of Bath really does have a joke against the official culture: she has much more fun. Chaucer's genius is such that both kinds of laughter can coexist in the same passage. The portrait of Alison in *The Miller's Tale* is funny because Alison is a ridiculous low-class imitation of a great lady of romance: but the parody also mocks the rhetorical abstractions of formal descriptions. Such two-way action is the essence of mock-rhetorical writing, not limited to Chaucer, but found extensively in *The Nun's Priest's Tale*, where there is also ambivalent humour over the subjects of serious speculation—fate, free will, fore-knowldege absolute. Both *The Friar's Tale* and *The Summoner's Tale* are mockery by unofficial secular cultures against important aspects of the dominant ecclesiastical official culture. To be laughed at is the forfeit which the official culture may have to pay for dominating the unofficial; or which the unofficial may pay for being unpunished. The greatness of the poetic humour of Chaucer consists in the variety and complex blends of contrasts of several different kinds which he combines in one poetic narration, but the key lies in the fundamental contrasts between various kinds of official and unofficial cultures. Most laughter arises, however, when the balance between the official and the unofficial is fairly even.

To return to the general interplay between the two in Chaucer's works, the balance between official and unofficial culture may well be very unequal. The 'Retracciouns' reveal a very heavy preponderance of the official, and there is, in consequence, no humour, irony or ambivalence. Much of the writing about women, on the other hand, is somewhat weighted towards the unofficial. In the use of language, since the vernacular was Chaucer's sole choice, and was essentially the language of women, the mother-tongue in every sense, the linguistic balance is almost entirely against the official, and there is nothing intrinsically comic in his using the vernacular. Yet a major comic paradox of *The Wife of Bath's Prologue* is that while almost the whole of its content is derived from official clerical Latin writing against women, the work itself is in English and in several ways asserts the rights of women. Very few women in fourteenth-century England, if any at all, knew Latin—not even nuns who entuned the Latin offices full seemly through their noses every day. The Church had always had occasional recourse to the vernacular for preaching to the laity and for a few didactic works aimed at the laity and at religious women. But the serious central developing thought and work of the official ecclesiastical culture was only in Latin, restricted to men.The intimate clash in Chaucer between the two language cultures and their intrinsic attitudes is beautifully and comically illustrated in *The Nun's Priest's Tale*:

> For al so siker as *In principio*,
> *Mulier est hominis confusio*—
> Madame, the sentence of this Latyn is,
> 'Womman is mannes joye and al his blis'.
>
> <div align="right">(<i>CT</i>, vii, 3163–6)</div>

There could be no neater illustration of the contrast (which is also found in one or two macaronic lyrics outside Chaucer). Which version is correct, or preferred by Chaucer? For if the English is a mistranslation of the Latin, the Latin is also in a sense a mistranslation of the English, and each language has its own characteristic validity. History and natural feeling are all nowadays on the side of the vernacular, secular, unofficial version. The story and the poem give no answer one way or the other. In a sense Chauntecleer—like Chaucer, perhaps—believes both, without insincerity. So sharp a juxtaposition of opposites creates a sense not so much of the relativity or fluidity of truth as of the limitations of any specific formulation of it, and the consequent call for a complementary formulation. Interpretations of *The Nun's Priest's Tale* as being an intentional allegory of the Fall, that is, as a conscious instrument of the official culture, are surely wrong, but an echo of Eve's delinquency may legitimately be heard in the passage just quoted. If so, then Adam's fault must be remembered too, and Chauntecleer's silliness is evidently masculine enough. Moreover, women do indeed bring men *joye* and *solas* (though this is rather an egotistical way of praising them), as well as trouble. Both the Latin and the English 'sentences' are extremes, and one extreme calls for the other as modification: *pro* needs *con*. Once again, there is no compromise, no grey middle term between black and white, but the sentences when set side by side, for all their logical incompatibility, express in a way a complex truth. Unity is found in the complexity, as achieved by juxtaposition, by the metonymy of close association itself, by the complementarity of the pattern, and by the fact that it is contained by one speaker. If the speaker, Chauntecleer or Chaucer, is prepared to entertain both terms at once, even with apparent self-contradiction, that may be unity enough. The English language also asserts some capacity for containment, for in this very poem it demonstrates an ability to handle the topics of the official culture. The vernacular is now adequate to convey complex thought and feeling, and has absorbed terms taken directly or through French from Latin into the English stock, so that it can handle much—not all—of the intellectual material normally treated in Latin. Chaucer necessarily withdraws from a full takeover of the Latin intellectual culture by the vernacular: 'I wol nat han to do of swich mateere' (*CT*, vii, 3251). The time was not yet ripe and the official intellectual culture remained mostly Latinate though on an ever narrower basis until the eighteenth century. Chaucer had all the same made an important advance of the vernacular.

He was also associated with another development of the vernacular which was apparently more hostile to official Latin culture. This was Lollardy. The early celebrated group of Lollard knights were close courtly associates with each other; one of them, Sir John Clanvowe, was a poetic disciple of Chaucer's, and presumably a friend, as others may well have been. The complications of and the changes in Lollardy need not be discussed here. It is enough to recall that it was variously hostile to many beliefs and institutions of varied importance, like the doctrine of transubstantiation, the wealth and political power of the Church, marriage, Sunday observance, pilgrimage, as well as to a lot of general jollity. The demand to have the Bible, the central official sacred Latin book, in the 'unofficial' vernacular, proved to be Lollardy's most explosive characteristic, and developed into its principal requirement and defining quality. For all the scholastic Wyclif's importance, the movement was essentially secular in origin. At first the gentry adhered, but persecution shook most of them off, and in the fifteenth century Lollardy was almost entirely a lower-class movement. It was thus doubly unofficial. Early in the fifteenth century the very use of English, let alone the possession of a Bible in English, was regarded by the Church as presumptive evidence of dangerous heresy.[13] The opposition of Lollardy to the official culture is also paradoxical, as can be expected from the paradoxical nature of Christianity, because much of Lollardy arose from simply taking literally certain parts of the Church's own message. The presence of Wyclif and other priests in the early days of the movement helps to mark its equivocal nature. Yet it was a real development in spiritual culture, aiming, like many such movements, even in our own day, at a new sincerity, spontaneity and inwardness of spiritual life in the world, a new but not unspiritual secularity that has obvious parallels with that overwhelming interest in personal human relationships, in the uninhibited movements of the human heart, especially sexual love, that characterises so much of Chaucer's work, and the unofficial secular culture.

Chaucer's unofficial vernacular culture also carried, what was very different from Lollardy, some elements of folk-culture, that is, of oral tales, and their inherent concepts.[14] There is a strong folk-element seen especially clearly in the plots of several of the *Canterbury Tales*, notably the comic and improper *fabliaux*. To speak of folk-tale in the fourteenth century does not exclude courtly or clerical participation and the situation cannot be read along class-lines. The folk-tale plots of *The Miller's Tale* and *The Reeve's Tale* are widespread through Europe in several languages and well established in writing. The earliest account of the folk-tale pear-tree episode of *The Merchant's Tale* is the twelfth-century Latin *comoedia Lydia* written in a highly elaborate literary style. Like other such episodes it is also found in the East and may have originated in India. Nevertheless, the official culture as represented so conveniently for us in Chaucer's understanding by *The Parson's Tale* did not approve such frolicking even when its indecency was concealed within the learned language, and though it may occur in Latin it must be regarded as 'unofficial', in opposition to the dominant notions of what was right and proper. Yet Chaucer in *The Canterbury Tales* invokes these ribald elements more liberally, in terms of the number of tales (not of the actual bulk of material), than any others. They have a coarse and hearty humour that mocks pretensions to dignity, to justice and superiority (whether of age or learning) or to marital possession, or to official ecclesiastical position. They share with other folk-tale plots in *The Canterbury Tales* (*The Clerk's Tale* of Griselda, *The Wife of Bath's Tale*) a certain qualified optimism, a belief in 'joy after woe', more characteristic of the basic irrepressible humanity of uneducated folk the world over than of sophisticated clerks, who inclined to pessimism then as now. But these folk-tale plots may also be told in a way, characteristic of courtly 'folk', that satirises class inferiors, as *The Miller's Tale* and *The Tale of Sir Thopas* do. They are ambivalent.

The complex cultural pluralism here briefly and schematically sketched as it appears focused in Chaucer's works contains other pluralisms.

Fortunately we may disregard the political, legal, administrative and practical elements of Church and State, Latin and Anglo-French, since they hardly appear in the literature. The inner complexities of the official Latin culture have also necessarily been largely neglected, though the internal conflicts between multiple pagan sources of knowledge and the equally multiple elements of the specifically Judaeo-Christian sources and inspiration had once been severe, even if by the fourteenth century they were mostly reconciled. Some other characteristics of the official culture need to be mentioned. First it was historically based, and had an intense consciousness of time past and future. It saw a purpose in history, and was concentrated upon an end. Beginnings and ends were important, but especially the end. Doomsday was absolute judgment. The last moments of a completely ill-spent life might redeem it. 'Th' ende is every tales strengthe' (*TC*, II, 260). The 'Retracciouns' thus count in moral terms for more than all the rest of Chaucer's works. But this absolutism allows much flux, much divagation, before the end. Associated with the historical teleological pattern is an intense idealism. The end represented the achievement of the highest ideal. 'Be ye perfect' (Matthew 5:48). There was a purposeful seeking and a consequent tension in official culture. Since official culture was idealistic, the unofficial culture usually represents relaxation, recreation, sport, frivolity. If the official culture was a seeking, a straining after long-term spiritual benefit, the unofficial culture could only be a finding of short-term physical gratification. But it is worth emphasising that the official culture was intellectually optimistic, as on the whole the unofficial cultures, perhaps through mere unthinkingness, were also optimistic—folk-tales tend to have happy endings, and after the Crucifixion comes the Resurrection. Historians, with the exception of Professor Du Boulay,[15] have tended to emphasise the pessimism of the later Middle Ages, but this may well be to exaggerate certain tendencies in the image of modern literary despairs. If there was optimism, it did not imply a foolish blindness to misery and wickedness. There was often a rationally low estimate of the world, traditionally expressed by Chaucer:

> The world hath mad a permutacioun
> Fro right to wrong, fro trouthe to fikelnesse.
> (*Lak of Stedfastnesse*, 19–20)

But there is nothing in the Middle Ages to match both the sense of a purposeless, valueless, arbitrary, 'accidental' universe and the literally suicidal despair that mark so much of the literary (though not the scientific) culture of the West in the latter part of the twentieth century. For the official culture of the Middle Ages certainly the world of appearances, of naturalistic experience, just like the world of literature and our very thoughts, was not only corrupt but transient and ultimately unimportant, and

> al shal passe that men prose or ryme.
> Take every man hys turn, as for his tyme.
> (*Scogan*, 41–2)

There was no easy evasion of suffering: rather it was *through* suffering, through meeting the worst, that the best, which lay behind appearances, might be achieved, and which was all the time wanting us to achieve it, helping us.

> And trouthe thee shal delivere, it is no drede.
> (*Truth, Balade de Bon Conseyl*, 7,
> repeated at 14, 21, 28)

Truth is not only 'what is true', but God himself. The individual soul was offered in the long term a prospect of eternal delight, at what was in comparison a slight cost in short-term gratification. Boethius in *The Consolation of Philosophy* had expressed that duality most attractively to Chaucer, as he did to thinking laymen for a thousand years or more through the Middle Ages and later. Chaucer constantly draws on Boethius for material and attitude in what are nevertheless his most personally sincere lyrics, *The Former Age*, *Fortune*, *Truth*, *Gentilesse*, *Lak of Stedfastnesse*, whose uniqueness and success in the general body of English literature deserve more notice. It is also worth noting that Chaucer finds the secular Christian wisdom of Boethius more personally sympathetic, eight centuries after Boethius's death, than contemporary fourteenth-century ecclesiastical formulations of ordinary religious devotion, or than those expressions of transcendental mystical experience which in his very lifetime reached their greatest height in English with the work of Hilton, Dame Julian, and the author of *The Cloud of Unknowing*. Boethius, like Chaucer a Christian man of the world, admirably expresses the world's charm yet transience, the need for the individual's mind to rise above the most adverse immediate circumstances, even death by torture, and in so doing to express an ultimate optimism about the goodness and purpose of Creation. Granted many variations, this was the general temper of medieval official culture, that needs always to be borne in mind.

Finally, it must be remembered that the official culture was essentially intellectual, cognitive. I do not mean that it excluded feeling and imagination for it obviously did not, but that it primarily sought knowledge and truth. The nature of salvation was thought to depend on getting the truth about the universe, and about oneself. This was the reason for the passionate conviction of the importance and significance of life in general and of how the individual thought and conducted himself. This was why heresy was so important and so frightening, and why it was persecuted. It was no exaggeration to say at least in theory that the persecutor was being cruel to be kind. The modern abandonment of the sense of absolute truth in Christianity by so many modern Christians as well as by atheists should not make us forget that once all Christians felt as strongly about truth as scientists do now. It is well recognised that modern science arises from the medieval Christian view of the universe, even though it has broken that view.[16] Knowledge of the physical universe was not as important as theological knowledge, but it was part of that order. The unofficial cultures were of course unintellectual or anti-intellectual, and suffer for it, like the miller in *The Reeve's Tale*, who despises clerks.

It is clear that the literary form which could most fully realise the complicated cultural situation must be an encyclopaedic one, and we are not surprised to find various encyclopaedic forms dominating the literary culture of the time. The Bible has some claim to be regarded as encyclopaedic and it was basic and universal; the many *Summa* of the schoolmen offer an example of another kind; but more specific to the literature of the Gothic period in Europe are such encyclopaedic poems (to select only two examples that deeply influenced Chaucer) as *Le Roman de la Rose* and *La Divina Commedia*. The poems of his exact contemporaries, Gower's *Confessio Amantis* and Langland's *Piers Plowman*, are also encyclopaedic in scope. Chaucer's own personal taste clearly ran to learning, and he achieves an intellectual range greater than that of any other poet, let alone major poet, in English. The man matched the age. Such universality of interest and resource in a poet could not have occurred at any other period of our history. Even Milton is surpassed.

The encylopaedic tradition in literature has been identified by Professor Northrop Frye in *Anatomy of Criticism* as 'Menippean Satire' or alternatively 'Anatomy'. *The Canterbury Tales* contains even the mixture of prose and verse which Professor Frye shows is typical of purer elements of the genre. It is not surprising that, though he overlooks Chaucer's work when establishing his concept of the form, Professor Frye describes Chaucer's favourite serious reading, Boethius's *The Consolation of Philosophy*, as 'pure anatomy'.[17] Frye notes that Chaucer was one of the favourite authors of the writer of 'the greatest Menippean satire in English before Swift', Robert Burton (p. 311). Nigel Longchamp, whose work was known to, and which provides interesting comparisons with, Chaucer, wrote in the *Speculum Stultorum* a pure Menippean satire.

The terms 'Anatomy' and 'Menippean Satire', not quite synonymous, come together because a taste for widespread learning, combined with an interest in the world, seem to lead to satire. Satire is the natural product of an idealistic intellectual culture, simply because practically everything in this world is less than ideal.

The intellectual and idealistic bias of 'encyclopaedism' does not encourage mere 'imitation' in words of the social or natural world of experience, however great may be the interest in the world. Some of what Professor Frye writes of the genre admirably illuminates this aspect of Chaucer's work:

The Menippean satire deals less with people as such than with mental attitudes [e.g. *Troilus and Criseyde*]. Pedants, bigots, cranks, parvenus, virtuosi, enthusiasts, rapacious and incompetent professional men of all kinds [e.g. many of the Canterbury pilgrims, the Eagle of *The House of Fame*, the birds of *The Parliament of Fowls*] are handled in terms of their occupational approach to life as distinct from their social behaviour. The Menippean satire thus resembles the confession . . . [as of the Wife of Bath and the Pardoner].[18]

Though it would be fruitful to continue to analyse Chaucer's works, severally or generally, as 'Menippean Satire', or 'Anatomy', it is important to note the other literary form which is so influential in Chaucer: that of romance. Though the origins of romance are earlier than the Middle Ages, romance is the dominant form of Gothic secular literature, though its religious form was even more widespread, as Saint's Life. Secular romance is a courtly form which lives almost entirely in the vernacular, and to that extent has strong unofficial elements, seeking satisfaction in the world here and now, especially in sexual love. The mainspring of Chaucer's early poetry, as I have shown elsewhere, is to be sought in the English vernacular romances current in his boyhood.[19] Romance may be defined by reference to its interest in individual satisfactions and personal relationships (of physical love or physical contest) and also by its happy ending, its optimism, in which it reflects not only popular but official culture. Furthermore, in its typical form, the Quest, romance clearly images the idealistic, purposeful, even yearning, strain of the official culture. Romance also has two aspects, inner and outer. The outer aspect, of arms and adventure, hardly interests Chaucer at all. The inner aspect, of the hero's quest for a love which shall be a spiritual, imaginative and emotional adventure, not merely sexual, absorbs Chaucer deeply, and develops into something more in himself and in his culture; a quest for knowledge, of tidings, stories, people, intellectual matters, an inclusiveness of human experience, leading eventually to a concern for the highest spiritual achievement, for salvation, as imaged rather indirectly in the apotheosis of Troilus and more directly, but alas, all too negatively, in the Parson's 'meditation' about the way to the 'Jerusalem celestial'. Thus do romance and anatomy in the end unite, with the inclusiveness of anatomy and the happy ending of romance.

The combining of anatomy and romance produces further ironic developments in later romance, and especially in Chaucer. The analytical mind fostered by anatomy, which juxtaposes so many miscellaneous elements, causes them to interact. If anatomy is sustained by the long-term optimism of romance, romance is also subjected by anatomy to corrosive comparisons and hence qualifications. Spontaneity is shown not to last: transience begins to look like lack of value. Anatomy and romance may come to seem mutually incompatible and hostile. The classic confrontation of romance with anatomy, in Chaucer's work before *The Canterbury Tales*, though often foreshadowed in shorter poems, is *Troilus and Criseyde*, that ironic romance, where confrontation as well as salvation is at last focused in the ending. Troilus finds his happy ending, intrinsic to romance, and, it seems, in accord with the official culture: but it has been postponed till after death, and by comparison his earthly love-affair shrinks a little; its gratifications were immediate, but transient, as of the lower culture.

The Canterbury Tales offers other confrontations, and the final disastrous victory in the 'Retracciouns' for the severest aspect of the official ecclesiastical culture. By a paradox, anatomy in this conclusion is denied its inclusiveness, romance its happy ending in this life. Satire itself turns into outright condemnation.

Yet this last word is again paradoxically not final to later time. The process of time which brings such transmogrifications also, in literature at least, preserves them. The works of intervening time are not destroyed, but coexist with the end that denies them, as was characteristic of the sustained tensions of the culture of the time and to be expected from the human condition. Neither flux nor stasis has absolute rule, but must coexist in a state of ironical tension. Given the nature of Gothic literary culture, its supreme expression must be an irony.

The peculiar precarious balances, inconsistencies and tensions of the Gothic period are not unique. They arise out of the human condition, are endemic within it, and are found in all periods. This is one reason for the continuous relevance of the major and indeed minor works of the Gothic period. It seems, however, that Gothic art in general, and the verbal art of the late fourteenth century, and of Chaucer, in particular, were at a point of balance between a multiplicity of forces, new and old, that was able to contain unusual diversity. Langland, the *Gawain*-poet, and to a less extent Gower, all witness to this multiplicity, but none so fully as Chaucer. (The others all have rather less detachment, rather more urgency to find and communicate a view, a certainty, a commitment, than Chaucer has except at the very end of his writing career, but they are all sufficiently ambivalent.) Irony is the very literary figure to express, even to create, this ambivalent culture. Irony being the statement of two different, often opposing meanings, in one set of words, it conveys both the oppositions, or incompatibilities, or inconsistencies, and their yoking together, that we find everywhere in Chaucer. Unity may sometimes seem no more than mere contiguity, but the acceptance of contiguity expresses an attitude that is itself a unifying; it is that toleration, that love, which so many critics have rightly found in Chaucer. There were other attempts to unify, important over large areas, made by the age itself. The construction of hierarchies of value that allowed for that 'principle of plenitude' explored by Professor Bennett[20] is one of the most important. And it must be emphasised that by no means all that Chaucer writes is to be taken as ironical at the literal level. There is a very great deal that we are meant to accept simply and as it were naively in its literal obvious sense. If in the end we fail to find a completely watertight general scheme to express our understanding, we need not be surprised. Neither Chaucer, nor English Gothic literature, nor human life, is to be so contained. A pregnant phrase has been attributed to Professor Noam Chomsky: 'All grammars leak'. All systems of thought are inadequate to contain the richness of human life.

For a poet to reflect (or create) so fully such a cultural situation brings some losses, or rather, involves the absence of some literary pleasures. The inconsistencies and discontinuities noted in Chaucer at the beginning of this essay, while they can reflect and create a valid sense of life even more penetratingly by the absence of organic or logical connection and of overall naturalistic representation, nevertheless cannot give us the sort of realistic representations bound by chains of cause and effect which the novel provides, and for which, especially when we are young, we naturally hunger. Chaucer's own advances in naturalistic realism are huge, and deserve recognition, but they are still set against a conceptual abstract view of 'reality', and are therefore still a part of his *pro* and *con*, and he writes no satisfactorily complete novel. There is another absence, perhaps more serious, though again more important when we are young. That 'sober certainty of waking bliss' (or, as usually preferred nowadays, certainty of brutal disaster), that guidance and sense of exalted commitment, given by some Neoclassical, but especially by Romantic and post-Romantic writers, up to D. H. Lawrence and beyond, who assume the heavy responsibilities of the imaginative verbal artist to be more than philosopher, historian or priest, is not much to be found in Chaucer's contemporaries, as Mr Burrow has pointed out, and least of all in Chaucer himself.[21] Such commitment is a Neoclassical and later, not a Gothic, function of the poet. We return to Chaucer's 'irresponsibility' as a poet, only qualified when he himself condemns all his best imaginative work. He only takes absolute responsibility, only offers guidance and absolute commitment and exaltation, in a rejection that we ourselves can only—supreme paradox!— reject. Within his imaginative work, he takes no responsibility. He throws it on to the reader. We are treated as equals. This is why we can reject his rejection and remain true to the experience of reading him. Chaucer requires, and we must supply, not disciples, not partisans, but responsible readers.

11 Chaucer and Chrétien and Arthurian Romance*

Some evidence has already been noticed[1] that suggests that Chaucer had read Chrétien. The evidence is Chaucer's use of the word *vavasour* to describe the Franklin (*CT*, I, 360)—the only occurrence of that word in his writings. It is possible however to argue that two other references by Chaucer also reveal a knowledge of Chrétien's works. Consideration of these possible points of contact between two very different yet very medieval poets suggests some fruitful contrasts and comparisons.

The word *vavasor*, Frankis states, is not much more common in French than in English, and is also of somewhat vague significance as to social status in both languages. Chrétien uses the word in only two poems.[2] In each case *li vavasors* is a man notable for hospitality, and in *Erec et Enide* he has white hair and a good cook, which further associate him with Chaucer's description of the Franklin. Frankis suggests that Chaucer is saying that the Franklin was the sort of person whom Chrétien refers to as a *vavasor*, and one may emphasise that the unusual word occurs fairly frequently in Chrétien's two poems, and so might well stick in the mind. Chaucer may not have known *vavasor* as a legal term in English, since it is only so employed in northern texts. The existence of the Middle English *Ywain and Gawain* witnesses to the availability of Chrétien's work in the fourteenth century in England, but it is notable that the romance, which is northern in language, does not repeat the word *vavasor* from Chrétien. The translator uses the more general and colourless word 'knight'. Frankis also notes that there seems no other certain evidence that Chaucer knew Chrétien's work.

A reference to Chrétien may however lie behind the rather strangely pointed joking remark in *The Nun's Priest's Tale*:

---

* First published in *Chaucer and Middle English Studies: In Honour of Rossell Hope Robbins*, ed. B. Rowland (London, 1974) pp. 255–9.

> This storie is also trewe, I undertake,
> As is the book of Launcelot de Lake,
> That wommen holde in ful greet reverence.
>
> (*CT*, vii, 3211–13)

This could be just a light-hearted anti-feminist squib, possibly with some contemporary reference, and also an example of Chaucer's scepticism towards several aspects of contemporary chivalric ideals. Yet it is peculiar that it should be directed specifically against women because, as far as can be judged from what little evidence there is, men were quite as much interested in Arthurian story, and in Launcelot, as were women. The Order of the Garter was founded by Edward III on the Arthurian model about 1350, as is well known; Arthur had a firm place in British-English history; and there is nothing effeminate about the contemporary poems, the alliterative *Morte Arthure* and stanzaic *Le Morte d'Arthur*, both of which mention Launcelot. If Malory, writing about the middle of the fifteenth century, may be cited as circumstantial evidence, Launcelot is his great hero, and there is again nothing particularly feminine about Malory, his work, or, finally, his printer Caxton, and the 'noble gentlemen' who asked Caxton to print Malory's *Morte D'Arthur*. It may be that there is some specific femininity associated with the vast body of French Arthurian romances, unknown to the present writer. But before hunting for that particular needle in the haystack it is worth noticing that the introductory remarks of Chrétien's own *Lancelot*, or *Le Chevalier de la Charrete*, pay very specific tribute to 'my lady of Champagne's' interest in the story of Launcelot, since she provided the poet with the story and asked him to write the romance. Chrétien specifically says that her command has more to do with the work than any effort he himself may expend upon it:

> Puis que ma dame de Champaigne
> vialt que romans a feire anpraigne,
> je l'anprendrai molt volentiers . . .

[Praise of the lady]

> Mes tant dirai ge mialz oevre
> ses comandemanz an ceste oevre
> Del CHEVALIER DE LA CHARRETE
> comance Crestiens son livre
> matiere et san li done et livre
> la contesse, et il s'antremet
> de panser, que gueres ni met
> fors sa painne et s'antancïon.
>
> (*Lancelot*, 1–29)

If we accept that Chaucer could have known this passage the point of his reference in *The Nun's Priest's Tale* at once becomes plain and sharp. He has read the beginning of Chrétien's *Lancelot*, has at least glanced at the rest, seen what a farrago of nonsense it is, and makes his passing joke for those in the know. We may also note that in his remarks there is no dramatic implication of the character of the Nun's Priest as ostensible narrator. The poet's own *persona* has taken over.

We may put this reference beside Chaucer's only other mention of Launcelot, also a light-heartedly sceptical dismissal; this time a joke at the expense of Launcelot's expertise in 'deerne love' (as hende Nicholas would call it):

> Who koude telle yow the forme of daunces
> So unkouthe, and swiche fresshe contenaunces,
> Swich subtil lookyng and dissymulynges
> For drede of jalouse mennes aperceyvynges?
> No man but Launcelot, and he is deed.
>
> (*CT*, v, 283–7)

This is very much a flippancy by the poet in his own *persona*, as are the lines immediately preceding this passage, where the poet disqualifies himself from being just such a man as he has represented the Squire, the ostensible narrator, to be. The Squire's own character, were it 'organically' presented, would surely be an enthusiast for Arthurian knighthood, just as surely as he is not the 'dul man' (*CT*, v, 279) who is at this stage the poet, in a favourite mock-modest *persona*, telling *The Squire's Tale*. Both references to Launcelot clearly hang together as characteristic of the narrating *poet* (*not* the Narrator), whom it is convenient to call Chaucer; who often likes to describe himself as 'dull'; and who has a fresh and cheerful scepticism about many of the fashionable sentiments of his day—love of sport, of animals (as Professor Rowland has recently shown us[3]), of adultery and of Arthurian romance.

Indeed, one might almost go so far as to argue (broadening the issue when we recollect Chaucer's 'realism' and his obvious pleasure in *fabliaux*) that Chaucer in his poetical character is decidedly anti-romantic. He could take his place in an Auerbachian procession towards ever greater realism, naturalism and tragedy, whose ultimate historical climax might be found in the literary culture of our own age, which certainly sees itself very often as 'realistic', 'frank' and 'tragic'. *Troilus and Criseyde*, the first self-aware tragedy, so to speak, in English, being named as a tragedy within the text (*TC*, v, 1786), would be an important stage in this progress. Chaucer's sarcasm about Arthurian romance, and about Chrétien's own *Lancelot*, would testify to the incompatibility of a great master of the realistic with Chrétien, the great master of symbolic fantasy. Chaucer's passing mockery of Chrétien might then be paralleled with the much more extensive and absolutely unquestionable mockery of the English romances which is found in *The Tale of Sir Thopas*. The English romances are mocked, we may think, not only for their verbal incompetence and general silliness, but because they are *romances*, which to Chaucer means silliness.

Plausible as such an argument would be, and indeed partially true, it would be over-simple. The nature of the mockery in *Sir Thopas* itself witnesses to a deep engagement on the poet's part at an earlier formative time in his life with his later victims. I have shown elsewhere how Chaucer's own development is grafted on to the rough stock of earlier native English romance.[4] It may be argued that *Troilus and Criseyde*, for all its rejection of the supernatural and of the unmotivated events of much romance, nevertheless has the intrinsic quality of romance, though it is 'tragic' or 'ironic' romance. Chaucer's deep ambiguities and ambivalences are not easily resolved. Such thoughts may also be prompted by another possible reference to Chrétien's work. In his 'Retracciouns' Chaucer mentions 'the book of the Leoun'. The traditional speculation is that this lost work may have been a version of Machaut's *Dit dou Lyon*, though Deschamps' *La Fiction* (or *Le Dict*) *du Lyon* has also been mentioned. Chaucer probably knew the poem by Machaut, but doubt has reasonably been felt about the identification. It seems not to have been noticed that Chrétien's *Yvain* is primarily known in French as *Le Chevalier au Lion* and the beast plays a notable part in the poem. 'The book of the Leoun' was probably an early work, since it has been lost. We know that *Yvain* was current in England in the fourteenth century as *Ywain and Gawain*, and we may imagine it popular. Chaucer's 'book of the Leoun' might have been a version of Chrétien's *Le Chevalier au Lion*.

Chaucer of course knew about Gawain, though he refers only once, and again flippantly, to 'Gawain with his olde curteisye' (*CT*, v, 95);[5] just as he refers only once, and of course in a flippant way, to King Arthur (*CT*, iii, 857). In these two instances we again have evidence of the poet's poetical character, not of the so-called Narrator, nor of individual pilgrim-narrators, all casual two-dimensional masks to be raised or lowered as the poet feels inclined. Not Narrator nor narrators but Chaucer the poet derides Arthurian romance—it is one of his constant and notable though minor traits. And yet we must allow that Chaucer's derision for the English romances that preceded him is based on an earlier knowledge that was surely product of a youthful love. It would not be the only youthful infatuation repudiated in maturity yet always influential. These Arthurian references, derisory though they are, suggest that Chrétien's Arthurian stories may have been another passing attraction.

It would not be profitable to claim a deep or lasting affinity between Chaucer and Chrétien. But once some relationship is granted as a possibility, comparisons and contrasts may be fruitful. The two poets share some commonplaces, such as the detailed description of the beautiful heroine. A reading of *Troilus and Criseyde* in the light of *Cligès* gives further depth to some of Chaucer's unexpressed or lightly expressed significances, most notably Criseyde's refusal to elope with Troilus (cf. *Cligès*, 5232 ff, where Fenice also says that Cligès will be her lord and her servant, as Aurelius is to Dorigen in *The Franklin's Tale*). Chrétien is more explicit than Chaucer on the topic of honour, the sentiment which underlies so much of Criseyde's behaviour.[6] Chrétien comments on the unreasonableness of love, yet finds in love his most fascinating subject-matter: here again is a parallel with the more enigmatic, less explicit Chaucer. In such cases Chrétien seems to express fully certain values which Chaucer takes for granted, or, for his own purposes, leaves under the surface.

12   The Arming of the Warrior in European Literature and Chaucer*

I

It is notable that both Chaucer and the *Gawain*-poet have a formal arming-passage amongst their works—but with how different a hero in either case! To compare Sir Thopas with Gawain is to get a glimpse into the abyss which separates their great contemporaneous authors. A little further acquaintance with European literature soon discovers a very considerable number of other formal arming-passages, strongly resembling each other in structure, though curiously enough no scholar or critic, even amongst those who have commented on the possible allegorical significance of Gawain's armour (which it is not my purpose to discuss here), appears to have remarked upon this phenomenon. The first purpose of this essay is to establish the existence and suggest the varying uses of this formal device, though there is no attempt to list every occurrence. The second purpose is briefly to examine Chaucer's use of it in comparison with that of the *Gawian*-poet and the ancient tradition. Chaucer by his use effectively destroys this tradition in English, as he does others. From this point of view he may be regarded as one of the last traditional poets and the first modern poet in English; or, as I have tried to express it elsewhere, as being both 'Gothic' (i.e. traditional) and 'Neoclassical' (i.e. modern, naturalistic). I use the term 'Neoclassical' to include much of Romanticism.[1]

Chaucer and, to some extent, the *Gawain*-poet, are our principal destination, but the long journey will be clearer if we start as far back as we can. There are three references to arming in Babylonian epic, where heroes are armed by gods for battles with monsters.[2] The details are a strange mixture of realism and cosmic hyperbole without (as far as I can judge) the formulaic structure of later armings, but they suggest the potent emotional and psychological forces, with cosmic mythological resonances, that the

* First published in *Chaucerian Problems and Perspectives: Essays Presented to Paul E. Beichner C.S.C.*, ed. Edward Vasta and Zacharias P. Thundy (Notre Dame and London, 1979) pp. 221–43.

physical preparations for battle involved. The primitive quality of Babylonian epic is approached only by the Irish example referred to below.

Our first clear view of the formalised description of the arming of the warrior occurs in the *Iliad*. It is a literary ritual corresponding, I presume, to a solemn and impressive ritual in real life, and the arming marks out both the hero and a combat of some particular importance. A. B. Lord comments briefly upon the arming, and connects it with similar formalised passages in early twentieth-century Yugoslav folk-epic. Thus our topic spans a period from the earliest records to almost the present day in European terms, though in England it faded out in the early fifteenth century.

A question of nomenclature arises here. Lord, followed by Homeric scholars, calls such formal passages 'themes'. Celtic folklorists, to be referred to later, call them 'runs'. They may equally well be referred to by the term used by Curtius—*topoi*; or by the Elizabethan term, 'commonplaces'. Each name emphasises a certain aspect of the phenomenon and implies a critical point of view, none of which I wish to exclude, but I shall in general use the term *topos*.[3]

II

There are four extended passages of arming in the *Iliad*;[4] when Paris arms for single combat against Menelaus (III, 328–38); Agamemnon arms to lead the Greeks (XI, 15–46); Patroclus arms himself in Achilles' armour (XVI, 130–44); and Achilles arms himself in new armour (XIX, 367–91). Each of the passages begins with the same three lines, which themselves being highly formulaic, clearly signal the recognised theme or topos. Homer had a basic theme for arming, which is given in its normal form in the arming of Paris and Patroclus. The theme is adjusted in the case of the other two heroes to fit the particular circumstances.[5]

The arming of Paris is translated thus by Richard Lattimore:

First he placed silver fastenings to hold the greaves at the ankles.
Afterwards he girt on about his chest the corselet
of Lykaon his brother since this fitted him also.
Across his shoulders he slung the sword with the nails of silver,
a bronze sword, and above it the great shield, huge and heavy.
Over his powerful head he set the well-fashioned helmet
with the horse-hair crest, and the plumes nodded terribly above it.
He took up a strong-shafted spear that fitted his hand's grip.
In the same way warlike Menelaos put on his armour.[6]

The general significance of the arming is as a ritual, 'probably one of dedication to the task of saving the hero's people, even of sacrifice. Each of these men is about to set out upon a mission of deep significance, and the "ornamental" theme is a signal and mark, both "ritualistic" and artistic, of the role of the hero.'[7] Each description follows the same order, often marking the pieces of armour with identical adjectives; greaves, corslet, sword, shield, helmet with crest, spear. This order is practical. It is probable that once the corslet was put on, a man could not bend over sufficiently far to tie on his greaves (and it may be noted that the heroes arm themselves). At the same time, one should not over-emphasise the practicality and potential naturalism at any stage. First, Greek armour of the heroic age appears to have included, besides the items mentioned, footguard, ankleguard, thigh-piece, belt, fore-armguard, and upper-armguard.[8] None of these is mentioned. A literal, realistic, naturalistic or mimetic presentation of 'how things actually are' is not the primary aim of traditional literature. Second, though the 'framework' of the arming topos in the *Iliad* is invariable, and to some extent expressed in unchanging verbal formulae, variations may be introduced in a manner familiar in traditional (including folklore) literature. In the *Iliad* the variations are mostly additions, of an elaborate kind, which are slotted into appropriate parts of the framework, on their minute scale quite comparable with the way Chaucer 'slots in' additions to the framework provided by *Il Filostrato* when he composes *Troilus*. Such additions both enrich and subtly change the received standard. It may be that the great poet reveals himself by the way he accepts with all its advantages of accumulated feelings the traditional topos, and yet adapts it to the purposes of his own poem, or to the limited context of one small section of his own poem. Such adaptations require a response in the reader or hearer different from that evoked by passages which claim to be both original and naturalistically mimetic, as in such 'Neoclassical' writing as the novel.

III

Before the advent of gunpowder the basic armour of the warrior was the same at any period, as Stubbings remarks,[9] so that local inconsistencies and anachronisms, in a traditional style of writing or speaking which does not primarily cherish naturalistic accuracy, were easily accepted even when not understood. The basic similarity is illustrated from a source perhaps even older than the *Iliad*, and much better known in the Middle Ages, where the topos had apparently not developed so far:

And Saul clad David with his apparel, and he put an helmet of brass upon his head, and he clad him with a coat of mail. And David girded his sword upon his apparel, and he assayed to go, for he had not proved it. And David said to Saul, I cannot go with these; for I have not proved them. And David put them off him. (1 Samuel 17:38–9, Revised Version)

Even here there is clearly a ritual as well as a practical element in the deed, if not in the literary treatment, and that the armour is borrowed is a curious coincidence with the armour which is borrowed in the first three instances of the topos in the *Iliad* (and in the fourth it is new).

Arming has an intrinsic significance, and so in Isaiah it is said of the Lord that:

he put on righteousness as a breastplate, and an helmet of salvation upon his head; and he put on garments of vengeance for clothing, and was clad with zeal as a cloak. (Isaiah 59:17)

This is taken up by St Paul—thus we see a topos growing—in the famous passage in Ephesians:

Wherefore take up the whole armour of God, that ye may be able to withstand in the evil day, and, having done all, to stand. Stand therefore, having girded your loins with truth, and having put on the breastplate of righteousness, and having shod your feet with the preparation of the gospel of peace; withal taking up the shield of faith, wherewith ye shall be able to quench all the fiery darts of the evil one. And take the helmet of salvation, and the sword of the Spirit, which is the word of God. (Ephesians 6:13–17)

Commentators refer us to the Isaiah passage and Wisdom 5:17–20, as part of Jewish apocalyptic, but surely St Paul is also here revealing the influence of both the primitive and the secular Greek topos.

IV

Virgil in the *Aeneid* (Book xii) has one relatively full example of the arming of the hero, though he curiously enough applies it to Turnus rather than Aeneas. He uses it as a marker of heroic magnitude, but possibly with some sense of its primitive quality, since it is not applied to Aeneas. The reference to horses precedes the arming of the hero, and the whole description has a more literary flavour. The greaves are omitted; but the corslet is followed

by sword and shield and helmet with crest and spear, as in Homer, though
Turnus then addresses a speech to his spear:

> Ipse dehinc auro squalentem alboque orichalco
> circumdat loricam umeris, simul aptat habendo
> ensemque clipeumque et rubrae cornua cristae,
> ensem quem Dauno ignipotens deus ipse parenti
> fecerat et Stygia candentem tinxerat unda.
> exin quae mediis ingenti adnixa columnae
> aedibus astabat, validam vi corripit hastam,
> Actoris Aurunci spolium, quassatque trementem
> vociferans . . .[10]

[Then he places on his shoulders his corslet stiff with gold and pale
orichalc. At the same time he ably adjusts his sword and shield, and his
red-plumed helmet. The sword (was that) which the god of fire had made
for his father Daunus and had dipped white-hot in the river Styx. Then
he vigorously seized a strong lance which stood propped against a huge
column in the middle of the palace—it was spoil from Auruncan Actor.
He shook the quivering shaft.]

It is to be remarked that the passage seems to have given a slight unease
even to Servius, who comments on line 88, 'non armatur hac loco, sed
explorat, utrum arma apte et congrue ejus membris inhoereant'. [In this
passage he is not armed, but seeks to discover whether the arms fit his limbs
suitably and conveniently.] Servius shows no knowledge of the topos and
consequently attempts to rationalise the oddity of Turnus apparently
putting on his armour a day too early. J. W. Mackail felt the same difficulty
fifteen hundred years later.[11] Traditional and especially oral poetry,
necessarily formulaic, often gives rise to such inconsistencies.

Virgil was of course constantly and deeply studied throughout the
Middle Ages, and no doubt this passage had its influence and effect, but it
seems hardly likely that it itself was the source of such frequent use as will
be shown to occur. No doubt there are other instances of the topos in
Classical Latin, but we may also posit a general oral tradition.

V

This general oral tradition may perhaps be seen to exist in the early period
of Irish literature. The *Táin Bó Cúalnge* is very early, though its history and

the manuscript tradition are exceedingly complex.[12] It may go back as far as the second century BC though perhaps first written down in the seventh century AD, and then subsequently rehandled after the normal manner of traditional literature. The most recent edition is of the twelfth-century Leinster MS, representing the second recension, said to be more literary than the first, though still extraordinarily grotesque. In the passage concerned, regrettably too long to quote,[13] the charioteer first arms himself, then (as in *Iliad*, XI, XVI and XIX) harnesses the horses to the chariot—perhaps once part of the topos. Then Cú Chulainn arms himself. The mixture of militaristic fantasy and hyperbole is characteristic of Old Irish and extraordinarily different from other examples in this chapter, which makes the fundamental similarity all the more striking.

The topos is followed by another set piece, even more grotesque, Cú Chulainn's 'first distortion'. These passages each have the effect of marking out the significant hero and by hyperbole emphasising his importance.

The latest example of arming the hero in Irish that I happen to have come across is in the probably seventeenth-century tale of decidedly literary flavour entitled in English *The Pursuit of Gruaidh Ghriansholus*,[14] which relates exploits attributed to Cú Chulainn. The author may have known Classical Greek tales, according to the editor, as well as traditional Irish tales, and we see here that characteristic intermingling of written and oral elements that marks 'traditional' literature (and perhaps, did we but realise it, even some 'Neoclassical' and 'modern' literature).

Between these two points in Irish literature, however, comes an extensive literature, and for information here, since I do not read Irish, I follow the learned work of Alan Bruford,[15] who has placed in his debt students of literature beyond his specific subject. Bruford's special interest lies in the relationship between oral tales presumed to be of great antiquity in Ireland (but which can be known only in quite recently collected versions), and the medieval Irish romances of a literary kind which date from around the late fifteenth to the late seventeenth century. The relationship is complex and does not concern us here, though we note again the interplay, and two-way influence, between oral and written work. Since Bruford approaches the subject from the folk-tale he refers to the topos of the arming of the hero as 'the arming run', which establishes its highly formulaic nature.

According to Bruford 'the arming run is the most celebrated run of all in Ireland. . . . Folk versions may expand the framework of literary arming runs in two ways: by adding extra articles of clothing or weapons (boots, breeches, knife), and by adding clauses—rather than adjectives—describing the history and properties of the article and how it was put on.'[16] The literary Romantic tales of the fifteenth century retain the 'basic equipment of warriors in Old Irish tales—a pair of javelins, sword and shield, and sometimes a helmet'.[17] There may or may not be a tunic or breastplate mentioned, or other weapons. In late literary or in oral versions there may be exchange of formulae between 'runs', and even the inclusion of actual nonsense. 'Any verbiage will do to fill out a run.'[18] Even in the literary tales, however, Bruford detects something of the same tendency. In his valuable chapter on runs, where he distinguishes between folk runs and literary runs, he concludes that at least they have in common that they were intended for oral delivery. 'The big set pieces are rhetorical purple passages, designed to sweep away the hearer in a sonorous wash of verbiage whose actual meaning was of little importance. They could well have been the high points of the story if read by a good performer, though the silent reader is likely to skip them.'[19] (Here is one of the origins of the differences between traditional, whether oral or written, and 'Neoclassical' literature: that is, the ultimately oral origin of traditional literature, to be contrasted with the more fixed nature of 'Neoclassical' literature, as determined both by its own theory and the dominance of its origin in print, and which leads to an attempted close correspondence between 'word' and 'thing'.) It is important to recognise Bruford's thesis that in many cases his 'oral' examples derive from earlier 'literary' ones, though both are traditional. There are complex processes at work of both decay of meaning and rationalisation.

VI

As might be expected, the topos appears in both *Beowulf* and *Le Chanson de Roland*, the two major 'epics' (if rightly so called) of medieval European vernacular literature. Since *Beowulf* was not known in Middle English literature we can regrettably do no more than notice the passage (ll. 1441–64), substantial as it is.[20] It is admirably assimilated to the style and structure of the poem. First we have the corslet (*here-byrne*) characteristically described, then the *hwita helm*, again adorned, and then the *hæft-mece, Hrunting nama*. The poet selects the essentials and weaves around them potent words that evoke the notes of ancient power and splendour. The passage occurs just before Beowulf's fight with Grendel's mother and thus shows that for the poet this is the key battle of the poem, undertaken voluntarily and solemnly by the hero, no mere response to an attack, as was his encounter, however heroic, with Grendel when Grendel came to the hall. But it has been pointed out to me that Beowulf's taking off his armour in the hall, when he goes to bed on the evening of Grendel's attack, is as it were an inversion of the topos. Beowulf takes off corslet and helm, neither qualified by so much as an adjective, and his *hyrsted sweord*, *irena cyst*, and gives them to a servant (ll. 671–4). This inversion of the topos is of great originality and power, of a kind hard to describe. Perhaps it is designed to show Beowulf's fundamental lack of aggressiveness, in that he is attacked as a defenceless sleeping man before moving to the offensive himself— though he knows very well how to be heroic when need be, and is then heroically armed. Such would fit in well with the poet's Christian yet heroic temper.

Le Chanson de Roland makes a surprisingly less specific use of the topos. It occurs, probably, in the *laisses* 55, 79, 136, 217, 231 (ed. F. Whitehead, Oxford, 1942), but it is used indiscriminately for pagan and Christian and certainly does not mark the hero. The passages are very brief with only minimal formulaic usages.

The topos is much more obvious in such poems as *Le Couronnement Louis* (ll. 405–13). It has been pointed out that it occurs with the same vocabulary and in the same order of corslet, helmet, sword, mounting a horse, taking a shield, then another sword, and a standard, as in many other *chansons de geste*.[21]

Even more striking than the topos in the *chansons de geste* is the use made of it by Chrétien in *Erec et Enide*. The first occasion is early in the poem when Erec is to defend the hawk on behalf of Enid, and is betrothed to her. Already armour has been mentioned by his host, Enid's father, in the conversation of the previous night. At dawn Erec, who has slept little, arises and hears mass. He is impatient for the battle, calls for his armour; Enid herself arms him:

> Les armes quiert et l'an li baille;
> la pucele meïsmes l'arme;
> n'i ot fet charaie ne charme,
> lace li les chauces de fer
> et queust a corroie de cer;
> hauberc li vest de boene maille
> et se li lace la vantaille;
> le hiaume brun li met el chief,
> molt l'arme bien de chief an chief.
> Au costé l'espee li ceint.
> Puis comande qu'an li amaint
> son cheval, et l'an li amainne;
> sus et sailliz de terre plainne.
> La pucele aporte l'escu

        et la lance qui roide fu;
        l'escu li baille, et il le prant,
        par la guige a son col le pant;
        la lance li ra el poing mise,
        cil l'a devers l'arestuel prise.[22]

[Erec was eager for the battle, so he asks for arms and they are given to him. The maiden herself puts on his arms (though she casts no spell or charm), laces on his iron greaves, and makes them fast with thongs of deer-hide. She puts on his corslet with its strong meshes, and laces on his ventail. The gleaming helmet she sets upon his head, and thus arms him well from tip to toe. At his side she fastens his sword, and then orders his horse to be brought, which is done. Up he jumped clear of the ground. The damsel then brings the shield and the strong lance; she hands him the shield and he takes it and hangs it about his neck by the strop. She has placed the lance in his hand and he has grasped it by the butt.][23]

Here we have the order: greaves, corslet, helmet, sword, horse, shield, spear, which is slightly different from that in the *Iliad*, but is clearly required by practical necessity. Chrétien uses the topos, but has brought it back into line with the facts of the case. Chrétien is both realistic and traditional. Erec is successful in his battle and marries Enid, to their mutual joy. That his beloved should arm the hero is an important contextual addition, giving the topos an emotional power and direction very characteristic of Chrétien's genius.

The second arming is even more elaborate and is also a significant marker. It occurs soon after Erec has overheard Enid bewailing the reproaches he has incurred for his uxoriousness. He orders her to dress in her finest robes, and she does so, lamenting. Then Erec summons a squire, not Enid, to arm him, and the elaborations underscore the ominous yet splendid style of the occasion, as music might sound a rich foreboding bass figure (ll. 2620–60). It is somewhat too long to quote, though its variations, to properly constituted minds, ensure that it is not to be skipped. The arms are brought and laid upon a Limoges carpet, where Erec also sits upon the image of a leopard which is portrayed on the carpet. Then greaves are laced, corslet (not at all rusty), helmet, sword (which he girds on himself); and then he calls for his horse. The order of arming is the same, notwithstanding the rich elaborations.

The formality of the topos, as opposed to its realism, is here noticeable in that neither shield nor lance is mentioned and must be taken for granted, because Erec certainly has them when he is soon attacked by three robber knights. Yet realism is perhaps not quite abandoned, if we reflect that after this arming Erec has elaborate conversations in the courtyard with his father and other persons, during which scene to have had him holding his shield and certainly a spear would have been otiose. That he has been formally armed guarantees that we feel, when the occasion soon after arises, that he has the necessary weapons.

Chrétien does not seem to make use of the arming topos in his other poems. If *Erec et Enide* is a relatively early work, as is usually supposed, he may have felt he had used the topos enough, or that it was too crude; but he used it well in this poem.

If a conjecture that I have made elsewhere has any substance, Chaucer may have known Chrétien's work, which was certainly available in England in the fourteenth and presumably thirteenth centuries.[24] The French and Anglo-Norman works referred to were certainly known in England, though it is interesting that the thirteenth-century English *King Horn*, for example, does not take over the arming topos. There was however another literary channel which leads directly into English, to which we now turn.

VII

It would be wrong to distinguish this channel clearly from that of the works discussed in the previous section, for this other channel is the Arthurian series emanating from the *Historia Regum Britanniae* of Geoffrey of Monmouth, which was certainly known to Chrétien, and which could easily have at least encouraged his own use of the arming topos.

In Book ix Arthur succeeds to the kingdom and is attacked by the Saxons, who after a setback return with renewed strength. The Archbishop addresses the army who then, cheered by this, all rush to arm themselves. There is a detailed description of the arming of Arthur, of a kind now familiar to the reader:

Ipse vero Arthurus, lorica tanto rege condigna, indutus, auream galeam simulacro draconis insculptam capiti adaptavit. Umeris quoque suis clipeum, vocabulo Prydwen, imposuit, in quo imago sanctae Mariae, Dei genitricis, inerat picta, quae ipsum in memoriam ipsius saepissime revocabat. Accinctus etiam Caliburno, gladio optimo, in insula Aval(l)onis fabricato, lancea dexteram suam decorat, quae Ron nomine vocabatur: haec erat ardua lataque lancea, cladibus apta.[25]

[Arthur himself, however, having put on a corslet worthy of such a king, drew upon his head a golden helmet carved into the likeness of a dragon. Also he placed on his shoulders the shield, Prydwen by name, inside which the image of Mary, mother of God, was painted, which very often recalled the memory of her to him. He was also girt with Caliburn, best of swords, made in the vale of Avalon; and the lance which was called Ron adorned his right hand. It was a tall, thick lance, well suited to slaughter.]

The greaves have got lost again; corslet, helm, shield (called Prydwen), sword (Caliburn), and spear (Ron) are the usual significant items, with the French order of accepting shield and sword. Hammer notes Geoffrey's debt to Virgil's account of the arming of Turnus (part of a very extensive verbal borrowing by Geoffrey from Virgil and other classical Latin authors), but the names of the weapons may suggest that Geoffrey knew other armings, in Welsh. The names may be a clue to the vexed question of Geoffrey's sources—to what extent they were Welsh, to what extent oral—which cannot be followed here. The topos once again marks the hero, and marks a very significant stage of his career. It seems not to be used by Geoffrey elsewhere. He seems to have given it a literary flavour, whatever his oral sources. He is interested in adorning his narrative, but not much interested in armour.

Geoffrey seems also to have invented the detail of the picture of the Virgin inside the shield, which is in the characteristic manner of local adornment of the given basic structure of a topos. Unlike most of the description it may be a rare example of Geoffrey borrowing from contemporary practice. If he did so he perhaps changed a secular and coarse chivalric joke to a pious and serious use. Joan M. Ferrante notes that the so-called first troubadour, Count William IX of Aquitaine (1071–1127), is reported by William of Malmesbury as having the picture of someone else's wife (whom he had seduced after rejecting his own wife) painted on his shield so that he could carry her in battle as she carried him in bed. Ferrante also notes that in the twelfth-century *Roman de Thèbes* Ethiocles, one of the heroes, rides a horse given him by one of his mistresses, whose legs he has painted on his shield as a joke (l. 6273).[26]

We look forward now to those texts which were based on Geoffrey. The literal translation from the Welsh text in Jesus College, Oxford, MS 61 printed by Griscom[27] shows the topos taken back into Welsh in a fairly close version. Since the names given in the Welsh text are fuller, it may be that the translator knew some general Welsh tradition that Geoffrey might himself have drawn upon.

Wace seems to have translated the *Historia* with an interesting independence, though lack of space forbids quotation. We may note immediately that he reveals acquaintance with the topos from sources other than Geoffrey's *Historia*, and since he finished *Le Roman de Brut* in 1155 these must be earlier than Chrétien. Wace's influence on Chrétien is held to be doubtful by his editor,[28] so that it is likely that both draw on a common tradition. Wace's order of arming is slightly different. The greaves come back and are put on first, then corslet, sword, helmet, horse, shield, lance. The inversion of sequence between sword and helmet recalls the *Iliad*. There seems no special reason for it. Otherwise, Wace's adornments are of the usual kind. He takes 25 lines, so he does not spread out unduly. His rapid narrative has had no time for the good Archbishop's allocution reported by Geoffrey, so that the arming stands out a little more vividly as a marker.

It is even more vivid when we at last come to English with the translation in its turn of Wace by Laȝamon. Here is a different world, wilder and stranger; and the topos looks different.[29]

> Þa he hafde al iset and al hit isemed,
> þa dude he on his burne ibroide of stele,
> þe makede on aluisc smið mid aðelen his crafte;
> he wes ihaten Wygar, þe Witeȝe wurhte.
> His sconken he helede mid hosen of stele.
> Calibeorne his sweord he sweinde bi his side;
> hit wes iworht in Aualun mid wiȝelefulle craften.
> Halm he set on hafde, hæh of stele;
> þeron wes moni ȝim-ston, al mid golde bigon;
> he was Vðeres þas aðelen kinges;
> he wes ihaten Goswhit, ælchen oðere vnlic.
> He heng an his sweore ænne sceld deore;
> his nome wes on Bruttisc Pridwen ihaten;
> þer wes innen igrauen mid rede golde stauen
> an onlicnes deore of Drihtenes moder.
> His spere he nom an honde, þa Ron wes ihaten.
> Þa he hafden al his iweden, þa leop he on his steden.
>
> (ll. 2828–44)

[When he had arranged all, and everything was satisfactory, then he put on his corslet of woven steel, which a smith with magical powers made by his noble skill; it was called Wygar, which Widia made. He covered his legs with steel stockings. Caliborn his sword he hung by his side; it was made in Avalon with magic skills. His tall helmet of steel he set on his head: there were many jewels on it, and it was encircled with gold. It was the noble king Uther's; it was called Goosewhite, and was unlike any other helmet. He hung a precious shield around his neck: in British it was called Pridwen. On the inside was engraved with red-gold markings a precious likeness of God's Mother. He took his spear, which was called Ron, in hand. When he had all his equipment then he leaped on to his horse.]

The order has been changed: corslet, greaves (*hosen of stele*), sword, helmet, shield, spear, horse. What strikes one immediately is that Laʒamon cares little or nothing for armour, and pays little attention to the topos. This seems a strange omission, since Laʒamon normally expands Wace by choosing topics from Old English poetry, namely journeys, arrivals and feasts.[30] Why should he not use the arming topos? The reason may partly be that it is of the essence of the medieval topos that it should normally be used only once, in a single work, in order to emphasise the role of the dominant hero and his first significant battle. Laʒamon liked to use topoi several times. But the omission remains effectively unexplained.

We may briefly note that the topos appears in medieval German at least once, and other instances may well be known to the learned. Gottfried von Strassburg has a most elaborate account of the arming of Tristan before the battle with Morold. The basic order is greaves, corslet, sword, helmet, shield, horse, though the passage is remarkable for the elaboration with which they are described the addition of spurs and tabard, presumably correctly after the greaves and corslet, and for the tone of the whole.[31]

VIII

The lines established by Geoffrey and the French texts generally are continued in English in the fourteenth century in the two main streams of alliterative poetry and rhymed romance (especially tail-rhyme romance). The alliterative tradition may be taken first, as somewhat more closely associated with the Arthurian series initiated by Geoffrey, and less near to Chaucer. Without attempting to list occurrences we may select the striking example found in the alliterative *Morte Arthure*, probably to be dated roughly in the second half of the fourteenth century. As is usual (but not inevitable) the arming topos occurs early on to mark and establish the hero.[32] (The topos does not occur in the corresponding passage in Geoffrey or Wace because they have already had the arming in the earlier episode.)

Arthur has dreamed his first dream and now proceeds to Mont St Michel to accomplish the heroic deed which establishes him in the poem, the killing of the giant. He orders Sir Cayos and Sir Bedbere to be armed after evensong, then proceeds to arm himself.

The editor considers this arming to be an example of descriptions of dress, which may have influenced it, but the framework and placing show that it is specifically the arming topos. The elaborations, it can now be easily recognised, are of a kind very familiar from the *Iliad* onwards. The order is corslet (elaborated by mention of the preliminary jacket and tunic and the subsequent surcoat of Jerodyne), helmet (with crest and additions), gloves, shield, sword, horse—in other words, the usual, or, as we may even say, the correct order. The gloves and other garments are unusual additions, but not out of the way. The greaves, as so often, have been lost. There is nothing in this passage that is strange to either courtly or 'heroic' poetry, and it can hardly be used, in the way that the editor suggests, to determine the level of audience or the turn of the author's mind, except to establish both in the broad category of 'traditional'.

The other notable passage in alliterative verse is the arming of Sir Gawain in *Sir Gawain and the Green Knight*, which is so well known and easily available that I shall not quote it here.[33]

The passage is placed, as we should expect, to mark the hero and his beginning on the great adventure. But it is better integrated into the narrative than is usual, for before Gawain comes to his horse he hears mass and takes leave of the king and his courtly companions. The order is elaborated. Gawain is dressed in the necessary preliminary clothing (as is Arthur in the *Morte Arthure*) but then proceeds to the steel shoes and greaves (elaborated with realistic detail of knee pieces and cuisses), corslet (with more detail), gloves, surcoat, spurs and sword. Then, as remarked, he must hear mass and take leave before he is presented with his horse, which is almost as elaborately attired as himself. The poet has of course not forgotten helmet and shield, or omitted them as Chrétien omitted shield and spear in the second arming of Erec. The helmet, very practically, is not put on until he has finished leave-taking. The shield, now so famous in academic discourse, is offered to him quite realistically after he has mounted, and the separation of the shield from the rest of the armour allows the poet to elaborate the shield's description—an extreme case of the normal licence to adorn exercised from Homer onward. No other arming that I know has so elaborate a description of the sheild. The *Gawain*-poet has presumably developed it from Geoffrey's detail of the picture of the Virgin on the inside of Arthur's shield, which the *Gawain*-poet also takes over. Finally, Gawain takes his lance (l. 667) and gallops vigorously away, as he and the court believe, to his doom. Without losing the formality of the topos the poet has wonderfully well integrated it with his narrative, to the gain of both realism and splendour. Yet it remains the local 'marker' topos it has been since the *Iliad*. The shield is only briefly mentioned later in a purely practical way. The pentangle and the picture of the Virgin are never mentioned again. They are the local adornments of the given basic structure of the topos, emblematic of Gawain's goodness, as the poet makes clear, but are in no way incorporated into the general narrative with an organic, thematic or allegorical function. The absence of a second formal arming is in no way significant. It would distort and overload the poem without adding anything useful. The shield, incidentally, was going out of practical use in the second half of the fourteenth century.[34] The *Gawain*-poet is deeply traditional.

Nothing better illustrates the difference of attitudes between those two contemporaries of supreme genius, the *Gawain*-poet and Chaucer, than their respective treatments of the arming topos. One might say of the *Gawain*-poet that he finally naturalises the literary topos, while Chaucer, naturalistic, or realistic in a quite opposite way, effectively kills it. The *Gawain*-poet was as old-fashioned in his day as Shakespeare was in his; in contrast to both, Chaucer holds 'with the newe world the space'.[35]

As already noted, *King Horn*, amongst the earliest of the vernacular English rhyming romances, does not take over the arming topos from his Anglo-Norman source. The vernacular romances of the fourteenth century, deriving from the Midlands and south-east England, including the tail-rhyme romances, at least reach out to the topos. They may be represented by the romances in the Auchinleck Manuscript, usually dated about 1340, which it has been argued that Chaucer knew.[36] That he knew this particular manuscript may not be quite certain, but what is beyond doubt is that he knew very well similar versions of such romances as it contains, and initially derived from them not the least effective part of his style. His parody of them is in part the witness of his deep and early engagement, but there is other evidence also.[37]

The Auchinleck MS offers a formal arming in the romance of *Sir Beues of Hamtoun* (ll. 969–88), which is adapted from the French.[38] Here it follows the dubbing of hero as knight, and therefore presumably emphasises his prowess, but it also immediately precedes the battle, which is the right place. Possibly the dubbing affects the order, which is shield, sword called Morgelay, then gonfanoun (brought by his lady Josian). Beues then puts on his 'actoun', followed by corslet and horse named Arundel. No helmet is mentioned. It is on the whole a feeble performance. The Manchester MS, which Kölbing prints beneath Auchinleck, is more 'correct', having habergeoun, corslet, helmet, sword, horse, in that order (ll. 739–52), but is not much more impressive. The translators have hardly got hold of the formal topos, and Chaucer would not have learned much about it from *Beues*.

The Auchinleck *Guy of Warwick* does rather better, and may be quoted.[39]

> He oxed his armes hastiliche,
> And men es him brouȝt sikerliche.
> Hosen of iren he haþ on drawe,
> Non better nar bi þo dawe.
> In a strong hauberk he gan him schrede,
> Who so it wered, þe ded no þurt him drede.
> An helme he haþ on him don:
> Better no wered neuer kniȝt non;
> The sercle of gold þer-on was wrouȝt,
> For a half a cite no worþ it bouȝt:
> So mani stones þer-in were,
> þat were of vertu swiþe dere.
> Seþþe he gert him wiþ a brond
> þat was y-made in eluene lond.
> His scheld about his nek he tok,
> On hors he lepe wiþ-outen stirop,
> On hond he nam a spere kerueinde,
> Out of þe cite he was rideinde.
>
> (ll. 3849–66)

This is much better. The presence of the greaves as usual for some reason suggests that the writer has a better grasp on both the realistic and the formalistic elements. Here we have greaves, corslet, helmet, sword, shield, horse, spear, with admirable vigour and a small amount of adornment, and in the right place, just before a major battle with the Saracens. The other parallels between *The Tale of Sir Thopas* and *Sir Guy* that Loomis presents in *Sources and Analogues* are not of actual armings, and the diction is so commonplace that it must be risky to suppose borrowing of any specific kind on Chaucer's part. Loomis also quotes an arming topos from *Libeaus Desconus* from British Library MS Cotton Caligula A. II.[40] Three others are quoted by Irving Linn from the fifteenth-century version of the fourteenth-century English rhyming romance, *Otuel and Roland*.[41] They all follow the usual general pattern, with individual (but still highly typical) adornments: aketoun, habergeon (Clarel only), corslet, shield, sword, helmet, saddle (Roland only), spear, horse, spurs. Different characters bring various parts of the armour to the various heroes, and it is clear that this is as usual a commonplace device for enriching but also individualising the use of the topos to make some point about the hero's relationships.

Another instance where the topos is well handled (doubtless thanks chiefly to a French original) is *Octavian*, where Clement arms his foster-son (who like Sir Thopas is to encounter a giant) so sorrowfully with rusty old armour: 'hacton', corslet, shield, spear, sword. Perhaps the disorder, with sword last, expresses the unfamiliarity of armour to Clement, but it is more likely to be due merely to the exigencies of the rhyme-scheme.[42]

These are all poetic uses of a poetic topos, but it will be well to remind ourselves just before turning at last to Chaucer that an actual everyday reality was not far beneath the topos. We have a genuine practical fifteenth-century set of instructions how to arm a man.[43] This work concerns complete plate-armour, which was only beginning to be used late in the fourteenth century, and there are two swords. The order is usual, except for the second sword, and there are practical additions that few poets (except in part the *Gawain*-poet) concerned themselves with, such as vambras and serebras; but even so the list is not complete, for there are, for example, no spurs. There is also no shield.

It will not do, then, when we come to Chaucer, to argue that the omission of spurs is part of the absurdity of the description.[44] Even at the risk of anti-climax that description need not be quoted here, since every likely reader of this essay no doubt has a copy of Chaucer at his 'beddes heed' and in every room.

The arming of Sir Thopas contains a very usual selection of usual elements, with the quite reasonable and realistic addition of breeches and shirt beneath. Even the coat-armour and bridle can be found elsewhere. The greaves are present, but they indeed are in a wrong and silly place. What is ridiculous is the presentation of the details with certain modifications, exaggerations and oddities such as, possibly, the white surcoat; certainly the shield of *gold*, so soft and heavy; the leathern, not steel, greaves; the sword-sheath of ivory yet no sword mentioned; the helmet of the cheap soft metal, latten; the shining bridle; the mild horse. The placing and pomposity of the arming, the prelude of the wine (of which I have noticed no precedent), Sir Thopas's swearing on ale and bread, are all splendidly absurd, and even more so when read against the long tradition of solemn splendour. Though the English verse romances are certainly mocked in the arming of Sir Thopas, it seems hardly likely that the topos would have made such an impression on Chaucer if he had not known it elsewhere in European literature, for it is not so exceptionally frequent in the English romances themselves. Chaucer was mocking, no doubt, the

Flemish bourgeoisie, and aligning himself with courtly sneers at lower classes. But he was also mocking, it would seem, the whole ancient formal aggrandisement of fighting, Arthurian bravery and bravado, 'and al that longeth to that art'. In *The Knight's Tale* Chaucer does not mock chivalry, but it is notable that though he had in it some fine opportunities for the arming topos, one, especially good, when Palamon and Arcite arm each other before their fight in the grove (*CT*, I, 1649–52), there is nowhere the least hint of the traditional formulae. When Chaucer describes Troilus in his armour as a knight, he shows him *returning* from battle, with much damage to his armour (*TC*, II, 624–44). There is no arming topos attached to Troilus. Yet, as we see from *The Tale of Sir Thopas*, Chaucer knows the topos perfectly well. Both his treatment of it and his refusal to use it elsewhere are significant. What Chaucer finds moving is suffering, not aggression. Even the Knight in *The Canterbury Tales*, hardbitten fighting-man that he is, and is praised for so being, is shown in his habergeon, without armour, seeking forgiveness for sin.

IX

The topos soon disappeared in English literature. Chaucer and the *Gawain*-poet have been contrasted. Chaucer as usual is the more modern. Use of the topos gives us some insight into the character of an author. Recognition that a description of arming is a topos guides us to a correct understanding of its literary function and meaning. As already noted above, the topos continues in folk literature in Ireland and Yugoslavia until the twentieth century. In England, no major author uses it seriously, to my knowledge, after Chaucer—nor any minor author either, apart from scribes and translators. Here it is interesting to note Malory. The critical cliché about Malory is that he is 'nostalgic'. Such a view should have been long dispelled by Vinaver's demonstration of Malory's forward-looking rationalisation of the excessive complexities of the French cyclic romances. Malory rationalises the arming topos almost to the point of extinction. When he is turning into prose the alliterative *Morte Arthure* and comes to the arming topos he practically demolishes it, simply referring to three items that Arthur took for his fight with the giant—gesseraunt (or corslet), bacinet (helmet) and shield. No sword is mentioned, no formality of diction is used. Even this residuum is reduced by Caxton, who tells us simply that Arthur 'armed hym at alle poyntes and took his hors and his sheld'.[45] Shakespeare does not appear to use the topos, though there is probably an echo of it when Cleopatra attempts to arm Antony. This will be Antony's first battle in the play and thus the arming comes in the 'right' place. Although Antony is at first successful in the battle he ultimately fails, and it is significant that in helping him to arm, Cleopatra is conspicuously inept. There is a light-hearted burlesque of arming in *The Rape of the Lock*, I, 121–48 ('Now awful beauty puts on all its arms'), and an even more light-hearted inversion of the topos by W. S. Gilbert with Arac's song in *Princess Ida*, Act III, where the greaves as so often give difficulty: 'These things I treat the same/(I quite forget their name)/They turn one's legs/To cribbage pegs/Their aid I thus disclaim.'[46]

Yet one final piquant use remains to be noted. In Ariosto's *Orlando Furioso*, that immensely long, half-mocking, half-self-indulgent romance, coming towards the very end of the whole tradition of romance, there are surely hundreds of armed encounters between outstanding heroes. In not one case is there a formal arming, until the very end, almost the last page (quite the 'wrong' place), when Ruggiero, who is the hero Ariosto most wants to exalt (despite the name of the poem), comes to his greatest and final battle. Then his famous armour is brought that was won from the realms of Tartarus; Orlando puts on Ruggiero's spurs; Charlemagne girds on his sword; Bradamante (his newly-wedded wife) and his sister Marfisa bring the corslet, with the rest of the harness; and that famous English duke with the well-known English name of Astolfo brings the horse. Ogier the Dane holds the spear for him.[47] The order is different, but the passage seems as serious as anything in the poem can be. It is strange to find so archaic a topos in so sophisticated a poem; its presence illustrates that deep ambivalence of Ariosto towards the subject-matter and manner of romance, ostensibly mocking it in order to indulge it, which was no doubt the reason for the enormous popularity of the *Orlando Furioso* in Europe in the sixteenth century. Ariosto pretends to be more modern than he is—surely an infallible recipe for a best-seller. For once, Chaucer seems less ambivalent, sharper, less sentimental.

Notes

Notes to Chapter One: The Archaic and the Modern

1. Derek Brewer (ed.), *Chaucer: the Critical Heritage* (London, 1978) vol. I, Introduction.
2. For example, Frank Kermode, *Romantic Image* (London, 1957) ch. 8.
3. J. R. Goody, *The Domestication of the Savage Mind* (Cambridge, 1977) p. 148. Professor Goody considers the debate extensively and offers some modifications of the dichotomy, together with a useful bibliography.
4. A. MacFarlane, *Witchcraft in Tudor and Stuart England* (London, 1970).
5. Cf. Ernest Gellner, 'The Savage and the Modern Mind', in Robin Horton and Ruth Finnegan (eds), *Modes of Thought* (London, 1973) pp. 162–81.
6. Cf. ibid. and E. Neumann, *The Origins and History of Consciousness*, trans. R. F. C. Hull, Bollingen Series, no. XLII (Princeton, 1954; repr. New York, 1964) p. 368.
7. 'The World is too much with us'.
8. Gellner, 'Savage and Modern Mind', p. 178.
9. Ibid.
10. Samuel Johnson, 'Preface to Shakespeare' (1765).
11. Derek Brewer, 'The Nature of Romance', *Poetica* (Tokyo) 9 (1978) 9–48, and *Symbolic Stories* (Cambridge, 1980).
12. See Goody, *Domestication of the Savage Mind*, for recent discussion and bibliography.
13. A. B. Lord, *The Singer of Tales*, Harvard Studies in Comparative Literature, no. 24 (Cambridge, Mass., 1960).
14. P. A. M. Clemoes, 'Action in Beowulf and Our Perception of It', in D. G. Calder (ed.), *Old English Poetry: Essays on Style* (Berkeley, 1979) pp. 147–68.
15. Mary Douglas, *Implicit Meanings* (London, 1975) p. xi.
16. Brewer (ed.), *Chaucer: the Critical Heritage*, vol. I, Introduction, and 'Some Observations on the Development of Literalism and Verbal Criticism', *Poetica* (Tokyo) 2 (1974) 71–95. See also Derek Brewer, *Chaucer: the Poet as Storyteller* (London, forthcoming).
17. Ruth Finnegan, 'Literacy versus Non-Literacy: the Great Divide', in Horton and Finnegan (eds), *Modes of Thought*, pp. 143–4.
18. Jill Mann, *Chaucer and Medieval Estates Satire* (Cambridge, 1973) p. 202 (my italics).
19. Chaucer seems not to have been very closely read for the *Oxford English*

Dictionary, which is strange, since Furnivall, for long the principal mover behind the *OED*, was also devoted to Chaucer. The eccentric and inconsistent method of dating Chaucer's poems in the *Middle English Dictionary* also obscures the novelty of his diction in poems other than *The Canterbury Tales*.

20. I make this and similar large-scale cultural speculations in my *Chaucer and his World* (London, 1978).

21. See *Chaucer and his World*.

Notes to Chapter Two: Love and Marriage in Chaucer's Poetry

1. As this does not seem to have been pointed out elsewhere I give the relevant references: *LGW*, 615 (Cleopatra); 729 (Thisbe); 1179 (Dido); 1559–60 (Hypsipyle); 1636 (Medea); 1686 (Lucretia); 2152 (Ariadne); 2259 (Philomela); 2465–6 (Phyllis); 2587–8 (Hypermnestra).

2. J. W. H. Atkins, *English Literary Criticism: the Medieval Phase* (Cambridge, 1943) also notes the teaching of the distinction.

3. Cf. Boccaccio, *De Genealogia Deorum*, book III, ch. 22.

4. It is liable to occur with any author who starts with a plot as his source of inspiration. Even Shakespeare is not free from this kind of defect. Bassanio's *actions* in seeking to marry Portia, for example, are those of a cynical fortune-hunter. But his *character* (which is of more importance) is that of a noble and virtuous gentleman.

Notes to Chapter Three: Chaucer's *Complaint of Mars*

1. Poetica astronomica, II, 42, in T. Munckerus (ed.), *Mythographi Latini* (Amsterdam, 1681).

2. F. N. Robinson (ed.), *The Works of Geoffrey Chaucer* (Boston, Mass., 1933).

Notes to Chapter Four: The Ideal of Feminine Beauty

1. In the Classical period formal description was employed first in legal and practical connections, and then in satire and especially history and biography, though there are also a few traces in poetry. See G. Misener, 'Iconistic Portraits', *Classical Philology*, 19 (1924) 97–123; and E. C. Evans, 'Descriptions of Personal Appearance in Roman History and Biography', *Harvard Studies in Classical Philology*, 46 (1935) 43–84, and 'The Study of Physiognomy in the Second Century AD', *Transactions of the American Philological Association*, 72 (1941) 96–108. As in the earlier period, description in the Middle Ages was intimately related both to rhetorical teaching, as will be shown, and to the science of physiognomy. The presence of a certain 'physiognomico-moral' basis, if I may be permitted such an expression, in descriptions should be remembered, though it is not a simple matter. I hope to treat it in a later article.

2. See F. Meister (ed.), *De Excidio* (Teubner, 1873) pp. 14, 16, 17.

3. N. E. Griffin, 'Chaucer's Portrait of Criseyde', *Journal of English and*

Germanic Philology, 20 (1921) 39–46, shows that joined eyebrows were regarded as a mark of beauty by the Greeks, but not by medieval men. To some medieval physiognomers, moreover, joined eyebrows 'significant levem et subtilem et studiosum in omnibus operibus suis' (Albertus Magnus, *De Animalibus*, ed. H. Stadler (Münster, 1916–20) vol. I, pp. 2, 3, 138).

4. That is, unless we count the descriptive elements found in *Canticum Canticorum*, IV. Perhaps the favourite comparisons in medieval writers of the neck to a tower, and the references to the sweetness of the mouth, are to be attributed to this source, but not the formal elements of the medieval descriptions.

5. *Elegies*, vol. I, p. 93 ff., quoted by E. Faral, *Les Arts poétiques du XIIe et du XIIIe siècle* (Paris, 1924) p. 80. That Maximian was well known and admired in the Middle Ages needs no emphasis. Faral's statement that the first formal description known is that of a parasite by Sidonius Apollinaris needs modification.

6. *Ars Versificatoria*, I, 56, 57 (Faral, *Arts poétiques*, pp. 129–30).

7. This is also the characteristic female figure of medieval art, though space is lacking to pursue the comparison. Since this example occurs in the twelfth century it is not likely that this form reflects the ogival curves of late Gothic art, as suggested by Sir Kenneth Clark in 'The Naked and the Nude', *Cornhill Magazine*, 1000 (1954) 296–7.

8. *Poetria Nova*, ll. 544 ff. (Faral, *Arts poétiques*, pp. 214–15).

9. *The Nun's Priest's Tale*, *CT*, VII, 3347.

10. It may be noted that Geoffrey adds a description of the lady's clothes and especially of her jewels. Such descriptions do not come within the scope of this article, but they are frequently important in later authors, and are, of course, important for rendering the lady's quality. A green dress seems to be the favourite in the thirteenth and fourteenth centuries, though not in Geoffrey: thus Idleness (*Romaunt*, 573), Beatrice (*Purgatorio*, xxx, 32), Emilia (*Teseida*, XII, 65), Alceste (*LGW*, *Pro*. F, 214, G, 146), the ladies in Dunbar's *Goldyn Targe* (*Poems*, ed. W. M. Mackenzie, 1932) 60. With this often goes a garland of flowers for the head, a 'tressour' of gold or a coronet of gold, or a gold thread to bind the hair.

11. *Opera*, I, ed. J. S. Brewer, RS (1861) pp. 349–52.

12. Cf. F. J. E. Raby, *A History of Secular Latin Poetry in the Middle Ages* (Oxford, 1934) vol. II, pp. 237 ff., 244–5. Other references, especially to twelfth-century *comoedia*, are given by L. A. Haselmayer, 'The Portraits in Chaucer's Fabliaux', *Review of English Studies*, 14 (1938) 310–14. Miss Misener, 'Iconistic Portraits', refers to the *Carmina Burana*, 118, 4, etc.

13. *Le Roman de Troie*, ed. L. Constans, SATF (Paris, 1904–12) I, 5541 ff., 5119 ff., 5275 ff.; *Erec et Enide*, 411 ff.; *Cligès*, 1553 ff.

14. Good examples may be found in Guido delle Colonne, *Historia Destructionis Troiae*, ed. N. E. Griffin, Medieval Academy of America Publications, no. 26 (Cambridge, Mass., 1936) pp. 71–3, 85.

15. *Le Roman de la Rose*, ed. E. Langlois, SATF (Paris, 1914–24) 525 ff.; *Romaunt*, 539 ff.

16. It does occur in the conventional description of the lady in *De Venus la Deesse d'Amor*, ed. W. Foerster (Bonn, 1880) 158a, which is considered, though rather improbably, by Langlois to be a source for *Le Roman de la Rose*.

17. *Le Roman de la Rose*, 989 ff.; *Romaunt*, 1006 ff.

18. Sculpture sometimes shows Eve covered only by her hair, e.g. in twelfth-century Moissac. There is no note of any clothes in this passage of *Le Roman de la Rose*, and in the light of the line 'I saw Beute withouten any atyr', *PF*, 225 (which is not quite as Boccaccio describes her in *Teseida*, VII, 56), this is perhaps how she is thought of here.

19. *Le Roman de la Rose*, 832 ff.; *Romaunt*, 848 ff.

20. *Le Roman de la Rose*, 1173–4; *Romaunt*, 1196.

21. *Le Roman de la Rose*, 1191 ff.; *Romaunt*, 1211 ff.

22. *Le Roman de la Rose*, 1240–1; *Romaunt*, 1262–3, follows this.

23. G. L. Brook (ed.), *The Harley Lyrics* (Manchester, 1948). A. K. Moore, *The Secular Lyric in Middle English* (Lexington, Mass., 1951), also notes the convention.

24. Brook, *Harley Lyrics*, vii.

25. Brook, *Harley Lyrics*, ix.

26. *Le Roman de la Rose*, 1067–70; *Romaunt*, 1085 ff.

27. E. K. Chambers, 'Some Aspects of Medieval Lyric', in E. K. Chambers and F. Sidgwick (eds), *Early English Lyrics* (London, 1907) p. 275.

28. 'Blow Northerne Wynd' is in Brook, *Harley Lyrics*, xiv. Compare vii, 5, 31, 55 with xiv, 10, 14, 55. Other lines or ideas in vii shared with other lyrics (not an exhaustive list) are ll. 8, cf. v, 11 and vi, 6; 10, cf. v, 31–2; 16, cf. ix, 24; 17, cf. iv, 15; 18, cf. ix, 26; 43, cf. iv, 28. This is enough to show the conventional nature of the poems. The lady in vii is compared to the phoenix, as are the ladies in *The Book of the Duchess* and in *Pearl*—not to mention the lady in Shakespeare's *The Phoenix and the Turtle*.

29. Brook, *Harley Lyrics*, Introduction, p. 6.

30. Maximian of course desired his beauty. But he was regarded as obscene, and can hardly be classed as a love-poet.

31. J. L. Lowes makes a few observations in *Geoffrey Chaucer* (Oxford, 1934) pp. 176–8, supplemented by Haselmayer, 'Portraits in Chaucer's Fabliaux'. I have not seen W. Curry's *The Middle English Ideal of Personal Beauty* (Baltimore, 1916).

32. For references see F. N. Robinson, *Works*.

33. See *Oeuvres de Machaut*, ed. E. Hoepffner, SATF (Paris, 1908–21) I.

34. 'Behaingne', 300 ff.

35. A girl beloved of a priest in a thirteenth-century fabliau 'n'ot mie passez douze ans' (*Fabliaux et contes*, ed. E. Barbazan, rev. M. Méon (Paris, 1808) IV, 429, l. 72). But Machaut's is the earliest example of age mentioned by a courtly writer that I have noticed.

36. *The Book of the Duchess*, 855–8. The suggestion for this turn of phrase is probably to be found in *Le Roman de la Rose*, where Guillaume describes Fraunchyse (see above, p. 32).

37. 'Behaingne', 302–3.

38. Cf. L. A. Haselmayer, 'The Portraits in *Troilus and Criseyde*', *Philological Quarterly*, 17 (1938) 220–3, whose conclusions are different.

39. *Ars Versificatoria*, I, 38 ff. (Faral, *Arts poétiques*, p. 119).

40. *TC*, v, 806–19.

41. C. S. Lewis, *A Preface to Paradise Lost* (Oxford, 1942) pp. 53 ff.

42. E. T. Donaldson, 'Idiom of Popular Poetry in the *Miller's Tale*', in A. S. Downer (ed.), *English Institute Essays, 1950* (New York, 1951), repr. in *Speaking of Chaucer* (London, 1970), has shown that the vocabulary of *The Miller's Tale* has much in common with the Harley Lyrics, unlike Chaucer's other poems, and that he probably used 'an outworn poetical fashion' with a deliberately comic intent.

43. See *The Merchant's Tale*, *CT*, IV, 2202, and *The Manciple's Tale*, *CT*, IX, 211–20.

44. Thus the rhetorical joke of the whole of *The Nun's Priest's Tale*; cf. *The Rape of the Lock*, alongside Pope's Homer. Absolom in *The Miller's Tale* is equally a burlesque of the courtly hero, whom I hope to treat in a later article.

45. W. A. Turner, 'Chaucer's "Lusty Malyne" ', *N&Q*, 199 (1954) 232.

46. Cf. *Canzoniere*, 11, 12, 71, 127, 146, 213.

47. Lydgate, *Troy Book*, II, 3642 ff., 4736 ff.; Dunbar, *Goldyn Targe*; Wyatt, *Poems*, ed. K. Muir (London, 1949) pp. 67, 81; Sidney, *Astrophil and Stella*, 7, 9, 32; Spenser, *Amoretti*, 15.

48. Sonnets 20, 98, 106, 127, and, most important, 130. Editors have accumulated useful contemporary or near-contemporary parallels for the traditional attributes which Shakespeare rejects. As H. Rollins notes in the Variorum edition of the *Sonnets* (Philadelphia, 1944), the tradition of cataloguing the ugliness of one's mistress, found in Horace, but most noticeable in the fifteenth and sixteenth centuries, is not the tradition Shakespeare follows here. Shakespeare intends no disparagement of his mistress.

49. *Poems*, ed. H. J. C. Grierson (Oxford, 1912) I, 12.

50. It is curious to reflect that just as the medieval love-tradition derived so much from Ovid, so the new flippancy stems from such a poem as the *Amores*, II, 4: 'Quod amet mulieres, cuiuscunque formae sint.'

51. There are of course exceptions to this generalisation. It is perhaps most true of the fourteenth century, and, in that century, of Chaucer's heroines of romance.

Notes to Chapter Five: Children in Chaucer

1. If we look at adjectives qualifying persons, *dear* is used about 90 times to qualify the person the speaker loves, who is usually a lady; then it is used about 30 times of a social relationship, usually to a superior (lord, master, etc.); then it is used of the word 'brother', partly a family and partly a social word, about 30 times. Next, *dear* is used of a daughter 16 times, niece 12, mother (often the Mother of God) 10 times, wife 9, friend 9, sister 8, uncle 7, child(ren) 6, cousin 6, religious usages (only once of God) 5, father 3, son 3, husband 1. The trend clearly shows that Chaucer's interest is away from the masculine side of the family in terms of affectionate interest.

    If we consider what adjectives may be applied to the nouns, we find that a mother is *dear* 8 times, *maiden* (referring to the Virgin Mary) 2, *sweet* 2, *lief* 2, *blissful* 3. The following adjectives are applied once each and make a pleasant composite image: *free* (i.e. generous), *meek*, *kind*, *woeful*, *benign*, *blessed*, *verray* (i.e. true), *rich*, *gay*. A father shares of these epithets only *dear* 3 times, and *free*, *benign* and *woeful* once each. Parents were obviously much more widely separated than today. The adjectives which can qualify 'father' give a very different image; *old* 6, *first* (of Adam or God) 3, *wise* 3, *spiritual, fleshly, cruel* 2 each; and once each *ready, argus-eyed, hoary, stern, hard, wretched, . poor, jealous, false.*

2. See Derek Brewer, *Chaucer*, 3rd edn (London, 1973) p. 79.

Notes to Chapter Six: Class-Distinction in Chaucer

1. See, however, J. S. P. Tatlock, 'Interpreting Literature by History', *Speculum*, 12 (1937) 390–5; M. Schlauch, 'Chaucer's Doctrine of Kings and Tyrants', *Speculum*, 20 (1945) 135–6; M. Emslie, 'Codes of Love and Class Distinction', *Essays in Criticism*, 5 (1955) 1–17, with comments by Cecily Clark, Derek Brewer and M. Emslie, ibid., 5 (1955) 405–18.
2. Details concerning Chaucer's own life are taken from M. M. Crow and C. C. Olson, *Chaucer Life-Records* (Oxford, 1966).
3. See E. T. Donaldson, 'Idiom of Popular Poetry in the *Miller's Tale*', and ch. 4 above, 'The Ideal of Feminine Beauty'.
4. This point is made, in a more general context, by Sylvia L. Thrupp, in her valuable *The Merchant Class of Medieval London* (Chicago, 1948; repr. Ann Arbor, 1962) p. 302.
5. The author of *Pearl* treats the problem of degree in heaven. See Derek Brewer, 'Courtesy and the *Gawain*-Poet', in J. Lawlor (ed.), *Patterns of Love and Courtesy: Essays in Memory of C. S. Lewis* (London, 1966) p. 65.
6. Derek Brewer, *Chaucer*, 2nd edn (London, 1960) pp. 160 ff.
7. *The Parlement of Foulys*, ed. Derek Brewer (London, 1960) pp. 34 ff.
8. See P. Nykrog, *Les Fabliaux* (Copenhagen, 1957), who effectively disproves the widely accepted implication of J. Bédier, *Les Fabliaux* (Paris, 1893), that because of their coarseness they are essentially 'bourgeois'.
9. A useful and perceptive general account is given in A. C. Spearing (ed.), *The Franklin's Prologue and Tale* (Cambridge, 1966), Introduction. See also G. H. Gerould, *Chaucerian Essays* (Princeton, 1952) pp. 33–54.
10. Cf. R. Blenner-Hassett, 'Autobiographical Aspects of Chaucer's Franklin', *Speculum*, 28 (1953) 791–800, who, however, concentrates on the possible similarity of legal experience.
11. T. F. Tout, *Chapters in the Administrative History of Medieval England*, vol. iii (Manchester, 1928) pp. 201–2.
12. Ch. 2 above, 'Love and Marriage in Chaucer's Poetry'.
13. Chaucer thought it socially absurd to use words like *gent, hende, derne*, as Donaldson, 'Idiom of Popular Poetry', points out, while *wench, lemman, popelote, gnof* seem to be loaded with class-feeling.

Notes to Chapter Seven: *The Reeve's Tale* and the King's Hall

1. For a list of their appointments and activities see A. B. Emden, *A Biographical Register of the University of Cambridge* (Cambridge, 1963).
2. See Crow and Olson, *Chaucer Life-Records*, pp. 98, 106, 108–9.
3. See Derek Brewer, *Chaucer in his Time* (London, 1963) pp. 61–2, 179–80.
4. Ibid., pp. 141–4.

5. See W. W. Rouse Ball, *The King's Scholars and King's Hall* (Cambridge, 1917) p. 25.

6. Statutes in ibid., p. 68.

7. A. B. Emden, *A Biographical Register of the University of Oxford to AD 1500* (Oxford, 1959).

8. *Calendar of Close Rolls*, p. 408, quoted by C. E. Sayle, 'King's Hall Library', *Proceedings of the Cambridge Antiquarian Society*, 24, o.s., no. 72 (1923) 54–76.

9. John M. Manly and Edith Rickert (eds), *The Text of the Canterbury Tales* (Chicago, 1940) vol. I, p. 60.

10. Ibid., pp. 287–8.

11. Ibid., pp. 349–55.

12. Ibid., pp. 381–6.

13. G. Kane (ed.), *Piers Plowman: The A Version* (London, 1960), esp. pp. 143–9.

Notes to Chapter Eight: The Ages of Troilus, Criseyde and Pandarus

1. *Scriptores Rerum Mythicarum Latini Tres*, ed. G. H. Bode (Cellis, 1834) no. I.184, p. 56 (Ganymede); no. I.210, p. 66 (Troilus).

2. *The Story of Troilus*, ed. R. K. Gordon (New York, 1964) p. 6.

3. *Le Roman de Troie*, ed. L. Constans I, 5417–20.

4. *Historia Destructionis*, ed. N. E. Griffin, p. 44.

5. Ibid., p. 164.

6. *The Story of Troilus*, p. 28.

7. Proem, *The Filostrato of G. Boccaccio*, ed. N. E. Griffin and A. B. Myrick (Philadelphia, 1929; repr. New York, 1936) p. 126.

8. J. D. North, 'Kalenderes Enlumyned Ben They, I', *Review of English Studies*, n.s. 20 (1969) 129–54, esp. p. 149.

9. *1 Henry IV*, II.ii.82, *Works*, Tudor edn, ed. P. Alexander, 1951.

10. Crow and Olson, *Chaucer Life-Records*, pp. 370–1.

Notes to Chapter Nine: Honour in Chaucer

1. The study of the treatment of honour in English literature was introduced into English criticism by Professor E. M. Wilson in 'Family Honour in the Plays of Shakespeare's Predecessors and Contemporaries', *Essays and Studies of the English Association, 1953*, ed. G. Bullough (London, 1953) pp. 19–40. There is more extensive study of honour in Spanish literature (cf. M. R. L. De Malkiel, *La Idea de la Fama en la Edad Media Castellana* (Panuco, Mexico, 1952)—a reference I owe to Professor Wilson). But Wilson shows that honour in Spanish differs in important ways from that in English sixteenth-century drama. C. L. Barber makes a valuable survey, *The Idea of Honour in English Drama, 1591–1700* (Göteborg, 1957). G. F. Jones comments on some aspects of honour from St Augustine onwards as a background to his discussion of Lovelace in 'Lov'd I Not Honour More: The Durability of a Literary Motif', *Comparative Literature*, 11 (1959) 131–43. See also C. B. Watson, *Shakespeare and the Renaissance Concept of Honor* (Princeton, N.J, 1960), and the suggestive essay

by Professor J. Pitt-Rivers, 'Honour and Social Status', *Honour and Shame: The Values of Mediterranean Society*, ed. J. G. Peristiany (London, 1966) pp. 21–77, on honour in Spanish literature. The introduction to Gavin Douglas, *Shorter Poems*, ed. P. J. Bawcutt, Scottish Text Society (Edinburgh, 1967) pp. xxix–xlv, has valuable comments on the background to Douglas's *Palice of Honour*. Derek Brewer studies honour in Malory in the introduction to Sir Thomas Malory, *The Morte Darthur*, Parts Seven and Eight (London, 1968) pp. 25–35. W. Héraucourt, *Die Wertwelt Chaucers* (Heidelberg, 1939), offers some brief interesting comments.

2. *OED* is useful, and reveals the range of concepts, but not surprisingly may often be questioned in its allocation of significances of this extraordinarily slippery word. The notion of Jones, 'Lov'd I Not Honour More', that a single vocable expresses two dissimilar concepts, avoids rather than solves the problem.

3. *Sermo* CCLV, Migne, *Patrologia Latina*, XXXIX, col. 1568.

4. *A Lexicon of St T. Aquinas*, ed. R. J. Deferrari *et al.* (Washington, 1948–9) p. 489.

5. Donne, 'To the Countesse of Bedford', *Poems*, ed. H. Grierson (Oxford, 1933) p. 193. l. 7.

6. Ch. 6 above, 'Class-Distinction in Chaucer'.

7. *Chaucerian and Other Pieces* (Oxford, 1897) pp. l–li, 297.

Notes to Chapter Ten: Gothic Chaucer

1. The Gothic analogy is now something of a commonplace. It was introduced into Chaucer criticism by C. A. Muscatine, *Chaucer and the French Tradition* (Berkeley, 1957), following German art and literary historians. R. M. Jordan, *Chaucer and the Shape of Creation* (Cambridge, Mass., 1967), and D. W. Robertson, *A Preface to Chaucer* (Princeton, 1962), valuably though at times controversially extend it. A salutary warning against misuse is given by E. Salter, 'Medieval Poetry and the Visual Arts', *Essays and Studies of the English Association 1969*, ed. F. Berry (New York, 1969) pp. 16–32.

2. Also noted by N. E. Eliason, *The Language of Chaucer's Poetry*, Anglistica 17 (Copenhagen, 1972).

3. E. H. Wilkins (trans.), 'Petrarch's Coronation Oration', *Publications of the Modern Language Association of America*, 68 (1953) 1241–50.

4. *De Planctu Naturae*, Migne, *Patrologia Latina*, CCX, col. 451 bc.

5. Derek Brewer (ed.), *Chaucer: the Critical Heritage* (London, 1978) vol. II.

6. Cf. Colin Morris, *The Discovery of the Individual 1050–1200* (London, 1972), who shows how modern individualism develops from and in the culture of the twelfth century.

7. The problems of analysing the nature of Chaucer's work more closely than as analogy or reflection of social pressures are very difficult. Cf. F. R. H. Du Boulay, 'The Historical Chaucer', *Writers and their Backgrounds: Geoffrey Chaucer*, ed. Derek Brewer (London, 1974) pp. 33–57, and ch. 6 above, 'Class-Distinction in Chaucer'.

8. For an introductory discussion of the Lollard knights in relation to Chaucer see Derek Brewer, *Chaucer in his Time*; for the latest detailed historical account,

K. B. McFarlane, *Lancastrian Kings and Lollard Knights* (Oxford, 1972). See also Derek Brewer, *Chaucer and his World*.

9. In Paradise, says Aucassin, are only old priests and cripples crawling in front of altars, etc., dying of hunger and thirst and cold and disease; while in hell are the fine clerks, and the knights killed in tournaments and 'rich wars', and other worthy men, and beautiful courteous ladies who have had two or three lovers; and there are gold and silver and fine furs, harpers, minstrels and the kings of this world. *Aucassin et Nicolette*, ed. M. Roques, CFMA 41 (Paris, 1925) VI, 24–39.

10. It has long seemed to me probable that the relative dulness of English literature of the fifteenth century (for all the important developments and expansions that took place at that time, and with the interesting special exception of Malory's *Morte Darthur*) is a dulness caused by the successful imposition of the criteria of the dominant ecclesiastical culture, with its absolutist claims. This dates from the successful quelling of Lollardy in the University of Oxford by Archbishop Courtenay in 1387, but extends more widely as the fifteenth century progresses (see Brewer, *Chaucer in his Time*, pp. 228–35). Malory was probably saved by his sturdy lack of intellectual interests, by his practicality, and by his firm grounding in the old-fashioned courtly secular culture of the Arthurian romances, operating in subtle relation with a simple but profound moral concern which is indeed part of his fifteenth-century ambience.

11. According to F. Bond, *Wood Carvings in English Churches*, vol. I: *Misericords* (1910) p. 150.

12. It may be that the most satisfactory, though still crude, method of distinguishing between higher and lower cultures, or official and unofficial cultures, is the degree to which they encourage long-term views and deferred benefits. Short-term gratifications, on the other hand, such as involve spontaneity, gathering rose-buds while we may, seizing the passing joy as it flies, taking no thought for the morrow, all seem to be characteristics of what are at least historically unofficial, or popular, cultures, and are not all unchristian. Some of these are negative, mere reluctance to be organised, but others are positive, which is why popular culture always has some real value in itself.

Medieval official ecclesiastical culture took an extremely long view in postponing all benefits till after death, and in positively avoiding, at least in theory, short-term gratifications. (A full treatment of this topic would have to consider how strong a short-term gratification is the act of postponement; as well as many other problems. All that can be made here is a general suggestion.)

13. For Clanvowe see McFarlane, *Lancastrian Kings*, p. 12; V. J. Scattergood, 'The Authorship of "The Boke of Cupide" ', *Anglia*, 82 (1964) 137–49; B. Cottle, *The Triumph of English 1350–1400* (London, 1969). For the heresy, see M. Deanesly, *The Lollard Bible* (Cambridge, 1920) pp. 319, 352, 366. I am obliged to Dr T. J. Hefferman for drawing my attention to these last references.

14. A largely unexplored subject, but see F. L. Utley, 'Folklore, Myth and Ritual', *Critical Approaches to Medieval Literature: Selected Papers from the English Institute, 1958–9* (New York, 1960) pp. 83–109. There is useful material in *Sources and Analogues of Chaucer's Canterbury Tales*, ed. W. F. Bryan and G. Dempster (Chicago, 1941), and *Originals and Analogues of Some of*

Chaucer's Tales, Chaucer Society Publications, pt 1 (1872), pt 2 (1875), pt 3 (1876), pt 4 (1886), pt 5 (1887). See also *The Literary Context of Chaucer's Fabliaux*, ed. L. D. Benson and T. M. Anderson (New York, 1971).

15. See F. R. Du Boulay, *An Age of Ambition* (London, 1970).
16. For one of the latest accounts see R. Hookyas, *Religion and the Rise of Modern Science* (Edinburgh, 1972).
17. Northrop Frye, *Anatomy of Criticism* (Princeton, N.J., 1957) p. 312.
18. Ibid. (insertions mine).
19. Derek Brewer, 'The Relationship of Chaucer to the English and European Traditions', *Chaucer and Chaucerians*, ed. Derek Brewer (London, 1966) pp. 1–38; reprinted as ch. 2 of Brewer, *Chaucer: the Poet as Storyteller* (London, forthcoming).
20. J. A. W. Bennett, *The Parlement of Foules: An Interpretation* (Oxford, 1957).
21. J. A. Burrow, *Ricardian Poetry: Chaucer, Gower, Langland and the 'Gawain' Poet* (London, 1971). See also Derek Brewer, *Chaucer*, 3rd edn, suppl. (1973) pp. 165 ff.

Notes to Chapter Eleven: Chaucer and Chrétien and Arthurian Romance

1. P. J. Frankis, 'Chaucer's "Vavasour" and Chrétien de Troyes', *N&Q*, 204 (1968) 46–7.
2. M. Roques (ed.), *Erec et Enide*, CFMA 80 (Paris, 1952) and M. Roques (ed.), *Le Chevalier au Lion*, CFMA 89 (Paris, 1960).
3. B. Rowland, *Blind Beasts: Chaucer's Animal World* (Kent, Ohio, 1971).
4. Derek Brewer, 'The Relationship of Chaucer to the English and European Traditions'. The point has been repeated by P. M. Kean, *Chaucer and the Making of English Poetry* (London, 1972) vol. ii, p. 61.
5. B. J. Whiting, 'Gawain: His Reputation, His Courtesy', *MS*, 9 (1947) 189–234, argues that Chaucer may have read *Sir Gawain and the Green Knight*. If so, he may well have thought poorly of it, as we may guess both from the flippancy of the reference to Gawain in *The Squire's Tale*, and from the contempt for 'rum, ram, ruf' of alliterative verse that is put into the Parson's mouth (*CT*, x, 43), though indeed he holds rhyme to be 'but litel bettre'.
6. See ch. 9 above, 'Honour in Chaucer'.

Notes to Chapter Twelve: The Arming of the Warrior

1. See ch. 10 above, 'Gothic Chaucer'; 'Towards a Chaucerian Poetic', Sir Israel Gollancz Memorial Lecture, *Proceedings of the British Academy*, 60 (1974) 219–52, and reprinted as ch. 4 of Brewer, *Chaucer: the Poet as Storyteller*; and 'Some Observations on the Development of Literalism', *Poetica* (Tokyo) 2 (1974) 71–95.
2. I am much indebted to Professor Canon J. R. Porter of the University of Exeter for references to arming in Babylonian epic: first, the *Eruma elish*, telling how the god Marduk was armed by other deities for his fight with the female chaos-monster Tiamat (J. B. Pritchard (ed.), *Ancient Near Eastern Texts Relating to the Old Testament*, trans. E. A. Speiser, 2nd edn (Princeton, N.J., 1955) p. 66);

second, two passages from the Epic of Gilgamesh, telling how the two heroes Gilgamesh and Enkidu are armed for combat with a monster (*The Gilgamesh Epic and Old Testament Parallels*, trans. A. Heidel, 2nd edn (Chicago, 1944) pp. 36–9).

3. A. B. Lord, *The Singer of Tales*, esp. pp. 68–98. I am generally much indebted to this remarkable book, of such importance for the study of medieval and folk literature. When, however, Lord associates the formalised description of dressing in the medieval Greek epic *Digenis Akritas* with the arming (p. 89) I believe he is confusing two different types of formalised topic. For use of the term *topos*, see E. R. Curtius, *European Literature and the Latin Middle Ages*, trans. W. R. Trask (London, 1953).

4. Lord, *Singer of Tales*, pp. 89–92; M. Bowra, 'Style', *A Companion to Homer Studies*, ed. A. J. B. Wace and F. H. Stubbings (London, 1962) pp. 26–37, at p. 30; A. B. Lord, 'Homer and Other Epic Poetry', *Companion to Homer*, pp. 179–214, at pp. 190–1; F. H. Stubbings, 'Arms and Armour', *Companion to Homer*, pp. 504–22, at pp. 504–14. I am also indebted to my colleague Dr Stubbings of Emmanuel College for personal advice on this topic. See also Harald Patzer, *Dichterische Kunst und poetisches Handwerk in homerischen Epos*, *Sitzungsberichte der Wissenschaftlichen Gesellschaft an der Johann Wolfgang Goethe-Universität, 1971*, x.1 (Wiesbaden, 1972). I am indebted for this reference to Dr A. M. Bowie, Lecturer in Classics at the University of Liverpool.

5. Lord, 'Homer and Other Epic Poetry', p. 191.

6. *The Iliad* (Chicago, 1951) iii, 330–9.

7. Lord, *Singer of Tales*, p. 91.

8. See the museum at Olympia in Greece where there are actual pieces of armour used and pictorial reconstructions, which I follow. There is also a portrayal of a warrior arming on a vase in the Greek National Museum, Athens, item 363. He appears to be putting on his greaves.

9. Stubbings, 'Arms and Armour', pp. 504–5.

In one of the tombs, the 'Giglioli', of the great Etruscan Necropolis at Tarquinia in Italy, dated about the third century bc, the painted decoration on the walls consists of the armour of warriors, painted as if hanging by nails from the wall. The only items represented are helmet, corslet, greaves, sword, spear, shield. These, it would seem, constitute the intrinsic 'idea' of armour, to which the smaller practical necessities, real pieces to cover feet, joints, thighs, such as are preserved in the museum at Olympia in Greece, are quite irrelevant.

Pictures of ladies saying goodbye to armed knights, especially if handing them a helmet or a weapon, probably reflect the topos, with some extra meaning associated with love, as occurs in Chrétien. A clear example occurs in the Luttrell Psalter (British Library Add. MS 42130, fol. 202, reproduced in Derek Brewer, *Chaucer in his Time*; cf. also the Bermondsey Dish of *c.* 1325, in the Victoria and Albert Museum, reproduced in Derek Brewer, *Chaucer and his World*; and Bibliothèque Nationale MS Fr. 2186, fol. 8v, reproduced in R. W. Barber, *The Knight and Chivalry* (Ipswich, 1974).

10. *Aeneid*, ed. J. W. Mackail (Oxford, 1930) xii, 87–96.

11. Ibid., p. 468.

12. *Táin Bó Cúalnge from the Book of Leinster*, ed. and trans. Cecile O'Rahilly

(Dublin, 1967). See also *The Táin*, trans. Thomas Kinsella (London, 1970).

13. *Táin Bó Cúalnge*, pp. 200–1.

14. *Tóruigheacht Gruaidhe Griansholus*, ed. and trans. Cecile O'Rahilly, Irish Texts Society, no. 24 (1924 for 1922) pp. 44–7.

15. Alan Bruford, 'Gaelic Folktales and Medieval Romances', *Béaloideas: The Journal of the Folklore of Ireland Society*, IML 34 (1966). I am indebted for this reference to Mr Patrick Sims-Williams.

16. Bruford, 'Gaelic Folktales', p. 184; see also p. 36. The author, unfortunately for our purposes, gives no list or specific example of arming runs.

17. Ibid., p. 27.

18. Ibid., p. 199.

19. Ibid., p. 37. In concluding the Irish references it may be noted that the arming of the hero probably lies behind the popular hymn attributed to St Patrick and known as 'St Patrick's Breastplate' (e.g. *Hymns Ancient and Modern*, no. 162).

20. I am grateful to Professor E. Vasta and Professor E. Thundil for calling this passage in *Beowulf* to my attention.

21. J. E. Martin (now J. E. Weiss), 'Studies in Some Early Middle English Romances', dissertation, University of Cambridge (1967) pp. 80–2. As examples she refers to the Anglo-Norman *Horn*, ll. 1408–81; *Raoul de Cambrai*, ll. 4934 ff.; *Roland*, ll. 3140–56; *Guillaume de l'Angleterre*, ll. 132–40.

22. Chrétien de Troyes, *Erec et Enide*, ed. M. Roques, pp. 708–26.

23. Trans. W. W. Comfort, *Arthurian Romances* (1914) p. 10.

24. Ch. 11 above, 'Chaucer and Chrétien and Arthurian Romance'.

25. I quote from Geoffrey of Monmouth, *Historia Regum Britanniae, a Variant Version*, ed. Jacob Hammer (Cambridge, Mass., 1951) ix.2, 104–11 (pp. 154–5), corresponding to *Historia Regum Britanniae*, ed. A. Griscom (New York, 1929) ix.iv (p. 438), which has verbal differences insignificant for the present purpose.

26. *In Pursuit of Perfection*, ed. Joan M. Ferrante and George D. Economou (Port Washington, N.Y., 1975) pp. 138, 174.

27. See n. 25.

28. *Le Roman de Brut de Wace*, ed. I. Arnold, SATF 56 (Paris, 1938–40) pp. lxxviii (on the date); xlv (on Chrétien); the arming is on pp. 489–90 (ll. 9275–300).

29. *Selections from Laȝamon's 'Brut'*, ed. G. L. Brook (Oxford, 1963).

30. Håkan Ringbom, *Studies in the Narrative Technique of Beowulf and Lawman's Brut*, Acta Academiae Aboensis, series A, 36, no. 2 (Åbo, 1968) p. 154.

31. Gottfried von Strassburg, *Tristan*, trans. A. T. Hatto (Harmondsworth, 1960) pp. 129–30.

32. *Morte Arthure*, ed. John Finlayson (London, 1967) pp. 43–4 (ll. 900–16).

33. ll. 566–89, ed. R. A. Waldron (London, 1970), and ed. J. R. R. Tolkien and E. V. Gordon, 2nd edn, rev. N. Davis (Oxford, 1967).

34. May McKisack, *The Fourteenth Century, 1307–1399* (Oxford, 1959) p. 238.

35. Another example of the topos in alliterative poetry occurs in *Sir Ferumbras*, ed. Sidney J. Herrtage, *EETS*, e.s. 34 (1879) p. 8 (ll. 235–40). The hero Oliver is armed early in the poem just before the first major enterprise (as usual, a battle). The topos is not elaborated. The order is greaves (*hosen of mayle*);

hauberk of steel; helm (with *aventail*, as usual in the fourteenth century); sword (Hautecer); horse (Garyn).

36. L. H. Loomis, 'Chaucer and the Auchinleck MS', *Essays and Studies in Honor of Carleton Brown*, ed. P. W. Long (New York, 1940) pp. 111–28. See also her admirable chapter on Sir Thopas in *Sources and Analogues of Chaucer's Canterbury Tales*, ed. W. F. Bryan and G. Dempster (Chicago, 1941) pp. 486–559.

37. I have argued this fully and I believe conclusively in my 'The Relationship of Chaucer to the English and European Traditions'.

38. Ed. E. Kölbing, *EETS*, e.s. 46, 48, 65 (1885, 1886, 1894) pp. 45–6. The other MSS have corresponding passages. It derives from the French version; see *Der anglonormannische Boeve de Haumtone*, ed. Albert Stimming, Bibliotheca Normannica 7 (Halle, 1899) ll. 532–45.

39 *Guy of Warwick*, ed. J. Zupitza, *EETS*, e.s. 42, 49, 59 (1883, 1887, 1891) ll. 3849–66.

40. Ed. Joseph Ritson, *Ancient Englesh Metrical Romanceës* (1802) vol. II, 10 ff., 217–40.

41. Irving Linn, 'The Arming of Sir Thopas', *Modern Language Notes*, 51 (1936) 300–11; *Otuel and Roland*, ed. M. I. O'Sullivan, *EETS*, o.s. 198 (1937) ll. 282–320, 357–86, 1217–46.

42. *Octavian*, ll. 877–88, Maldwyn Mills (ed.), *Six Middle English Romances* (London, 1973) p. 99.

43. Harold Arthur, Viscount Dillon, 'On a MS. Collection of Ordinances of Chivalry of the Fifteenth Century, belonging to Lord Hastings', *Archaeologia*, 57 (1900) 29–70; the extract occurs on pp. 43–4, and I quote the slightly modernised version by Edith Rickert, *Chaucer's World*, ed. C. C. Olson and M. M. Crow (New York, 1948) p. 156. The MS is now New York, Morgan Library, MS 775.

44. S. J. Herben, 'Arms and Armor in Chaucer', *Speculum*, 12 (1937) 475–87, shows that the actual underclothing and armour of Sir Thopas are quite normal and accurate.

45. *The Works of Sir Thomas Malory*, ed. E. Vinaver, 2nd edn (Oxford, 1964) vol. I, p. 200.

46. *The Savoy Operas* (New York, 1967) p. 260.

47. *Orlando Furioso*, canto XLVI, ll. 109–10.

Index

Chaucer's works are indexed under their titles, and these entries include any references to the characters in the works. Works by other authors are indexed under the name of the author (where this is known).